EDUCATING CHILDREN AND YOUNG PEOPLE IN CARE

Learning Placements and Caring Schools

Claire Cameron, Graham Connelly
and Sonia Jackson

Jessica Kingsley *Publishers*
London and Philadelphia

Case study on pp.106–9 includes an extract adapted with permission from the editors of an article in the *Scottish Journal of Residential Child Care*.

Case study of 'A' on pp.209–10 reproduced by permission of the Coram Children's Legal Centre.

First published in 2015
by Jessica Kingsley Publishers
73 Collier Street
London N1 9BE, UK
and
400 Market Street, Suite 400
Philadelphia, PA 19106, USA

www.jkp.com

Copyright © Claire Cameron, Graham Connelly and Sonia Jackson 2015

Front cover image source: Kibble Education and Care Centre.

Library of Congress Cataloging in Publication Data
Cameron, Claire.
  Learning placements and caring schools : a practical guide
to the education of children in care / Claire
Cameron, Graham Connelly and Sonia Jackson.
    pages cm
  Includes bibliographical references.
  ISBN 978-1-84905-365-5 (alk. paper)
1. Children--Institutional care--Education--Great Britain.
2. Foster children--Education--Great Britain.
3. Children with social disabilities--Education--Great
Britain. I. Connelly, Graham. II. Jackson, Sonia. III.
Title.
  LC4096.G7C36 2015
  371.930941--dc23

                            2014043320

British Library Cataloguing in Publication Data
A CIP catalogue record for this book is available from the British Library

ISBN 978 1 84905 365 5
eISBN 978 0 85700 719 3

Printed and bound in Great Britain

ACKNOWLEDGEMENTS

This book is a collaboration between three highly experienced researchers at Thomas Coram Research Unit, Institute of Education, University of London, and the Centre for Excellence for Looked After Children in Scotland (CELCIS), University of Strathclyde. To both sets of employers, and our families who tolerated many weekends at the endeavour, we are grateful for the opportunity to write this practical guide.

More specific thanks are due to some individuals who volunteered their time to talk about their work and experiences. In late 2013, at a meeting of the UK Social Pedagogy Development Network in Kirkcaldy, Scotland, one of the authors (Claire Cameron) asked for volunteers who would like to share their practice about the education of children in care. Three foster carers, two in Scotland and one in Staffordshire, England, and one social pedagogue working in England, took up the offer and their perspectives enrich the book. Some of our case studies draw on specially commissioned material. Graham Connelly interviewed a mentor at Strathclyde University, and a young man who was a migrant from Africa. Sonia Jackson would like to thank Diarmid Mogg, Ellen-Raissa Jackson and Ruth Forbes for helpful advice and information. To all of them we are very appreciative of their time. Many thanks to the staff and young people in Kibble's Art department who produced art work for the front cover and in particular the artist whose work is shown.

Last, we would like to thank Ben Abrams for putting aside his PhD studies to give the text a final copyediting check.

CONTENTS

List of Tables

List of Figures

CHAPTER 1

Bringing Education into Care Placements and Bringing Care into Schools

This book is an evidence-informed practical guide to supporting the education of children and young people in public care, and those leaving care as young adults. Its main argument is that for children to thrive and flourish, and realise their potential, and particularly where they have had very difficult early childhoods, they need to be cared for in school and educated at home. The integration of care and education in daily life is key. The chapters in this book set out the argument in different ways. In the first chapters we focus on the idea of encouraging education in what we call 'learning placements' in foster care and residential care; in later chapters we examine the ways in which, in different phases of childhood, schools and other educational environments can be 'caring schools'.

In this chapter the education (school) systems in the UK are described, with particular focus on curricula and testing regimes in England and Scotland. Then, effective learning strategies are discussed, and learning profiles of children in care are outlined.

KEY POINTS

‣ Educating children in care is at last recognised as important; but to be effective, care and education need to be integrated in both placements and schools.

‣ There are two meanings of education: broadly based development and a narrow focus on performance. Children in care need both.

Introduction

The education of children in care is at long last in the foreground of policy attention. As Graham Connelly pointed out (2013, p.107), 'teachers, social workers and carers would need to confess to having lived on another planet' not to have noticed the plethora of information about the risks young people in care face of not getting an adequate schooling. The publication of statistical data showing the low level of educational attainment of children in care compared with other young people has helped to identify the extent of the problem in both Scotland and England. Nomination of 'designated teachers' has helped to provide support for children and young people in care in schools, yet the experience of far too many children in the public care system continues to be one of not getting sufficient knowledge through enjoyment of, or, ultimately, qualifications from, the education system.

Success in education is still one of the main means of prosperity as an adult. Being without educational qualifications or the wherewithal to attain them leaves young people highly vulnerable to unemployment and poverty as well as ill-health and diminished self-esteem. Ensuring young people in its care are educated is one of the most effective actions the state can take to protect them from further risks as adults and improve their quality of life. It is also their right. Article 28 of the United Nations Convention on the Rights of the Child (UNCRC), to which the UK is a signatory, states: 'Young people should be encouraged to reach the highest level of education of which they are capable.'

This guide provides evidence and practical support to practitioners whose role is to educate and care for children and young people in care (such as social workers, foster carers and residential care workers) or whose role includes the education of children in care within a broader remit (such as teachers, learning mentors and advisors).

The authors have worked in the field of research, practice and development of services for looked after children and their education in England, Wales and Scotland for, cumulatively, many decades. They have arrived at the conclusion that the continental European approach of social pedagogy has much to offer children's services in the UK. Social pedagogy, often translated as 'education in its broadest sense' is becoming better known in the UK, particularly among those working with children in public care, through training and development programmes, books, professional magazine articles and conference presentations.[1]

In this book, we introduce some ideas associated with social pedagogy. First, we argue that care and education are integral to each other: a conceptual and organisational split between care and education services is not helpful. Hence 'learning placements' and 'caring schools'. Second, we argue that the everyday environment of 'upbringing' and 'care' is just as important as the 'educational' environment. Indeed, the professionals charged with looking after young people in foster homes and residential care spaces are 'experts in everyday life'. We return to this idea of everyday expertise throughout the book. The third social pedagogic idea is that, following Pestalozzi, the practical (represented by hands) must be integrated with the relational (represented by a compassionate heart) and theoretical knowledge and empirical evidence (represented by the head). In this book we reflect this range of contributions to knowledge and practical guidance. We have used a range of sources: theoretical and empirical evidence; personal testimony; and accounts of doing and being together. We have interviewed some foster carers, social pedagogues, young people and others specifically for this book.

We have also drawn, to a considerable extent, on a research project that two of the authors (Cameron and Jackson) took part in between 2008 and 2010. The YiPPEE project was a five-country study of the post-compulsory educational pathways of young people who had some educational qualifications. It used multiple data sources, including detailed accounts of the lives of the young people aged 18–24, interviews with relevant professionals, a survey of local authorities and analysis of national statistics (Jackson and Cameron 2014). The experience of this study, carried out in parallel in Denmark, Hungary, Spain and Sweden as well as England, inspired us to write this practical guide. The third author, Connelly, brings an invaluable Scottish perspective. Perhaps starting later than England, Scotland has energetically pursued the issue of supporting the educational potential of young people in care, with a multi-disciplinary perspective that complements the social pedagogic approach. Since 1999, devolution of powers within the United Kingdom has meant

---

1   Thempra.org gives a good overview of social pedagogy resources in the UK.

diversifying policy and practice. While we would have liked to cover all four nations equitably, in reality most of our material has its origins in England and Scotland. We hope that practitioners in Northern Ireland and Wales can nevertheless take some inspiration from these pages.

This chapter provides a broad framework for thinking about the issue of education for children in care. First, we argue that there are two meanings of 'education', one broad and one narrow, and both are required for the fulfilment of young people's educational potential and wellbeing. This discussion includes an overview of the school systems in England and Scotland. Then we introduce the ideas at the core of the book: 'learning placements' and 'caring schools'. We discuss some factors that have a bearing on learning for the particular circumstances for children in care, who have often had traumatic and extended difficulties in their lives, and introduce the idea of the 'everyday expert' for children in care, who has a critical role in promoting and enriching learning.

Two meanings of education
Broadly based development or upbringing

In a broad definition of education, it is not the sole province of schools and classrooms but happens everywhere. Education is about helping people form their thinking and action. It is about learning, which happens through the everyday experience of being brought up in families and communities. According to the German social pedagogue, Klaus Mollenhauer, education is the central task of upbringing, which parents undertake on behalf of society. Upbringing is not well defined, but in the English language, in general terms, it refers to the effect of care and treatment on a person's moral codes. For Mollenhauer, upbringing means passing on 'valued cultural heritage' to the next generation through the actions of adults in relation to children. Such adults include parents, people undertaking a parental or upbringing role such as foster carers or residential care workers, youth workers, teachers and any other societal role models. Through their everyday educational actions, adults are helping young people form their values, views about the world around them and 'how to be' in relation to others. From this perspective, it is an educational upbringing act to show a young person how to behave in a shop queue or to greet a stranger in accordance with societal norms and expectations. For Mollenhauer, adults in general serve as both the midwives of children's development and their moral censors by opening up or closing down their opportunities (Smith 2013).

From this perspective, education is about enabling children to grow up as citizens of a country, equipped to take advantage of opportunities and realise ambitions, which may be both individual and social. By encouraging young people to adopt certain socially defined values and skills, education has a role in social cohesion, economic prosperity and in upholding democracy.

Wetz (2011) argues that this broad developmental role of educator as mentor to children's development was the primary underpinning or classical understanding of being a teacher in the UK for much of the twentieth century. No doubt there were exceptions, but on the whole, teachers understood their educational role as a developmental one.

Education as performance

In the UK, however, and particularly since the early 1990s, the definition of education has narrowed so that 'education' signals what happens in schools, and 'teachers' are responsible for education. Moreover, competency-based approaches have become dominant, and these define teaching as providing education in terms of subject knowledge, pedagogic strategies, orderly classroom management, assessment and recording, and continuous professional development. According to Wetz (2011), the role of the teacher has become a technical one, delivering the curriculum, and the mentoring relationship has become the province of specific specialists.

In 2009, the Cambridge Primary Review argued that an increasing emphasis on 'the basics' and 'standards' in primary schools was compromising the kinds of learning that require time for problem solving, dialogue and extended exploration of ideas. Being able to memorise facts was becoming more important than understanding the world around children. They recommended that children's wellbeing and active engagement in learning should be at the forefront of a renewed primary education, and the teaching strategies adopted should support this through a collaborative approach between teachers and children. Knowledge, they argued, was best acquired through a negotiated approach characterised by dialogue, by a teacher leading children to understand both past and present, going between personal and collective knowledge and between different ways of thinking (Cambridge Primary Review 2011).

Despite this high-profile review, the policy focus on education as meaning school performance in 'the basics', and in particular in terms of memorisable facts, has continued, certainly in England. In part, that has been driven by international comparisons, such as PISA (Programme for International Student Assessment). PISA is an ongoing, worldwide comparison of scores reached by 15-year-olds in three 'basic' subjects of maths, science and reading, in which UK students performed 'around average' in 2012, despite above-average spending on education (OECD 2012). Inevitably, by focusing on knowledge acquisition in these 'basics', other parts of education are not subject to comparison and are neglected, in order to improve the ranking in international league tables. Indeed, data recording and performance monitoring by schools is now central to a teacher's role.

School systems in England and Scotland

School systems in the four countries of the UK are distinctive, and are growing increasingly so. Characteristics such as degree of selection on entry, age of starting school, examinations undertaken and testing regimes differ, particularly between Scotland and the other countries of the UK; since the devolved system of government applied in 1999, education has been one of the major portfolios of responsibilities in the four nations. Here we focus on England and Scotland. Table 1.1 sets out the main structures of the school systems in the two countries. Although there are broadly similar educational phases, there are differences in the ages of transition between phases, and the degree of specificity of phases in the early years.

Table 1.1 The structure of educational systems in England and Scotland

Age phase	0–3/3/5 yrs	4/5–11/12 yrs	11/12–16 yrs	16–18/19 yrs	17/18/19 yrs onwards
Phase name	**Early years**	**Primary**	**Secondary**	**Upper Secondary**	**Higher Education**
England	• Early Years Foundation Stage (2–5) • Primary schools, nursery schools, private settings, voluntary settings	• Key Stage 1 (5–7) • Key Stage 2 (7–11) • Primary schools	• Key Stage 3 (11–14) • Key Stage 4 (14–16) • Secondary schools	• Secondary schools • Further education institutions • Specialist colleges including sixth form colleges	• Further education institutions • Higher education institutions including universities
Scotland	• Pre-school education centres (3–5)	• Primary schools (5–12)	• Secondary schools (12–16)	• Secondary schools • Further education institutions	• Further education institutions • Higher education institutions including universities

Source: Eurydice (2013)

Curricula and testing of performance of children in school in England and Scotland

Table 1.1 necessarily simplifies the actual educational system, particularly at the younger age phases. In fact, the arrangement of education into a system is complex and diverse in England, although less so in Scotland.[2] Early childhood education and care (ECEC) (0–5 years) is the first phase of education. Although this phase is non-compulsory, there is substantial evidence that attending high quality early education and care services has a positive benefit for children; however, the number of children who are in public care who attend is unknown. ECEC settings include family-based care with childminders (for children aged 0–7), and group-based care, either full-time or part-time, in nurseries or pre-schools, or in nursery classes in primary schools. At the time of writing, all three- and four-year-old children in England and Scotland are entitled to 15–16 hours of free early education for 38 weeks a year, as are two-year-olds from highly disadvantaged backgrounds including those who are looked after by local authorities. Over 90 per cent of children aged three and four attend some form of ECEC.

The ECEC curriculum in England is led by the Early Years Foundation Stage (EYFS). Monitoring of children's academic performance against a defined standard of development begins immediately. The EYFS includes a 'progress check' between the ages of 24 and 36 months and an EYFS 'profile' at age five, according to their accomplishments in relation to: communication and language; physical development; personal, social and emotional development; literacy; mathematics; understanding the world; and expressive arts and design.

Primary schooling begins formally at age five, but in practice nearly all children start school at age four in the reception class of primary schools. Once children are in Year 1, at age five, the national curriculum Key Stage 1 (KS1) applies; this is followed by Key Stage 2 (KS2) for children aged 7–11. During the first year of KS1, all children undergo a phonics screening test 'designed to confirm whether individual children have learnt phonic decoding to an appropriate standard' (DfE website, n.d.). At the end of KS1, there are statutory tests in reading, writing and mathematics designed to

---

2   We have not included the arrangement of private education in the table.

'provide a snapshot of a child's attainment' (DfE website, n.d.). At age 11, at the end of KS2, teachers administer nationally set tests of children's attainment in English, mathematics and science, the results of which are published. The grade that children acquire at primary school sets their Minimum Expected Graded (MEG) for secondary school and this grade acts as a benchmark for subsequent assessment of progress.

About 93 per cent of children in England, and 96 per cent in Scotland, attend state primary schools; the remainder attend privately run or independent schools, or, in the case of a small minority, are home educated. An increasing number of state primary schools in England are becoming detached from local authority support through the government's free schools and academies programme; around six per cent in early 2014. This means they are publicly funded and their governance arrangements are controlled by central government, but have autonomy about most aspects of the school's operation.

Once children enter secondary school at around age 11, they follow KS3 and 4 curricula and their performance is relentlessly assessed, against a wider range of subjects, culminating in GCSEs taken at age 16. It is compulsory to take English, maths and science subjects. Secondary schooling in England is undergoing rapid diversification. Around half of all secondary schools, which cater for young people aged 11–14 in Key Stage 3 and 14–16 in Key Stage 4, are academies or free schools. Some secondary schools have selection criteria based on entrance tests or earlier performance. The admissions code is legally binding, which gives children in care priority access to the school best suited to them, but academies and free schools are their own admissions authority and concerns have been raised as to whether they will, in future, adhere to the spirit as well as the letter of the code. There is also a small but influential private or independent secondary sector; around two thirds of students from independent schools went to prestigious universities in 2010/11 compared with a quarter of students from state schools (BIS 2013).

Upper secondary schools and colleges (16–19 years) may be academically focused school-based, or independent sixth forms or vocational colleges, or offer a mixture of academic and vocational qualifications. During upper secondary education, young people can study for a wide range of qualifications, such as AS/A-levels,

International Baccalaureate, BTECs or other vocational qualifications. If they have not achieved a 'good' grade in English and maths at age 16, they must repeat these subjects during the upper secondary phase. In 2014, the 'participation age' was raised to 17 and to 18 in 2015, elongating the school career, or the period of childhood subject to adult-led assessment of skills and competences, to 15 years or more.

In Scotland, there is a general political consensus about education provision, and relative popular satisfaction with the education system (Gillies 2013). For these reasons, there has been greater stability in the school system than in England in recent years, though the resulting lack of experimentation has also drawn criticism, particularly in respect of the inability to improve the school experience of the most disadvantaged children, including those in the care system (Bloomer 2013).

If the overall system in Scotland has remained stable, the curriculum has not. In 2004, following a national debate about education, a new curriculum, subsequently known as Curriculum for Excellence (often shortened to CfE), began to be designed and the process of implementation was still happening a decade later. A characteristic of the curriculum is the common aims for education across the child lifespan from 3 to 18, encapsulated in the four 'capacities' of becoming successful learners, confident individuals, responsible citizens and effective contributors. It is common to see the work of children displayed in Scottish nursery, primary and secondary schools captioned according to one or more of the capacities. A second feature of the new curriculum is that it is underpinned by theories of learning, such as those of Piaget, Bruner and Dewey, which emphasise the value of children engaging actively in knowledge construction. A third feature is the emphasis on cross-curricular learning, at least in the years before greater specialisation in what is known as the 'senior phase' of upper secondary education. Learning is measured by 'experiences and outcomes' which can be assessed in cross-disciplinary projects. This approach might be seen as less prescriptive and driven by performance than in England.

In the Scottish system, teachers assess children by a range of methods, including observation, coursework and standard tests, but test results are not published nationally. Standards of attainment are assessed by the Scottish Survey of Numeracy and Literacy, which samples the national performance of school children at three stages (approximately ages 8, 11 and 13) in literacy and numeracy in alternate years.

In summary, education in England and less so in Scotland is largely defined in terms of performance in school and is the responsibility of teachers and schools. Much assessment of education is in terms of 'core' subjects of maths, science and reading/writing. This is a very narrow definition of education. In this book we argue that children who are in public care are most likely to thrive if their care placement, or upbringing, is seen as educationally oriented – that there are opportunities for learning about themselves, about others, about the world around them. This is education in its broadest sense. At the same time, education in the narrow sense, attending school and acquiring educational qualifications, is best achieved if schools care about the individuals and their particular backgrounds. For children in care who flourish, it is often the care and commitment of an individual teacher or other adult which make the critical difference. Caring schools are fundamental to progress. We discuss 'learning placements' and 'caring schools' in later chapters. Here, we give some broad background for our main argument.

How children learn

In her principles of learning, gathered from international research, Vosniadou (2001) argues that children learn when they are actively involved in their learning, when the subject matter has real relevance for their lives, when new subject matter builds on existing knowledge, and when they have strategies for learning and can evaluate their learning. They also need to be open to challenge and be able to understand general principles rather than rely on memorisation. Learning takes time as new skills need to be practised, and individual differences matter. Fundamentally, the job of teachers is to motivate learners to want to push their learning further.

These principles coincide with the findings of Higgins and Elliott Major (2012), who argue, based on research in English schools, that effective feedback from teachers to pupils is one of the most successful ways to improve children's learning in school. Effective feedback is the production of information that relates to performance and guides what the teacher and the student must do next to reach a goal. Other effective strategies for classroom learning are learning with and through peers and being able to reflect on and evaluate one's own learning. These findings illustrate the social and interactive dimension of learning that Vosniadou referred to, and show that the broad definition of education (upbringing outside schools) is needed to support progress in the narrow definition (performance in schools).

To make the most of education in school, children need to have developed social skills to support working with peers and individual skills of documentation and reflection on both situations and learning. There are implications in these findings for the roles of teachers, foster carers, residential care workers and social workers. Young people who have missed out on, or never developed, social skills or have a low sense of their own worth will find effective learning hard and will need extraordinary efforts on the part of professionals to support their progress. For children in care, the contexts where such social skills are formed are the everyday living environments of foster care and residential care. The people who undertake foster care and residential care are 'experts in everyday life'. The upbringing offered by foster carers and residential workers, their judgements, actions and reflections on action are the basis of 'learning placements' that we foreground in this book.

Caring schools

At the same time, for children to learn in school, teachers have to recognise difference and motivate individuals. To appreciate and support individuals and their differences means to engage in a fundamental human ethic of caring about them, and, according to philosopher Nel Noddings (Smith 2004), caring for them too. While 'caring about' conveys a more general sense of justice, it is also a precondition for caring for others as individuals. Schools have a role to play in supporting care on behalf of society in the sense of developing the abilities of children to care for others and to feel cared for. For Noddings (1992), education from a care perspective requires teachers and other school staff to model care in their behaviour, engage in dialogue so that those they care for get feedback about caring and can evaluate it, encourage practice in caring and reflection on it, and affirm and encourage others' development. This last requirement, called confirmation, involves trust and continuity in teacher–student relations as knowledge of the individual is needed, and for such knowledge to be handled with sensitivity.

Noddings's work sets a high standard for an ethic of caring in schools that, as we have seen, are largely defined and evaluated in terms of the academic performances that students produce in tests and examinations. This book explores ways in which dimensions of caring in schools have been and can be demonstrated, particularly focusing on the experiences of children in care.

The implications for children in care

Children in public care form less than one per cent of the population of those under 18 years of age; in England the figure is just over half of one per cent and in Scotland it is approximately one-and-a-half per cent. This higher figure is partly due to the different definition of 'looked after children' used in Scotland, which includes children placed on supervision by a Children's Hearing while remaining in the family home. When this group is omitted, however, the proportion of the under-18 population in Scotland looked after 'away from home' has still been higher in recent years (at just over 1%) than in the other countries of the UK.

Among this relatively small group of young people, there is a wide range of what we might call 'learning profiles'. In 2002, Meltzer and colleagues reported that nearly half (45%) of young people aged 5–17 looked after by local authorities in England were assessed as having a mental disorder, mostly conduct disorders but also anxiety and depression and hyperactivity. For those in residential care the figure was higher, around seventy per cent of young people. For children of the same age in the general population, the rate of mental disorders was about ten per cent, indicating that many children in care are a group with a particular profile that will have an impact on their learning.

Indeed, nearly seventy per cent of children in care in England are defined as having special educational needs (SEN) either because they have an official Statement of Special Educational Need or they do not have a Statement but have a lower level of need defined by a school. This is more than three times the incidence in the general population (DfE 2013a). One might argue that the identification of special educational needs is dependent on context: schools know that they can access extra resources, so there is an incentive to define need in order to help children cope with the school environment. The figures indicate difficulties for many young people in the particular environment of schools but say relatively little about the actual learning abilities of students. In fact there is evidence from Sweden that most children in care are within the 'normal' range of intelligence (Tideman *et al.* 2013).

Learning profiles are also affected by the structural conditions of children's lives. Educational chances are highly influenced by social class and parenting background (Douglas 1964; Desforges with Abouchaar 2003: Cameron *et al.* 2012). Reviews of studies in the UK and the USA show that factors such as material deprivation were much worse for families in lower social classes; and home discussion of education, or parental involvement, much higher in middle class families, were very important factors in supporting educational success (Desforges with Abouchaar 2003). Furthermore, Feinstein (2003) found that children from lower social classes who were in early education and scoring low on cognitive measures at 22 months made less progress in school than children of higher social classes who achieved the same scores at that age.

Where a child lives and goes to school has an impact on their chances of educational success. Cassen and Kingdon (2007) found that young people with no or very low level qualifications at age 16 were concentrated in major urban conurbations of England where levels of deprivation were higher and the percentage of adults without qualifications was higher. As children in care very largely come from lower social classes, with higher levels of material deprivation, and from families where adults are also unlikely to have educational qualifications, they are likely to face barriers in school achievement without focused effort and support on the part of teachers, 'everyday experts' and social workers. Key resilience factors, which may enable children to take a different direction, include parental interest and involvement, self-belief, additional educational support at home or through a high quality ECEC provision, and the influence of a mother's educational level. These may need to be actively supported through everyday experts – such as having well-educated foster carers.

There is a further difficulty for many children in care in achieving educational success. This is the evidence from studies of brain trauma on children's development. Cairns (2013, pp.149–150) argues that 'horrific events in our environment produce an intense stress response in us…known as traumatic stress.' The 'levels of stress hormones produced are toxic' so 'we are poisoned by our own physiological survival response' with the effect of altering physical, psychological and social ways of functioning. Trauma may derive from separation from parents in early infancy or from abuse and neglect, the effects of which may be exacerbated if the abuse goes on for a long period of time or takes multiple forms. Without effective treatment, the effects of trauma can be considerable and act as barriers to learning, including impairments to language, memory and behaviour. Children with traumatic stress may be hyper-vigilant, perpetually scanning the environment for threats or jumping at every sound. They may have altered perceptions and find it hard to focus on tasks such as reading or listening. They may have poor physical coordination and poor self-image, or an elevated sense of numbness, making them at risk of injury or self-harming. They may be emotionally unresponsive or under-appreciative of the aesthetic or natural world around them. They find it hard to be in group situations as other people can be perceived as threatening, and can have difficulties constructing meaning (Cairns 2013).

For children who have suffered trauma to recover, their condition needs to be stabilised through being in a safe place with secure attachments to trusted people, they need to integrate or make sense of their experience of distress and trauma through communication of some kind, and then they need to adapt or reintegrate and 'experience the joy and delight' of being able to participate in families and society again. Successful treatment requires a multi-disciplinary approach involving 'safety, stabilisation, therapy, secure social attachments and the possibility of joy' in which all of these elements must be present (Cairns 2013, p.155).

To summarise, there are around 70,000 children looked after in England on any one day and 16,000 in Scotland, (including those supervised at home)the majority of whom will have been abused or neglected and come from family backgrounds characterised by material and educational disadvantage. They are likely not to have educational role models in their families or to have parental involvement in their early education. Their early education is unlikely to compensate for their material disadvantage.

Furthermore, they are likely to be identified as having special educational needs for behavioural reasons, and mental disorders, although there is a good chance they have cognitive abilities within the normal range. Educational progress is likely be hampered by the effects of traumatic stress caused by early neglect and abuse.

What this book will do

Chapter 2 sets out the legislative context for the education of children in care and leaving care in the four nations of the UK, with a particular focus on England and Scotland. We then turn to the two central themes of the book: learning placements and caring schools. Taking our cue from the experience of one young woman with a typical pattern of fragmented care and a determination, often thwarted, about education, Chapters 3–6 explore ways in which learning can be embedded in care placements and informal learning opportunities. Chapters 7–11 discuss how we might support young people through educational phases including early childhood education and care (Chapter 7), primary schools and the transition to secondary schools (Chapter 8), alternative provision (Chapter 9), upper secondary (Chapter 10) and higher education (Chapter 11). Chapter 12 gives space to the particular circumstances of young people who arrive in the UK as unaccompanied asylum seekers. Finally, Chapter 13 brings the book to a close and provides some recommendations for developing local and national strategy. In each chapter, we provide key points, theory and evidence, case examples from national and international sources, and some points for practice alongside resources for further reading.

Useful resources

+ Infed.org is a website about informal education, learning and community. It hosts profiles of influential thinkers in the field. Maintained by Mark Smith at George Williams College, London, it specialises in the theory and practice of informal education, social pedagogy, lifelong learning, social action, and community learning and development.

+ Human Scale Education (www.hse.org.uk) works with schools and parents to promote human scale learning environments where children and young people are known and valued as individuals. The website hosts publications and debates and seeks to generate a network of human scale educators.

+ Thempra (thempra.org) or 'theory meets practice' is a website forum for social pedagogy in the UK. It has a wealth of resources including academic papers and personal/professional testimonies, and acts as a noticeboard for the Social Pedagogy Development Network's twice yearly meetings.

+ The Rees Centre for Research in Fostering and Education, University of Oxford, carries out research and publishes reports and literature reviews on all aspects of fostering, with special reference to education. http://reescentre.education. ox.ac.uk.

+ More information about the Scottish curriculum, including the system of qualifications, can be found on Education Scotland's Parentzone website www.educationscotland. gov.uk/Parentzone; and about Scotland's system of school assessment on www.scotland.gov.uk/Topics/Statistics/ Browse/School-Education/SSLN.

CHAPTER 2

Legislation Supporting the Education of Children in Care in the UK

Principles and Provisions

KEY POINTS

‣ Knowing the law is an important aspect of supporting the education of children in care and advocating for their rights.

‣ Local authorities have a statutory duty to promote the educational achievement of children they look after.

‣ Children in care are entitled to attend the best schools even when they are technically full.

‣ All schools must have a 'designated teacher' with special responsibility for looked after children.

‣ Every local authority in England must appoint a Virtual School Head to take strategic oversight of the education of looked after children as if they were attending a single school, with responsibility for improving their experience and outcomes.

Introduction

The education of children looked after away from home was largely ignored by legislators until almost the end of the twentieth century. Earlier research by one of the authors suggested that this was mainly due to the division between education and social services, with children in care making up too small a proportion of the school population to attract any attention, while social workers took little interest in children's school experience or attainment (Jackson 1987, 2000). This division is also found in other European countries (Jackson and Cameron 2014). Countries with an established profession of social pedagogy take a broader view of the purpose and scope of education than the UK, where 'education' tends to mean what goes on in school classrooms, but everywhere the educational performance of children in public care and the opportunities open to them lag far behind those of children growing up in their own families.

This chapter discusses the main statutory provisions and policy initiatives relating to the education of children in care and considers how far they contribute to improving their experience and raising attainment. If, as we argue throughout this book, education is integral to promoting the welfare of children and young people, as set out in the UNCRC, all legislation designed to promote the best interests of the child is potentially relevant, but unless there is a specific focus on their cognitive development and school experience these aspects are always in danger of getting lost.

In addition to the primary legislation there is a long list of statutory instruments and guidance issued since 1989. Most of these are concerned with the social care of children looked after away from home, but of course looked after children are also affected by law relating to the education of all children. We have chosen to focus on those elements which have the most direct impact on everyday experts and professionals responsible for their care and upbringing.

For some time after devolution of powers in 1999, legislation and guidance for looked after children in Wales, Scotland and Northern Ireland followed that in England albeit with important historical differences (Jackson and Sachdev 2001). There are now increasing signs of divergence, some of which are discussed in later chapters, but we have avoided going into too much detail here. One important innovation in England is the requirement for every local authority to appoint a Virtual School Head (VSH). There are signs that this could make a real difference to the educational experience of looked after children, so we include an account of the development of the role as a case study in this chapter.

Law relating to the education of children in care
The Children Act 1989

The Children Act 1989, which covers all aspects of the social care of children, still provides the basis for children's care away from home in England and Wales. The Scottish and Northern Ireland equivalents are the Children (NI) Order 1995, the Children Act (Scotland) 1995 and from 1 April 2015, the Children and Young People (Scotland) Act 2014. Legislation on children's social care since then technically takes the form of amendments to these Acts and all guidance refers back to them. There are five main statutes:

+ Children (Leaving Care) Act 2000

+ Adoption and Children Act 2002

+ Children Act 2004

+ Children and Young Persons Act 2008

+ Children and Families Act 2014.

The general principle that underlies all these statutes is that the educational experience and attainment of children in out-of-home care should be as close as possible to that of children growing up in their own families.

At the time the Children Act 1989 came into force there was little interest in the education of children in care. In relation to future employment, education may have seemed less important because of the economic conditions of the time. Britain was still a very class-based society and the intense concern for their children's education, characteristic of middle class parents even then, was only shared by a minority of working class families (Jackson and Marsden 1962; Jackson 2010a). There were still plenty of unskilled jobs in manufacturing requiring no educational qualifications (Archer *et al.* 2003). The lack of attention by social workers and policy makers to educational matters may be partly explained by their failure to adjust to the entirely different employment environment of the late twentieth century (Jackson 2010a). By contrast, the high proportion of care leavers aged 19 not in education, employment or training (NEET) is currently a matter of great concern to government and local authorities. Among care leavers in England aged 19, 20 and 21, 38 per cent were NEET in June 2014, compared with a figure of 16 per cent for all young people aged 19–24.

EDUCATION IN THE CHILDREN ACT 1989

Although the Children Act 1989 could be seen as a first step towards ending the neglect of education within the care system, it still does not give it much prominence (Jackson 2010b). Almost the only reference in the Act itself is the duty (s.1.3 (b)) to meet the physical, emotional and *educational* needs of looked after children. Nevertheless, this is the basis for all measures taken by local authorities to improve the educational experience and outcomes of children in care.

The principles underpinning the Act are set out in the official publication, *The Care of Children: Principles and Practice in Regulations and Guidance* (HMSO 1989). It states that 'the various departments of a local authority (e.g. health, housing, education and social services) should co-operate to provide an integrated service and range of resources *even when such co-operation is not specifically required by law*' (Principle no. 28 – emphasis added). The only other mention of education is in the acknowledgement that 'change of home, caregiver, social worker or school almost always carries some risk to a child's development and welfare' (17 op.cit). Evidence cited throughout this book underlines the truth of this statement, and the need for professionals to give much greater emphasis to stability for looked after children.

The Guidance which accompanied the implementation of the Children Act 1989 goes into more detail about what 'having regard' to education might mean, although only Volume 6 on *Children with Disabilities* devotes a whole chapter to 'Working with Education Services' (Department of Health 1991a). The other relevant volumes, Volume 3 *Family Placements* and Volume 4 *Residential Care*, give it less than two pages each (Department of Health 1991b, c).

Since 1999, local authorities have been required to submit annual returns on the number and proportion of children achieving various qualifications by the end of Year 11, then the end of compulsory schooling, and it was this that first quantified the enormous gap in attainment between looked after children and others. This data provided local authority children's departments and looked after children education services (LACES) teams with a clear target: raising the proportion of their looked after children who achieve at least five GCSE passes at grades A*–C, and enabling them to compare their performance with that of other similar authorities. However, there is still no detailed statistical information on post-16 participation and qualifications achieved and no targets for upper secondary education other than to reduce the proportion of looked after children who are NEET at age 19.

At the individual level, five GCSEs including English and maths (and the equivalent 'National' qualifications in Scotland – for more information about the new system of qualifications in Scotland, see www.sqa.org.uk) is a vitally important target for young people themselves, since it is the key to most training and employment opportunities as well as the entry level to school sixth forms. That is recognised in the requirement to avoid placement moves in school Years 10 and 11, the run-up to GCSE, but this aim is often not achieved. There is no rule that GCSEs must be taken at age 16, and there may often be strong arguments for young people who have had a turbulent time in care to take an extra year to improve their chances of success. In future, schools may be more prepared to be flexible in allowing repeat years and offering further tuition to pupils who miss their grades as those who do not pass English and maths GCSE with a C grade at age 16 will be required to continue to study those subjects.

OPENING UP POSSIBILITIES FOR FURTHER AND HIGHER EDUCATION

Children Act Guidance on the education of children in foster care (Chapter 2, paragraphs 2.33–2.39) begins with the important statement that 'Children who are looked after or accommodated have the same rights as all children to education, including further and higher education and to other opportunities for development' (Department of Health 1991a). The parallel Guidance on residential care (Department of Health 1991c) acknowledges that young people accommodated in children's homes can be especially disadvantaged educationally and advises that they should be given every opportunity to take full advantage of educational opportunities. It urges staff working in residential homes to recognise and applaud a young person's achievements and provide support and encouragement when he (*sic*) encounters disappointments. They should be alert to the possibility that the child may be bullied or discriminated against at school, should work closely with teachers, attend school social events and parents' evenings and report back to the young person. There should be appropriate quiet conditions for homework and access to reference books. The statement in the earlier volume quoted above about further and higher education is repeated even more emphatically:

> It is sometimes too readily accepted that further education is not appropriate for young people in homes. This belief needs to be countered forcefully. Young people who have the ability should be encouraged most strongly to continue their education beyond compulsory school age. Staff in homes need to emphasise the value of education… Every encouragement should be given to young people to undertake higher education when they have demonstrated ability to benefit from it. (Department of Health 1991a, para 1.112)

Unfortunately a report on children's homes by the social services inspectorate found that these admirable exhortations were very remote from the reality of life in a children's home at the time (SSI/Department of Health 1993). This report was important as it was the first official use of the term 'corporate parent', emphasising the duty of all local authority departments and employees to co-operate to further the interests of children who were unable to live with their own parents.

The corporate parent has proved to be a useful concept, taken up with particular enthusiasm in Scotland where it has been given statutory force, and many local authorities now have corporate parenting committees with lead (elected) members taking special responsibility for looked after children. However, a consumer survey noted that 'efforts made over the last 15 years to create a system based around the concept of corporate parenting do not appear to have been fully successful with regards to education' (Who Cares? Trust 2012, p.5). In particular, foster carers and social workers said they did not have enough information on education to help looked after young people and care leavers. Over half the professionals who took part in this survey had not received any training relating to education in the previous three years.

Educational legislation during the 1990s was in complete conflict with the Children Act 1989 and had the effect of locking large numbers of children out of school and denying them access to education, sometimes for as long as a year at a time (Blyth and Milner 1996). The Education Reform Act 1988 and the Education Act 1993 decisively shifted power away from the local education authority in favour of individual head teachers. This orientation meant it was even more difficult for local education authorities to pursue their special obligations towards looked after children in England and Wales, as head teachers could make their own decisions about allocation of school places (Benson 1996).

Some children were refused places because of fears, often unfounded, that they would be a disruptive influence in the classroom and interfere with the work of better motivated students (Fletcher-Campbell 1997). For the minority who did have real problems the answer was to expel them with little concern for the effect on their educational opportunities or future lives (Firth and Horrocks 1996; Brodie 2001). At best they would be allocated to Pupil Referral units, where they might get more sympathetic treatment but would be 'categorised out of normal education', and have no chance of acquiring useful qualifications (Tomlinson 1982; Poyser 2013). Changes of placements in the middle of school years often meant that places in desirable schools were all taken up, so looked after children tended to find themselves in schools where no one else wanted to go. For this reason, the requirement in the Education Act 2005 to give preference to looked after children even when the most suitable school was officially full represented a very important advance.

A BETTER EDUCATION FOR CHILDREN IN CARE

The Labour Government elected in 1997 immediately declared the intention of raising educational standards and improving opportunities for all children, and the following year that aspiration was extended explicitly to looked after children in the form of the Quality Protects initiative (Department of Health 1998). Frank Dobson, then Secretary of State for Health, wrote to every local authority elected member in England and Wales emphasising that the most important thing they could do for children in their care was to give them a good education. New money (£885 million) was allocated to local authorities to improve the care of looked after children. Disappointingly, later research found that only a very small proportion of these funds was used for educational purposes (Berridge *et al.* 2008). Quality Protects, like the Children Act Guidance, explicitly linked educational attainment and future life chances, on which the British Cohort Studies provide conclusive evidence (Feinstein and Brassett-Grundy 2005; Jackson 2007).

This was why the government went on to commission an inquiry into the education of children in care by the Social Exclusion Unit (Social Exclusion Unit 2003). All schools now collect very detailed statistics on the progress of their pupils at different Key Stages, and carers should have no inhibitions about asking to see how their foster children are performing compared with others at the same stage. They are then in a good position to ask for additional resources, such as one-to-one tutoring, a laptop computer or a home broadband connection.

JOINING FORCES

Some provisions which remain part of standard practice were introduced by the first-ever joint Guidance issued in 2000 by the Department of Health (then the department mainly responsible for looked after children) and the Department for Education and Skills (DfES), with some of the provisions having statutory force (DH Circular LAC (2000) 13).The Circular was prefaced with the inspiring statement: 'Children in public care are our children. We hold their future in our hands and education is the key to that future.'

The Guidance introduced several important practical steps towards the aim of promoting good corporate parenting. These included the requirement to:

♦ provide every child in care with a Personal Education Plan (PEP) to be reviewed six-monthly

♦ appoint a teacher to act as a resource and advocate for children and young people in care (the 'designated teacher')

♦   secure a full–time, mainstream education placement within 20 school days of a change of placement.

Children (Leaving Care) Act (CLCA)2000

The CLCA 2000 gave legislative force to the aspiration in the Children Act 1989 Guidance for young people in care to continue their education beyond compulsory school age. It addressed many of the serious problems experienced by young people in transition from care to independence which had been identified by leaving care researchers since the 1980s (Broad 1998; Stein 2002). It resulted in the establishment of leaving care teams in almost all local authorities. Local authorities were obliged to provide financial support and vacation accommodation to eligible young people who wanted to go to college or university, whereas previously this had been done on an ad hoc basis so that prospective students were deterred from applying to university because they did not know how they would be able to support themselves. Even those who were offered places often failed to take them up for the same reason (Jackson *et al.* 2003). Those students who started their courses before the CLCA was implemented were four times more likely to leave prematurely than those who could claim local authority support as a legal entitlement (Jackson *et al.* 2005).

More policy initiatives

The Social Exclusion Unit Report, *A Better Education for Children in Care* (Social Exclusion Unit 2003) was published at the same time as the Green Paper *Every Child Matters* (DfES 2003), which set out five desirable outcomes for all children, two of which, 'enjoy and achieve' and 'achieve economic wellbeing', are clearly related to education. *Every Child Matters* (ECM) aimed to join up education, health, care and upbringing for all children, while recognising the particular needs of children in care.

The SEU Report set a revised Public Service Agreement (PSA) target 'substantially narrowing the gap between the educational attainment and participation of children in care and that of their peers by 2006'. This is still far from being achieved at the time of writing; and due to success in raising standards generally, until

2012 the gap in attainment actually widened, and there are wide variations in participation in post-compulsory education across local authorities (Hauari *et al.* 2010).

Prioritising education in the Children Act 2004

Evidence which showed the enormous costs incurred by the failure to educate children in care (Social Exclusion Unit 2003; Jackson *et al.* 2002; Jackson and Simon 2006) produced decisive government action. The Children Act 2004 (s.52) amended the Children Act 1989 s.22(3)(a) and for the first time placed a duty on local authorities to promote the educational achievement of looked after children (as opposed to 'having regard to their education'). The Statutory Guidance issued by the Department for Education and Skills stated:

> Local authorities as (their) 'corporate parents' should demonstrate the strongest commitment to helping every child they look after, wherever the child is placed, to achieve the highest educational standards he or she possibly can. This includes supporting their aspirations to achieve in further and higher education. (DfES 2005)

A fundamental change introduced by the 2004 Act was the joining up of education and care services in a single Department under a Director of Children's Services at the most senior level of the local authority, designed to overcome the divisions noted as preventing thinking about education within 'care' services and vice versa.

The education of looked after children rose still further up the policy agenda with the Green Paper, *Care Matters: Transforming the Lives of Children and Young People in Care* (DfES 2006), followed, after consultation, by the White Paper, *Care Matters: Time for Change* (DCSF 2007), which underpinned the Children and Young Persons Act 2008. The *Care Matters* papers carry forward the principles of the 1989 Act in their emphasis on the local authority's duty to support the education of looked after children as a good (and well-informed) parent would.

A range of ideas for improvement were put forward. Some were directly related to education; others, such as the right to remain in foster care beyond 18, had an important indirect impact, particularly on opportunities to continue in further or higher education. One of the most successful ideas was that local authorities should appoint a senior officer to take strategic responsibility for the education of all children and young people looked after in their area as if they were attending the same school, as described below.

The Virtual School Head for looked after children

The VSH is a local authority officer with responsibility for overseeing a coordinated system of support for looked after children and improving their educational achievements. Looked after children attend a range of local schools but the role of the VSH is to improve educational standards and access to educational provision as if they were in a single school – hence a 'virtual school', with a head teacher like any other school. The virtual school is not a 'teaching' institution but a model whereby authorities can provide services and support and hold to account those providing the services. The responsibilities of the post extend to pupils in care placed outside their home authority, as well as those looked after by another council but educated in the VSH authority. This is important because these children tend to get an inadequate service from both authorities.

The VSH was piloted in 11 local authorities and evaluated (Berridge *et al.* 2008). The findings were very positive. The existence of the role greatly increased the visibility of looked after children within corporate governance and in schools. In many areas there were measurable improvements in school attendance, reduced exclusions and better GCSE results, and much closer working relationships between different services. The VSHs also took on many other useful functions, such as training for designated teachers and foster carers. They arranged for collection of comparative statistics to see which schools did the best job of educating children in care in relation to attendance, exclusions and attainment and identifying where problems existed at school level.

A critical factor was found to be the level of seniority of the person appointed. They needed to be former head teachers or deputy heads, usually in secondary schools, who could relate to other senior staff in schools and to Directors of Children's Services and other council officers on a basis of equality.

A later report by Ofsted confirmed that the VSH was not only a very effective advocate for individual looked after children, but took an overview of their educational needs as the head of a multi-professional team (Ofsted 2012). Most authorities appointed VSHs who went on to form a strong, mutually supportive network (Parker and Gorman 2013) and the All-Party Parliamentary inquiry into the educational attainment of looked after children, *Education Matters in Care*, recommended that the appointment of a VSH should be a statutory requirement for every local authority (APPG 2012), which is now inscribed in law.

In many areas the virtual school and the LACES team have combined into one organisation under the leadership of the VSH. The VSH retains the strategic role but it is informed by the work of the educational support workers. Virtual schools are extending their previous remit to cover a wider age range, to include pre-school children and further and higher education. The VSH is also important symbolically as the champion for looked after children at the authority level, just as the designated teacher is at school level.

The Children and Young Persons Act (CYPA) 2008

The CYPA 2008 made it a statutory requirement for every maintained school in England to appoint a designated teacher (first proposed in the Joint Guidance issued in 2000) with special responsibility for supporting the education of any looked after child attending the school.[1] In primary schools this is usually the head teacher and in secondary schools a senior teacher. There is limited research on the effectiveness of this role, and it seems to depend how seriously it is taken. There is a danger that, if insufficient time is dedicated to the role, the teacher may not have enough time to become familiar with the care system and to understand the kinds of stresses it creates for pupils (Parker and Gorman 2013) or the impact of attending school on children in a state of distress. Another problem is if the person appointed does not have sufficient seniority in the school to act as an effective advocate or propose changes in policy or practice. However, when the role works well, the designated teacher is an important ally for carers and social workers. He or she is supposed to act as a 'champion' for the young person and help to sort out any problems. The CYPA 2008 includes several other provisions relevant to the

---

1   In Scotland, the role is 'designated manager', emphasising the seniority of the post.

education of looked after children. Followed by the Care Planning, Placement and Case Review (England) Regulations (DfE 2010), it strengthens the legal requirements for the support to be provided to 'relevant' young people. Sixteen- and seventeen-year-olds must have a pathway plan and a personal advisor; and 'formerly relevant' young people, that is, those over 18 who continue in education and training, are entitled to financial assistance, accommodation and a personal advisor up to the age of 25 (up from 21). (This was an amendment to the Children Act 1989 section 23C.)

Although the idea of pathway planning is well-intentioned, some young people have complained that starting to talk about leaving care at the age of 15 or 16 is very unsettling and anxiety-provoking at a time when their classmates are focused on working for their GCSE exams. As with the PEP, reviewing the plan can be treated as a routine bureaucratic chore or a real opportunity to sit down with a young man or woman and help them to think constructively about their future. The VSH research found that it was essential for a person with educational expertise to attend PEP and pathway planning meetings, along with the young person and their carer if he or she wishes. In some areas the virtual school has taken on the task of chairing PEPs; this task is supposed to be done by the child's social worker, but social workers often feel they do not know enough about the education system to be able to undertake the role effectively (Berridge *et al.* 2008).

National Minimum Standards for Foster Care 2011

Three-quarters of those in care are looked after in foster families, so these regulations, issued under section 23 of the Care Standards Act 2000 with statutory force, are very important and are used by Ofsted as criteria for its inspections. They are basically addressed to providers of fostering services, either local authorities or independent agencies. The second item in the opening statement of values states:

> Children should have an enjoyable childhood, benefiting from excellent parenting and education, enjoying a wide range of opportunities to develop their talents and skills leading to a successful adult life.

Standards 7 and 8 together describe what might be called a learning placement. Children, including pre-school and 'older' children, 'have a foster home which promotes a learning environment and supports their development' (p.20). They have access to educational resources and opportunities beyond the school day to engage in activities which promote learning. They are supported to attend school, or alternative provision, regularly. The foster carer works with the child's 'education provider' to maximise achievement. The fostering service has a written education policy that promotes and values children's education.

Children are supported to take part in 'school based and out-of-school activities' (7.1). Children should be able to pursue individual interests and hobbies and take part in leisure activities and trips and overnight stays in friends' houses. The regulations respond to past criticisms that over-rigid rules prevented children in care from enjoying these ordinary childhood experiences and give foster carers more freedom than in the past to use their own judgement to make decisions on these matters.

Foster carers maintain regular contact with the school, attend all parents' meetings and advocate for the child where appropriate (8.6). They should also have up-to-date information about each child's educational progress and school attendance record.

Standard 12, about moving to adulthood, includes supporting children to prepare for the world of work or further and/or higher education (12.1 c.) and includes requiring the fostering service to have policy and practical arrangements which enable children (*sic*) to remain with foster carers into legal adulthood, that is, after age 18, if they need more time 'to develop appropriate life skills'. However, it does not mention education in this regard.

Standard 13 on recruiting and assessing foster carers 'who can meet the needs of looked after children' makes no mention of any educational standard. Standard 20 does require the fostering service to provide training and for foster carers to have personal development plans which set out how they will be supported to undertake ongoing training 'appropriate to their development needs and experience'.

Standard 21 states that foster carers should receive the support and supervision they need in order to care properly for children placed with them. The social worker should provide assistance in dealing with relevant services, such as health and education.

The preamble to these standards emphasises that they are a minimum and that 'many providers will aspire to exceed these standards and develop their service to achieve excellence' (Ofsted 2011, p.4). It is still very concerning that foster carers do not need any qualifications at all, not even basic literacy and numeracy, and it is uncertain how far 'training' would enable them to provide an educationally rich environment as envisaged in Standard 8 if they have a very low level of education themselves.

We know that the educational attainment of all children is very strongly influenced by the educational level of their parents and the interest and encouragement they receive from home, and there is evidence that this is equally true of those in foster care (Bentley 2013). The main reason advanced for not setting any educational standards for the recruitment of foster carers is that it would reduce the supply of carers. In that case, fostering agencies would need to offer better terms and seek to access a wider pool of potential foster carers (Sinclair 2008). If that resulted in better educational outcomes for children, it would be a very good investment (Jackson and Simon 2006).

Children and Families Act (CFA) 2014

This very important Act provides young people with the option to remain in their foster homes with financial assistance to their former foster carers up to the age of 21 if all those concerned wish it (Children and Families Act 2014 s.98). This is likely to be helpful to them emotionally and should finally end the practice of suddenly cutting off funding for foster placements on the young person's eighteenth birthday, often in the middle of their A-level or BTEC course, with disastrous effects (Jackson and Ajayi 2007; and see Chapter 11).

The call for this right to be extended to those living in residential care homes was resisted by the then Secretary of State, Michael Gove, on the grounds that the quality of children's homes was not good enough. This seemed strange reasoning since the quality of children's homes was ultimately his responsibility, and has been strongly criticised by user groups and by the House of Commons Education Committee (2014).

The CFA 2014 also puts on a statutory basis the appointment of a Virtual School Head in every local authority. It is notable that this is one of only five such obligatory appointments. The intention is that the role should be at a senior level with direct access to the Director of Children's Services and the lead member for looked after children or corporate parenting. It is not yet clear how far councils will respect this requirement as they are increasingly subject to financial pressure and the need to make cuts. There are anecdotal reports of reduced staffing and demands for the VSH to take on additional responsibilities, work part-time or spend more time on individual casework as opposed to focusing on the strategic aspects of the role. Concerns about this were already expressed in the 2012 Ofsted Report.

The new statutory guidance for local authorities in England issued in July 2014 does not include the emphasis on the seniority of the role which both the evaluation of the pilot VSHs (Berridge *et al.* 2008) and the Ofsted Report (2012) considered essential. Also, exclusion, described under the previous government as the 'absolute last resort', is now 'just to be avoided as far as possible'.

In Scotland the Children and Young People (Scotland) Act 2014, came into force during 2015. It implements many of the recommendations based on the GIRFEC policy initiative (Getting It Right for Every Child 2008). The Act lays strong emphasis on children's rights under the UN Convention, including their right to education. It extends the powers of Scotland's Commissioner for Children and Young People to investigate individual cases. It stresses the local authority's duties as a corporate parent and extends the age to which care leavers can ask to receive support from their local authority to 26. It also includes measures designed to increase the number of adoptions from care and strengthens the support available to kinship carers, including support for education. Some of the provisions go beyond those in the English Act. For example, every child is entitled to a 'named person' as a resource from 0 to 18 years. Children looked after either in foster or residential care have a right to stay to age 21 if they wish. This represents a big change from the Commissioner for Children's report in 2008 which found that large numbers of Scottish children were still leaving care at 15 or 16 to live in very unsatisfactory accommodation with no concern for their further education (Scotland's Commission for Children and Young People 2008).

One further piece of legislation worth mentioning is the Legal Aid, Sentencing and Punishment of Offenders Act 2012 (LASPO) which amended the law to give all children remanded to youth detention centres and young offenders'institutions in England looked after status. This is important because many of them will previously have been in care (estimates vary between 30 and 50 per cent) and it means that the local authority will retain some responsibility for their wellbeing, both during and after their sentence. Taylor (2006), in a study of young people in care and criminal behaviour, found that being in custody, however undesirable, enabled many of her interviewees to engage with education for the first time, often because it was their first experience of stability and order. For Ben Ashcroft (2013), the education he received at a young offenders' institution after 51 moves in care completely changed his life trajectory.

Concluding thoughts

Great legislative strides have been made to recognise and address the education of children in care. However, education policy since the advent of the coalition government (2010–15) has begun to work in the opposite direction. The Every Child Matters agenda was sidelined, if not abolished, although the principle of requiring basic school-leaving qualifications to achieve economic wellbeing remains. The introduction of a Pupil Premium with specific funding for looked after children, managed by the Virtual School Head, ensures that there is some ring-fenced resource, but it is highly targeted on a narrow definition of improving educational performance.

Perhaps most difficult is the emphasis on the conversion of schools, and new schools, to academies and under great pressure to keep or improve their position in league tables, thus creating a fiercely competitive climate. Some head teachers see looked after children as a liability, with potential to undermine the school's average public examination scores. Guidance on Schools Admissions in July 2014 states that looked after children should be enrolled in schools assessed as good or outstanding by Ofsted. Carers and social workers may have to be very assertive to obtain a place in the best school for their looked after child, especially at a time when all places have already been allocated, seeking help from the Virtual School Head if necessary.

Overall, since 1997, education for children in care has received much greater attention from government both in England and Scotland, with several major policy initiatives focusing on the need to raise the attainment closer to that of their contemporaries not in care. Some of the fundamental weaknesses of the education and care systems for children looked after away from home have been addressed, providing a stronger legislative and regulatory basis for educational achievement and progression. The requirement for all young people to be in education or training up to the age of 18 will encourage social workers and carers to take a longer view and extend their opportunities.

The most significant legislative achievements are that: the care and education gulf has been bridged in the introduction of Departments of Children's Services with Directors at the most senior level; the corporate parent local authority is required to promote the attainment of all children they look after; and there are now specific champions of young people who are looked after in the education system, at the level of practice and strategy, in the form of designated teachers and Virtual School Heads. These actions are supported by extending the period of foster care beyond the age of 18 years. The Children and Young People (Scotland) Act 2014 takes a different tack, but displays a very strong commitment to improve educational outcomes and offer support for longer. The framework is in place in both countries to overcome the obstacles that have so long stood in the way of enabling children in care to achieve their educational potential. The following chapters discuss the practical measures that need to be taken to bring this about.

Practice points

- ♦ For carers and social workers, be aware of the legal entitlements of looked after children and be prepared to defend their rights.

- ♦ For foster carers and residential workers, arrange a meeting with the designated teacher as soon as possible after a child is allocated a school place. Give enough information about the child to engage the teacher's personal interest and sympathy.

- For everyday experts, find out how the school is spending the Pupil Premium and be prepared to ask for anything you think would be a useful contribution to the education and upbringing of the children you look after.

- Know the name and contact details of the Virtual School Head. The VSH is the person who has the power to challenge a school's interpretation of the admissions code or avert a threatened exclusion.

- For foster carers and social workers, you have a right to training on educational matters and should complain to the VSH if it is not provided.

- The Who Cares? Trust is an organisation that supports and campaigns for children in care and care leavers. It publishes a magazine for teenagers and Who Cares? Junior for 6-12 year olds. www.thewhocarestrust.org.uk

- Coram Children's Legal Centre, the leading children's legal charity, provides free legal information, advice and representation to children and young people, their families, carers and professionals. www.childrenslegalcentre.com

- All four nations of the UK have Commissioners for Children and Young People which have websites and Freephone numbers for children. They have a particular duty to provide advice and assistance to children living away from home or receiving social care, as set out (for England) in the Children and Families Act 2014.

CHAPTER 3

An Educational Journey
Children in Care in Context

The aim of this chapter is to explore, drawing on a range of sources, the characteristics of the education of children in care in the UK. We introduce the reader to Donna, and her educational journey, before examining the ways in which specific interventions may help children with similar characteristics.

KEY POINTS

- A commitment to and enjoyment of school can be strong even if parents and/or carers can only offer limited support.

- Children in care begin to lose ground in academic subjects compared with their age peers early in life and the gap widens as they get older.

- Young people in care often lose their way around the upper secondary phase, with multiple competing demands in their lives.

- Children in care are more likely to have special educational needs or mental health problems, which may lead to them being suspended or excluded from school and set them on a downward spiral. Schools need to find ways of enabling them to experience success and build their self-esteem and sense of competence.

> ▸ Effective education for children in care, as for other 'vulnerable' groups, shares many features found in 'good' schools: visionary leadership, high expectations, a culture of collaboration with parents and professionals, and enjoyment of educational opportunities.

Introduction to Donna

It is a common perception that children in care fail in education, but in fact many show considerable interest and sustain a commitment to education over time. By having a nuanced understanding of children in care as a group with diverse characteristics, it is possible to see how better to support them.

Donna was a participant in the aforementioned YiPPEE study. She was 22 when first interviewed, and had had a childhood in and out of the care of her mother and various foster carers under the auspices of the local authority. She was one of a number of young people in the study who had shown a capability to study to higher educational levels but had faced various difficulties along the way. Through the detailed portrait of her, and the following section showing how her experience and perspective relates to the position in national statistics, we illustrate an educational journey through care that was not untypical in the YiPPEE data.

Case study: Donna, age 22

Donna was first taken into foster care at the age of one year. Soon after she was born, her mother developed a relationship with a new partner and had another child by him. She no longer felt that she wanted Donna around and requested that Social Services take her into care. After a short time she was returned to her mother but was then taken back into care at age six when her mother suffered a mental breakdown as the result of a violent incident with a neighbour. Following a second return home, Donna reported a long history of neglect and of being singled out by her mother for different treatment from her two half-siblings. Donna felt that she was the 'odd one out' in the family and was made to feel isolated and excluded. The relationship between Donna and her mother continued to worsen until Donna requested to be taken into care again at age 15.

Donna's father moved to America very shortly after she was born and although she didn't have a particularly close relationship with him, she visited him once a year. When she was 12 he was diagnosed with cancer and he died when she was 19. Donna said that towards the end of his life her father would phone her nearly every day. He encouraged her to remain in school after 16 and to go on to further education rather than go straight into a job. In contrast, Donna's mother was very unsupportive of her education and wanted her to enter any form of employment rather than continue studying. Donna spoke about the importance of school as a place of escape from her life at home and because of this had a consistently good attendance record. Despite her chaotic home life and care history, Donna's schooling remained stable; she attended just one primary and one secondary school and went on to achieve five GCSEs with good grades.

At the age of 16 Donna was asked to leave her foster placement due to her difficult behaviour, which she attributed to being over-indulged by her foster carers. She was moved to another foster placement where she remained for three months before being placed in a shared house at the age of 17. At this point Donna's lifestyle descended into heavy alcohol use and drug experimentation, which caused her to drop out of her course at college. Donna spent a number of years attempting various further education courses but repeatedly gave up before completing them. She moved into supported accommodation at the age of 20 and then to a Housing Association flat where she was living at the time of her first interview.

When we first met her, Donna was halfway through a National Diploma in Dance which she was determined to complete despite having become pregnant as the result of a short-lived and abusive relationship. She had finally discovered what she really wanted to do thanks to the continuing belief and encouragement of the teacher in her leaving care team; he had never given up on her and provided uncritical, practical support through all her false starts. Despite the unplanned pregnancy, she continued on her dance course and successfully passed the first year assessment a few days before giving birth. She had some support from her mother, but wanted nothing to do with the baby's father and very rarely saw her sister.

However, by the second interview, around a year later, Donna was living in good quality privately rented accommodation and greatly enjoying her baby. Her mother was visiting regularly, although the relationship was still strained. Donna had made clear plans to continue on the second year of her Diploma, by obtaining letters of support from her tutors; she had arranged childcare which would be paid for by the leaving care team, and she was determined to complete the course even though she recognised that a career as a performer was no longer possible. She said she was prepared to do any kind of job as her top priority was to support her child but she might later take a qualification in social care.

An educational journey in care

In her account, Donna had two episodes of public care as a young child but did not go to school regularly until she was nine years old, as before that her mother did not regard school attendance as a matter of any importance. She said:

> 'I didn't really start school properly until the end of Year 4, start of Year 5 because previous to that I'd lived with my mother and she never made me go to school. So it was kind of, if we got up and strolled to school we went, if we didn't it wasn't a problem.'

Donna said she felt 'out of place' after her mother acquired a new partner and had two children with him. She said:

> 'But then me and my Mum never really had a very good relationship and my Mum didn't really get along with me very well because of my Dad. My Mum basically was still in love with my sister's Dad 'cos they had a son and daughter together and like they were quite happy and I was the odd one out.'

This feeling of being out of place or the odd one out was also reported by young people participating in the YiPPEE study in other countries, and was particularly highlighted in Sweden (Johansson and Höjer 2014). For Donna, emotional neglect extended from everyday food to school attendance. Her mother did not support her education and when she visited school antagonised the teachers by shouting at them:

> 'Oh, no, well she didn't even talk to me. She wasn't even interested in if I was eating. I don't even think she knew I went to school. She was banned from parents' evenings. She came in Year 7 when I was 11 and she got into a bit of an argument I think. I can't really remember but it was something to do with a disagreement.

Like a teacher had said that I was disruptive and my Mum like disagreed. And then she came to a parents' evening in Year 8 and she didn't, she just didn't pay any attention and stuff and was quite rude to most of my teachers so they asked her not to come back ever again.'

Although Donna's father lived in North America, he kept in touch and encouraged her to stay in school.

School was a haven for Donna as it represented security and predictability:

'I literally went to school to be like in that familiar place to me. Like I had the same friends, the same teachers, it was the same lunch... I reckon if I would've gone to jail I would've felt that same as well, just because it's like...it's weird not having anything in your life that's normal apart from one thing and it just happened to be school.'

School offered the opportunity to be good at something in the context of a home life where she did not feel she was valued. She recalls being 'quite good at school' and attending a 'really good school, you had to pass an entrance exam to get in, and I got in'.

At the age of 15, Donna entered foster care, and was fortunate in that it did not cause her to change secondary schools. She achieved what is now called 'the basics' of five grade A*–C GCSEs. From this age on, she had a number of placements, she spent a lot of time and money on drugs and alcohol, and she felt her energy was sapped by coping with the legal and emotional aftermath of her father's death. Looking back, she reflected that at this time in her life, 'I didn't really care about my education; I didn't really care about college or anything like that.' She attempted A-levels three times:

'I did it three times and quit three times...because every single time I started a course I'd get halfway through and then I'd quit 'cos I was lazy even though I really enjoyed it. I spent too much time partying and got tired and didn't want to go to college the next day and stuff like that.'

Living independently as she did, she had no one to get her up in the mornings for college. Her leaving care worker provided patient and consistent support and eventually she enrolled in a National Diploma in Dance and completed the first year. But after the birth of her child she said:

> 'I don't want to go any further with dance. My next plan is to get a part-time job, learn to drive and get a car. The job I'd like to get would be in some kind of social care, some facility that helps people, for example with mental health problems... The only job I've ever enjoyed was interviewing young people about work along with social services staff. I might go back and do NVQ level 3.'

She paid tribute to the support of the teacher attached to her leaving care team:

> 'He was the one that got me into dance classes and dance college. He helped me get funding for private lessons for an audition. He helps with everything really, he's more than a teacher... It's good that I've got him really.'

This journey, through early neglect and separation from birth family, feeling left out in the family and having a series of foster and supported living placements in late teenage years, is relatively common for children in care. Donna lost her way for some years but by the second interview, when she was 23, and had become a mother, she was getting to a more settled point in her life. Delay in acquiring further education qualifications and finding the right course or occupation to pursue is very common among young people from a public care background (see Chapter 10). There is an argument that Donna effectively left the upbringing orbit of a foster 'home' for the independence and responsibilities of a shared 'house' too early for educational support to have an impact. In her account, what helped Donna both achieve and return to education was remaining in the same school during the compulsory phase and finding that she enjoyed it, and above all the unstinting support of her leaving care worker during the more chaotic upper secondary education phase of her life.

Situating Donna's story in the evidence about improving educational achievement

Here we situate Donna's experience in the context of data about the academic performance of children in care in England, and research and practice evidence about what supports the education of children at various ages. Studies that focus on children in care are relatively rare, so we have turned to studies that involved 'vulnerable' groups, which included children who share many characteristics with children in care (Kendall *et al.* 2008). We have divided this section into educational phases, but the first phase, the pre-school years, is discussed separately in Chapter 7.

The primary years

Nearly all children (around 98 per cent in England and 96 per cent in Scotland) are attending some form of formal educational setting by the age of four, nearly all of them in reception classes in primary schools (England) or a mixture of centre-based nursery care and schools (Scotland), before the compulsory school age of five. During this year an assessment is made of children's learning and development, which in England is called an Early Years Foundation Stage profile. No information is available about how many children in care attend educational settings at age four and so have such profiles. What is clear is that by age seven children in care in England are not achieving as well as their peers not in care. At the end of Key Stage 1, aged seven, and after three (or more) years of education, children in care are likely to be 20 percentage points behind their peers not in care in teacher assessments of reading, writing and mathematics.

Table 3.1 Percentages of children in care and not in care attaining expected levels of attainment in reading, writing and maths at Key Stage 1 (England)

2013 % achieving expected level	Children in care	Children not in care	Attainment gap
Reading	69	89	20
Writing	61	85	24
Maths	71	91	20

Source: DfE (2013a)

At the age of seven, Donna was not even in school. She was living with her mother, whose priorities were elsewhere. However, the Effective Provision of Pre-School Education (EPPE) studies show that the home learning environment is very important at this age. Home learning environment was more important for intellectual and social development than parental occupation, education or income (Sylva *et al.* 2004). This means there is much parents can do to support education, and much that foster carers can do too, regardless of socio-economic status. In the EPPE study, features of the home learning environment that supported education included activities such as: teaching the alphabet; playing with letters and numbers; library visits; reading to the child; and teaching the child songs or nursery rhymes. The influence of a high-level learning environment continued to be evident in intellectual gains at the end of Key Stage 1 (age 7).

Specific literacy interventions can be an important means of accelerating progress among those with literacy difficulties (Brooks 2002). An example is 'Reading Recovery' where participants (aged six to seven years) doubled their reading progress by the end of the programme compared with a control group. It was found that the children whose reading skills had been in the bottom ten per cent when they joined the programme were still reading better than their opposite numbers in the control group at age ten (Sutton *et al.* 2004). There was a particular impact on the standard of boys' reading and writing skills at Key Stages 2 and 4. However, the gap between boys and girls was not narrowed as both benefited equally from the strategies to improve the attainment of the boys (Younger *et al.* 2005).

Nurture groups can also be effective in enabling pupils starting primary school with emotional and behavioural difficulties or at risk of educational failure to become integrated into mainstream classes without additional support (O'Connor and Colwell 2002; Goldschmied and Jackson 2004; Pugh and Statham 2006). Nurture groups are based on principles of non-judgemental responses to children, with dedicated staff focused on building trusting relationships with children and a specific space within a school to provide a secure base. They promote reciprocity in relationships between adults and children characterised by active listening and responding, helping children to verbalise feelings, trying to understand what children are communicating through their behaviour, and careful management of transitions (White, n.d.). The emphasis, in nurture groups, given to relationships and the links between emotional wellbeing and learning share an understanding with the broad definition of education discussed in Chapter 1.

Between the ages of seven and eleven the gap in attainment in English and maths begins to widen for children in care, to upwards of 25 percentage points (Table 3.2). Why this might be the case is not known. It may be that fundamental weaknesses in the children's understanding of mathematical concepts, dating from their earliest years, becomes critical at this age (Griffiths 2014). Another factor may be that foster family support may begin to weaken as the demands of homework reach the limits of foster carers' capabilities. A small research study by Brian Cairns and one of the authors found that some well-meaning carers might press children to do maths homework but if they were unable to help when the child got stuck, this would simply lead to conflict. Also, fostered children may be assumed to be non-problematic at this age and to fit in, so that no special help is provided. But, as Table 3.2 shows, the maths scores of children in care fall even further behind those not in care than their attainment in English.

Table 3.2 Percentages of children in care and not in care attaining expected levels of attainment in English and maths at Key Stage 2 (England)

2013 % achieving expected level 4+	Children in care	Children not in care	Attainment gap
English – reading test	63	86	23
Maths	59	85	26

Source: DfE (2013a)

Some studies have shown that educational attainment among specific groups can be supported through changing the environment, such as tailored interventions or whole school efforts, such as full service extended schools.

Strand (2010) pointed out that the educational achievement of black African children is generally higher than that of black Caribbean children in primary schools in England. This appears to relate to parental circumstances, such as poverty, educational qualifications and aspirations, rather than differences in the schools attended by children in each group. However, schools where children of African heritage prosper share many characteristics of good schools nationally: they have visionary leadership, good management, high quality teaching and learning, use performance data effectively, and manage behaviour in ways that promote children's motivation (Demie *et al.* 2006). In addition, these schools, according to evidence from a study of Lambeth schools (where more than 80 per cent of pupils are from black and minority ethnic groups), have high expectations of pupils, offer many within- and outside-school learning and enjoyment activities, and, crucially, they work in partnership with parents. African parents, who in Lambeth mostly come from Nigeria and Ghana, but also from across African countries, value education highly, and the schools were successful in finding ways to value the contribution of parents to children's upbringing (Demie *et al.* 2006). Successful schools for children of African heritage are offering a broad definition of education where enjoyment and participation in learning are to the fore.

The evaluation of a national pilot of intervention programmes designed to raise the achievement of children with English as an additional language (EAL) (Benton and White 2007) found that Key Stage 2 results, at age 11, improved in respect of attainment in English among those in pilot schools, probably as a result of intensive support from a consultant attached to each of the schools. But the improvement was equally good for non-EAL children, probably because of the wide reach of the programme. Teachers used the pilot programme materials to create new opportunities for all children, such as in speaking and listening, and use of targets to plan for language development (Benton and White 2007).

In keeping with the findings of Demie *et al.* (2006), full service extended schools (FSES), which offer a range of study support and family support services alongside school, improved children's attainment, especially among vulnerable groups. Particularly effective features of extended schools were where there was a culture of collaboration between agencies working in schools, where relationships with children on an individual or small group basis were fostered, and where there were opportunities to discuss pupils and reflect on their progress jointly. In an evaluation, the gap between those eligible for free school meals (FSM) and/or those with special educational needs (SEN) was smaller in FSES than other schools (Cummings *et al.* 2007). Again, this speaks to a broad idea of education as supporting children from vulnerable groups in all aspects of their lives.

For children in care, the role of relationships with teachers and other adults in school and the importance of forums for pupil participation in decision making is key. If teachers can get to know the perspectives of students through such methods, it helps to raise their awareness of the issues facing the young people and create the sense of a common endeavour in learning.

What seems particularly important for children in care in primary school is to sustain their learning over time, and to minimise changes of placement and school. The aspects of primary school that appear to make most difference to sustaining learning for vulnerable children, including those in care, are focusing on literacy, good behaviour and attendance, partnership with parents/carers, flexible class structures with additional support as needed, an engaging and active curriculum, and, critically, active help over the transition to secondary school. Such transitions have a positive impact on improved life chances (Wood and Caulier-Grice 2006).

Secondary education

Despite her disrupted childhood and late entry into regular schooling, Donna, with five good GCSEs, did better by the end of secondary school (Key Stage 4) than most children in care. Data collected by the English Department for Education records that of those young people who have been in care for 12 months or more at the end of Year 11, only 15 per cent have five GCSEs graded A*–C, which is generally set as the minimum benchmark for onward progression to (academic) upper secondary education. This is forty-three percentage points behind their peers not in care and represents a dramatic widening of the gap since the end of primary school (Table 3.3). Moreover, five GCSEs is a minimum: many young people take ten or more GCSEs and A* grades are common.

Table 3.3 Percentages of children in care and not in care attaining GCSEs (England)

2012 %	Children in care	Children not in care	Attainment gap
English and maths A*–C	16.1	58.8	42.7
5 or more GCSEs including English and maths A*–C	15.3	58	42.7
5 or more GCSEs	36.6	80.3	43.7

Source: DfE (2013a)

The effect of parental social class is marked at the GCSE stage, and parallels the attainment gap between those in care and not in care. Among the poorest one fifth of families, just 21 per cent of children achieve five good GCSEs, while among the richest fifth 75 per cent do so, making an attainment gap of 54 percentage points (Goodman and Gregg 2010). Although children in care usually have their origins in very socially and economically deprived families, only the examination results of young people who have been in care for at least 12 months are included in the data above, and these young people should, in theory, be living in families (or residential settings) which are less impoverished than their families of origin. Kirton's (2013, p.660) summary of foster carers' social class background is that they are a 'broadly representative population albeit with lower than average levels of educational qualification and household income.' The same could be said of residential care staff.

Goodman and Gregg point out that, among all children, the attainment gap between rich and poor increases less markedly in the secondary years, while the opposite is the case for young people in care, as we have shown. Nevertheless, Goodman and Gregg's (2010) analysis is useful in pointing out the importance of high expectations about further study for educational success at the GCSE stage. Young people whose parents and carers hope that they will go on to university have a goal to aim for and are likely to invest time and effort in study. Those who share family time such as meals and outings, in a household where quarrels are infrequent, and resources are devoted to supporting education, for example by paying for private tuition and providing computer access, are likely to do better in GCSEs. Individual characteristics associated with better GCSE results are that young people believe they can do well and that they are in control of events, in other words they have a sense of self-efficacy. Higher achievers find school worthwhile, expect to attend higher education, are not bullied and avoid 'risky' behaviours such as smoking, cannabis use, truancy and antisocial behaviour, which may lead to suspension and exclusion, cutting off educational opportunities.

Expectations can be effectively nurtured through school-based relationships such as those with mentors. Mentoring can be an effective means to overcome barriers to learning such as behaviour problems, especially if it begins early, in Year 7 (Kendall *et al.* 2005). Learning mentors were also associated with improvements in attainment at Key Stage 4 for particular groups of pupils, such as girls and Asian pupils (Kendall *et al.* 2005). We discuss mentoring in relation to children in care in Chapter 6.

Aside from the general characteristics of approach to learning and home environment, some specific interventions can be helpful in raising expectations and achievements during the secondary years. One example is In Care, In School (Parker and Gorman 2013). This project in south west England involved the production of ten short filmed sequences and accompanying materials of everyday scenarios about how it feels to be in school when you are in care. The films were based on the experiences of members of the In Care Council (a forum in each local authority designed to give voice to children in care, and to influence local policy and practice in relation to looked after children by providing them with a direct link to the Director of Children's Services and the Lead Member). Each film was designed to prompt discussion among the audience, and they were aimed at teacher trainees, teachers and other staff, in order to raise awareness about the particular life circumstances of children in care and the issues they face in going to school.

Initial evaluations showed that the involvement of young people in the construction of the materials, and in some cases their involvement in lessons in schools, had a very powerful and positive impact on their own sense of self as experts and on their self-esteem. Some school heads and teachers had expressed reservations, but the films and the issues raised had made a deep impression on the teacher trainees, suggesting a lasting awareness of the issues when the next generation of teachers take up their posts (Parker and Gorman 2013).

CHILDREN WITH SPECIAL EDUCATIONAL NEEDS

As noted in Chapter 1, children in care are much more likely than others to be designated as having special educational needs. In 2013, 28.5 per cent of children in care had a Statement of Special Educational Need (referred to as a Statement), and a further 39.3 per cent had a special educational need at School Action Plus level but no Statement, meaning that additional support would be required in school. Over half of these special educational needs were categorised as behavioural, social or emotional and a further twenty per cent were categorised as a moderate learning difficulty (DfE 2013a).

This is more than three times the level in the general population of young people, where about 20 per cent of children are identified as having special educational needs. There is a gap of 52 percentage points between children in care and not in care.

From 2014, there are new arrangements in England for arranging support for children with special educational needs. Now, children who are identified as having a Statement and young people over 16 with a learning difficulty will have an integrated assessment and a single Education, Health and Care Plan. In addition, funding for supporting children with special educational needs will come from school budgets. Schools have a duty to identify, assess and make special educational provision for all children with SEN and the local authority has a duty to set out what schools are expected to provide from their delegated budget. Schools can review the support they allocate to children with SEN and make changes in line with changing needs, but they cannot make changes in support because of changes in funding they receive (Council for Disabled Children 2014).

Closer examination of the examination results for children in care shows that nearly half of the children in care with special educational needs attained the expected school performance level at age 11 (46% English, 43% maths). Moreover, at age 16, 40 per cent attained five or more GCSE grades A*–C. Just 12 per cent obtained five or more GCSEs including English and maths. These proportions are similar to the attainments of the whole children-in-care group and may indicate that the designation of special needs has had a positive effect in terms of directing resources towards children in need of help. It also indicates that the issue for children in care is not necessarily specific learning disabilities so much as behavioural problems that act as a barrier to performance in school environments. A review of special needs provision (Ofsted 2010, p.5) asserted that 'as many as half of all pupils identified' for additional support (School Action) 'would not be identified as having special educational needs if schools focused on improving teaching and learning for all, with individual goals for improvement.' Thus, the identification of need is within a context of what is provided for all.

Among the general population, the Increased Flexibility for 14 to 16 Year Olds Programme (IFP), evaluated in 2006, enabled schools to establish effective working partnerships with institutions and external providers, with more frequent contact and formal mechanisms for sharing information. Students who were low attainers and those with special educational needs, at age 14, benefited from this programme in terms of their GCSE grades and the number of subjects studied at GCSE. These students were also more likely to continue into further education and training than their contemporaries not in the programme (Golden *et al.* 2006).

Given the high proportion of children in care among those designated as having special educational needs, the recommendations of the Ofsted review (2010) are particularly pertinent here. These were: (i) improving the quality of assessment; (ii) ensuring that additional support is effective; (iii) improving teaching and pastoral support early on; (iv) developing specialist provision and services strategically so that they are available to maintained and independent schools, academies and colleges; (v) simplifying legislation so that the system is clearer for parents, schools and other education and training providers; (vi) ensuring that schools do not identify pupils as having special educational needs when they simply need better teaching; and (vii) ensuring that accountability for those providing services focuses on the outcomes for the children and young people concerned.

THE MENTAL HEALTH OF CHILDREN IN CARE

All children in care in England are supposed to be assessed using the Strengths and Difficulties Questionnaire (SDQ) to ascertain their mental health status. Mental health is highly associated with educational progress. In 2014, this information was recorded for 68 per cent of young people who were looked after. Boys scored higher than girls at all ages, indicating an elevated cause for concern about their mental health. Children in care aged 8–14, on average, scored 14 or more, indicating borderline cause for concern, with boys aged 9–13 at particular risk of mental health having an adverse impact on learning (DfE 2014). This is further evidence of the need to focus early on the relational foundations of learning, from the point at which children come into care, when experiencing success at school and broader educational engagement and enjoyment must be a priority to help address low self-esteem.

The information about the secondary phase shows that while this is a crucial time for school performance, the educational journey for young people looked after is likely to be precarious. During these years, the attainment gap widens, the role of the home environment continues to be highly important for engagement in school, especially the ability of parents or carers to instil or maintain self-belief and high expectations in young people, and relational practice within schools is important in sustaining educational engagement. In addition, the role of outside-school activities in supporting self-belief and self-esteem is important. Young people in care, especially boys, are also likely to need additional support with mental health issues by the age of 12.

Evidence from school studies suggests that while the difference schools can make to children's performance and wellbeing is important, it is outweighed by the role of the home environment – its 'educational competence' as much as socio-economic factors.

Upper secondary education

In other European countries the years from 16–19 usually consist of a defined 'upper secondary' stage of education (Jackson and Cameron 2014). In the UK, this period has never been clearly delineated, except for the straightforward academic route, even since young people have been legally obliged to stay in education or training up to 18. Attempts to establish a unified and universal upper secondary education system (Hodgson and Spours 2011), leading to a recognised endpoint, have never been successful, so that formal education after age 16 overlaps with further education and embraces sixth form and equivalent vocational education in regional or city colleges. It can be a very confusing and poorly signposted route for students without well-informed guidance.

Donna was rather typical of young people in or leaving care in that she made muddled progress during her upper secondary phase (see also Chapter 10). At a period when she was living semi-independently she was distracted by a chaotic social life and her father's death in America, causing her to give up repeatedly on A-level study, despite her earlier enjoyment and appreciation of school.

In England, no national data is held on the educational performance of young people looked after in care after the age of 16 when compulsory school attendance formerly ended. There is no detailed information on participation or qualifications after that age, such as A-levels or equivalent Level 3 qualifications, presumably because in the past few looked after young people were expected to obtain them. Department for Education data tells us that around three-quarters of young people looked after who took GCSE qualifications participate in education in some form at age 16/17. Of the 5550 young people in care who left Year 11 in 2011, 71 per cent were enrolled in full-time education by 30 September that year, compared with 87 per cent of all young people, and a further ten per cent were engaged in some kind of structured training and/ or employment programme (DfE 2012a). However, we do not know what qualifications they achieved from this participation, nor how long they stayed in education. At age 19, 20 and 21 just seven per cent of young people who were in care at age 16 were participating in studies beyond A-level, as Table 3.4 sets out. In total, just 39 per cent were in some kind of part-time or full-time education, training or employment, and over a third (37%) were recorded as unemployed or inactive, a considerably higher proportion than among all young people: about one fifth of young people aged 16–24 years were unemployed in 2013.

Table 3.4 Educational and training activity among 19-, 20- and 21-year-olds who were looked after by local authorities when aged 16[1] (percentages)

| | (Formerly) looked after young people | |
	Full-time	Part-time
Studies beyond A-level	7	–
Other than higher education	10	2
Training or employment	13	7
Total	30	9

---

1   and at least 13 weeks after their 14th birthday (DfE 2014a).

In many of the accounts from the YiPPEE young people, it was accurate, well-informed guidance, carried out very patiently and often in the face of multiple distractions, that got them through the upper secondary phase. As Donna said of her leaving care worker, a trained teacher and committed lifelong learner, 'He helps with everything really, he's more than a teacher.' This statement underlines the 'wellbeing' aspect of educational support required by this group. But getting access to such a person was a matter of chance in the YiPPEE study. Chapter 10 details the important role of leaving care teams and educationally focused workers to encourage young people to stay in upper secondary education. It is becoming the norm for young people of all ages, in the face of very limited alternatives, to remain in education during the upper secondary phase: young people in care are part of this general trend, but the time is quite often used ineffectively. Most attention in this phase has been paid to raising the aspirations of young people in care in order to help them think about going to university (see Chapter 11).

Concluding thoughts

If we want the educational journeys of young people in care to become more straightforward than Donna's was, there is much to learn from the evidence pertaining to young people from a range of disadvantaged backgrounds. All the effective interventions discussed in this chapter give considerable emphasis to a broad definition of education in which:

+ relationships between adults and children must be responsive and reciprocal, characterised by valuing the expertise and voice of the child

+ education is enjoyable, engaging and has high expectations of students

+ there is a culture of constructive collaboration with professionals, parents, and those we have called everyday experts, such as foster carers and residential care workers

+ there is early intervention, both in terms of the educational phase and in a clear focus on education, right at the start of the care placement.

Practice points

+ Put participation in, and enjoyment of, school at the forefront of thinking when children come into care, even when there is or has been a lack of support for education from birth parents.

+ Avoid changing placements during secondary school years, and especially avoid changing schools during this time.

+ Think inclusion. The needs of looked after children in education have much in common with the needs of other vulnerable children.

+ Separate out behaviour from learning. A disproportionate number of looked after children are designated as having special educational needs, usually for behavioural reasons. To what extent does this designation disadvantage or advantage looked after children?

+ Think mental health. Attend to mental health issues early and address self-esteem barriers to learning.

Useful resources

+ Kendall, S., Straw, S., Jones, M., Springate, I., and Grayson, H. (2008) *A Review of the Research Evidence: Narrowing the Gap in Outcomes for Vulnerable Groups*. Slough: NFER. This volume brings together a range of practice-based evidence relating to addressing the education of children who are disadvantaged. Clearly explained and selected methodically, the review gives plenty of advice about effective interventions. Little, however, focuses specifically on children in care.

+ In Care, In School (www.incareinschool.com) seeks to 'help teachers and pupils understand, from a young person's point of view, what it is like being in foster care and having an education'. The website provides resources from the project in Bath and north east Somerset.

CHAPTER 4

Creating and Sustaining a Learning Placement

The aim of this chapter is to introduce ways of creating and sustaining a foster care or residential care placement as a 'learning' placement. A learning placement is one where learning, both formal and informal, is to the fore, whether in a family or in an institution.

KEY POINTS

▸ Learning placements enable children to develop a sense of belonging to place and people, which makes it more likely that the placement will last as long as they need it.

▸ The 'common third' is a way of thinking of what is in common between a carer and young person and building from a young person's interests.

▸ Learning placements offer the best conditions they possibly can for study and quiet, constructive activities as well as fun and enjoyment.

▸ In learning placements the carers are always aware of opportunities for learning that occur in the course of everyday life.

▸ Children should have plentiful supplies of stationery and books, regularly refreshed.

▸ Bedtime stories are a key element of household life, for children of all ages.

> ‣ Reflection is a key tool for making sense of a learning placement.

> ‣ Supporting learning in foster families or group homes should mirror the practice of committed and well-informed parents.

> ‣ Everyday experts need to be 'educationally competent' to enable children in care to fulfil their potential.

Introduction

In 2011, Eileen Munro's report on the child's journey in local authority care made clear that choosing the right placement, at the right time, is critical for children's success. She quoted one of the young people consulted for her enquiry whose view echoed that of many: 'Being in care can be OK, even a good experience, if you have the right placement and a good social worker. I think the care system's main priority should be making sure both those things are OK' (Munro 2011, p.27).

Research shows that stability is vital for a successful upbringing in care. Part of ensuring stability is the responsibility of the organisational environment (Ward 2009), which must see that there are enough foster carers and residential workers, and that social workers enjoy working conditions that encourage them to stay in post. Another part is matching the carer or care environment with the needs and capabilities of the child. In this chapter we focus on supporting the capabilities of a child or young person in a care placement, or what we call a 'learning placement'.

What is a learning placement?

A learning placement is one way of making placements meaningful and so rewarding for both carers and children. Whether in residential or foster care, a learning placement is one where curiosity is nurtured and learning is a joint activity. Both adults and young people are interested to find out facts, explore ideas and create 'products' –

whether music or mosaic pictures or maths. It is the process of doing things together, in dialogue, what EPPE, the renowned longitudinal early childhood research project, called 'sustained shared thinking', that creates the relationships and so the milieu in which self-identity as a learner grows (Sylva *et al.* 2004). Two features of learning placements are discussed in more detail here: the idea of the 'common third' and reflection on practice.

The common third

Continental European social pedagogy names the process of making meaning through doing things together as having a 'common third'[1] in which the focus of attention is on the 'thing' that is in common. There are numerous benefits to the common third. First, the focus on a 'third' object can relieve tension or awkwardness around talking as a way of establishing a relationship. By establishing a relationship around doing things together, each party, carer, child or group of children contributes to the whole. A second benefit is that doing things together creates the possibility of mutual respect for the part each person plays in creating the product or the memory. For example, going for a walk or a picnic or a day to the seaside, where each person's ideas about where to go and what to do are included in developing the plans, that may change as the day goes on, helps each person to feel that creating the day was something they had some influence on, something they can look back on. A third benefit is that the common third will give rise to conversations about 'remember when we…' or points of reference which will later contribute to jointly held memories about important places in children's lives.

The arts provide a rich milieu for developing common third relationships. Helen Chambers has been involved in working with arts practitioners and social pedagogues in the UK. She summarised the role of the expressive arts as an important opportunity to develop 'creative activities to build relationships and give a place for people to play, share and have "permission to fail", as well as create something tangible. The arts can provide fun and laughter, encourage another way of thinking, not as therapy but rather personal expression and

---

1   The 'first' and 'second' refer to the two parties in the relationship, that is, the adult and child.

achievement through a boundaried and meaningful relationship with others' (Chambers 2013).

A social pedagogue working in London who was interviewed for this book gave an example of creating a common third relationship with a young person who was not attending school. She said:

> 'It's really important to find out from an individual what their interests are and to form a learning journey with them. I was working with a young person who was living with an aunt, between placements, and did not have a school to attend. So I went to see him and found out that he liked football. We created a project together. This involved him using the internet to find out about his team, and about football, going to visit the Arsenal Museum with me, writing it up, taking photographs and doing a presentation to me on what he had found out.
>
> This project helped keep him engaged in learning, in the widest sense, while he was waiting for a school place. Social workers told me that he didn't want to engage, but the day we went to the museum he was all ready when I collected him. He was on his own in the house and could have refused. But he was there. Through doing the project he experienced what it was like to do something, at a time when he was permanently excluded from school. He gained confidence from doing it.'

Another example of a common third at work might be deciding to bake a cake together, finding a recipe, shopping, cooking and eating together, all the while finding out about each other's tastes and habits and cooking skills and knowledge. Further examples might be learning to fix bikes together or researching and planning holidays, or learning to play a guitar, as well as approaching homework as a shared task. Jointly held experiences and memories of a common third event, project or creation cement a sense of belonging to a place and time. Developing a sense of belonging, known to be very important in stable and successful care placements (Sinclair *et al.* 2004), is sometimes referred to as 'sedimented', as it takes place over time, with repeat events, routines and objects or markers that make up habits or 'pathways of habit' (Young 1997). This continuity and repetition gives meaning to the experience and anchors the self. According to Epstein (2003, p.8) there are also important learning experiences associated with planning and reflection. She says: 'Engaging children in planning and reflection makes them more than mere actors following prescribed roles. It turns them into artists and scientists who make things happen and create meaning for themselves and others.'

A learning placement is one where, through a jointly held focus on doing, thinking and being together, appreciating strengths of the other and respecting their viewpoints, children feel that their contribution is valued and rewarded. Through a learning placement, young people will feel that in some sense they 'belong' to the foster or residential setting.

A learning placement is not just a space where the emotional and relational foundations for supporting learning are in place. A learning placement is also one where carers puzzle over *how* children are learning and *what* they are learning, at home, in their social lives and in formal educational settings. Carers are, in fact, experts on everyday life and to be expert they must engage in reflecting on and analysing the behaviour, events and interactions that comprise everyday life together. In this sense, the work of everyday experts mirrors that of well-informed, warm-hearted and well-resourced parents.

Reflection

Reflecting on practice in order to make sense of it is a key skill of everyday experts and one that underpins a learning placement. It is a form of ongoing learning through gathering information and insights that guide decision making (Macfarlane *et al.* 2014). Thom Garfat (2005) argues that there are four stages of reflective practice. Being reflective requires (i) thinking seriously about one's actions; (ii) identifying the outcome of those actions; (iii) identifying the context within which the actions occur; and (iv) considering one's immediate experiencing of an event. Effective practitioners engage in reflective practice both to make sense of what is happening and to take action to improve practice the next time the phenomenon occurs.

Such 'reflection' may occur during (reflection in action) or after (reflection on action) an event or experience. The primary goal of reflection is to increase the practitioner's capacity for effective practice through a constant process of review. Reflective practice involves the cycle of Experience – Reflection – Action:

- ♦ *Reflection in action:* may involve thinking about what is happening, about previous similar experiences, one's own values and beliefs, possible outcomes or one's immediate internal experience.

- ♦ *Reflection on action:* occurs at some distance from the event in question, involves the possibility of the creation of theory for future practice. The goal is to improve one's future actions through the consideration and development of alternative ways of thinking and doing.

Reflection may be carried out on one's own or in a team. It will usually include taking into account the thoughts and ideas of self and others such as colleagues or family members, young people or other professionals concerned and knowledge from experience and theory.

METHODS OF BEING REFLECTIVE

There are a number of ways of carrying out reflection. One way is to ask questions about one's own practice, in an attempt to link one's own thoughts, feelings and actions with another's behaviour.

For example, you might first notice what you heard or saw, and note what you felt and thought about what you saw. Then you might ask what alternatives there were to what you said or did and why you didn't pursue them. Third, you might consider what effects your action had on the person or group concerned (Borders and Leddick 1987).

A second method is to keep a reflective journal. Here, one records a concrete experience, thinks about and records observations about the experience, and integrates the observation with abstract concepts or theories, and then uses the theories to make decisions or solve problems. Keeping a journal can be very rewarding and improves writing skills as well as critical thinking skills, but to do it well requires guidance about what to record and how best to record it. Making effective use of the reflection in the journal also benefits from it being shared, for example in supervision, or with trusted others.

Commonly we think of reflection as taking place face to face. It can also be carried out effectively using a third object, such as a telephone. This can work particularly well where there is a common agenda and the two parties are of equal status such as members of a team.

In one example, two doctoral students spoke regularly on the telephone to share ideas (Walker and Winter 2014). They recorded, listened to and transcribed short extracts of their conversations. They found that doing this enabled them to share helpful or difficult experiences, and by doing so could validate the other's experience by relating it to a similar experience of their own. The process of transcribing, listening and thinking through led them to 'echo one another's experiences because we are in similar boats but, of course, they are not exactly the same, [it was not simply validating] but learning from one another through thinking together'. The process of exchange and reflection allowed each to think through their approach and adapt what they had planned to do. This method may be particularly applicable to everyday experts who work on their own but have built up good working relations with colleagues, such as foster carers, who face challenging situations, such as advocating for children's education.

REFLECTION AND PROFESSIONAL STANDARDS

Being reflective in and on practice is well established in children's services work. One of the criteria to be an early years educator is to 'engage in continuing professional development and reflective practice to improve own skills, practice, and subject knowledge (for example, in English, mathematics, music, history, or modern foreign languages)' (National College of Teaching and Leadership 2013, para 4.3). In foster care, the Training, Support and Development (TSD) standards are a national minimum benchmark that sets out what foster carers should know, understand and be able to do. Standard 7.4b states that foster carers should 'understand and be able to reflect on how your day-to-day work as a foster carer is influenced by feedback from people you come into contact with and from children, young people and their families' (DfE 2012b). Staff working in children's homes are required, according to National Minimum Standards, to reflect on incidents of challenging behaviour and learn from them to inform future practice (standard 3.21) and to encourage children to reflect on and understand their history (standard 22.6) (DfE 2011).

According to Garfat (2005), 'acting without reflection raises the risk of the practitioner acting on their own business'. Failing to reflect on past actions denies the practitioner, and the field, the opportunity to benefit from learning from experience and leads to the old 'we do it this way because we always have' approach 'which is, unfortunately, far too common'. On the other hand, engaging in critical reflection, where one 'closely examines all aspects of events and experiences from different perspectives', has the potential to extend and transform practice through thinking otherwise (Macfarlane *et al.* 2014).

To summarise, learning placements are a useful way to think about both meaningful relationships between carer and child and about what actually happens in placements. The idea of placements as being places for learning gives a sharpened focus to setting goals for children in public care that are not just child-centred but build outwards from individual children and young people and their talents, strengths and capabilities. One example was a children's home where the staff wrote a charter for supporting education. They involved young people in the discussion and came up with practical ideas such as respecting others when they were doing homework, having a homework hour, and providing books, newspapers and magazines.

Supporting learning at home

Following the above, supporting learning at home for children in care should closely parallel what is known to be effective in families, where supporting learning often (but not always) occurs spontaneously. Desforges with Abouchaar (2003) reviewed the English language literature on the impact of parental involvement on children's achievements and found very large agreement that where children were intellectually stimulated at home, through parent–child discussions, where there were good models of constructive social and educational values and high aspirations relating to personal fulfilment and good citizenship, children were more likely to achieve educational objectives. Schools and parental involvement in schools were also important, but the most critical factor was active parental support. Parenting influences learning through shaping the child's self-concept as a learner and through setting high aspirations. But the extent and form of parental involvement is strongly influenced by family social class, maternal level of education, material deprivation, maternal psychosocial health and single parent status and, to a lesser degree, by family ethnicity. As children get older, the influence of parental involvement, unsurprisingly, weakens. But the extent of parents' involvement is related to children's attainment; where children get higher grades, the parents are more involved and vice versa. This may be related to social class in that well-educated middle class parents approach schools and teachers as equals whereas those who see teachers as different from or superior to them may feel inhibited in a school environment.

Parents' own experience of school is another important factor. Someone whose experience of school was of being repeatedly told off, mocked, punished or beaten may find the association of the institution and their memory make it near impossible to see their children's teachers as benign or well intentioned. This is one reason why some foster care agencies employ educational liaison staff to help broker links between home and school. In some areas there are home link teachers employed to do this for residential homes.

Although partnership with parents is often promoted as a positive way to improve learning, some parents are put off by feeling put down or humiliated by schools and teachers. Given that foster carers often hold lower than average educational qualifications, or none at all (Kirton 2013), it is likely that many foster carers feel uncomfortable in a school environment, and in particular negotiating with head teachers.

For one foster carer from Scotland interviewed for this book, who had originally been a dance teacher working in areas of high social disadvantage, the key to working with schools was:

'making sure they knew me as a foster carer. If [foster carers] have a looked after child, they should make an effort to go to school, to see the guidance[2] teacher, keep that connection with phoning or emailing, and they pass it on to teachers... [They need to be] listening to the child, not getting into arguments

---

2   A guidance teacher provides pastoral care support in secondary schools. In England this would be the designated teacher whose role, statutory since 2009, is to promote the educational achievement of looked after children on the school roll.

and screaming, not getting into that situation. What works for that child is not the same as the other 25 children in the class, but finding another strategy. [Foster carers should be] building relationships to help them.'

This requires a degree of tenacity, self-confidence and perseverance and, ultimately, believing that education is too important to leave to the teachers. Another foster carer, from Staffordshire, and an ex-secondary school teacher, talked about how education was part of everyday life with her foster child:

'It's about using every opportunity, so something that might not appear to be learning, cooking or making cakes, we talk about the numbers. So if we need 6 ounces and 3 ounces, ooh how do they relate, we talk about those things, not sitting down and having a lesson. One of the boys is 11 but academically he is 4 or 5, so he is learning to count. When we are out we look at door numbers, and see what they are. He can only really count to 20. We are trying to stretch that. Without saying let's learn numbers. For him that's a scary thing.'

One of the most important ways carers can support learning at home is enjoying reading together with children in their care. This is critical for later examination success as well as creating a rewarding 'common third' for the relationship. The Letterbox Club is a scheme, supported by Booktrust, to promote enjoyment of books among children in foster care and improve their educational outlook, or, we might say, to enhance their learning identity (Griffiths 2013). Local authorities pay a subscription depending on the number of eligible children. Originally aimed at primary school children aged 7–11, the scheme has now been extended into Years 8 and 9 and to younger age groups of children.

Case study: The Letterbox Club

Children who are members of the Letterbox Club receive a parcel of books, educational games, stationery and a personal letter once every month for six months, addressed to them in their foster homes. The books are very carefully chosen to appeal to children of different ages and reading ability and the activities can be done on their own or with their carer. Children make good progress in their reading through the scheme. A formal evaluation in Suffolk showed that in 2007 and 2008, children in Years 3 and 4 in primary school gained on average around four points over eight months on their standardised reading scores. The scheme has been rolled out and evaluated in Northern Ireland, Wales and Scotland. The children love getting parcels through the post and seem especially to enjoy the idea of being members of a Club.

Jamie was 10 years 5 months old when he was first tested. His reading age was 8 years 11 months (so he was about 18 months behind the average for his age; his standardised reading score was 92). A month after his last Letterbox parcel arrived he was tested again. He was now 11 years 1 month old, and had a reading age of 10 years 1 month (so he was now only 12 months behind, with a standardised score of 95). Jamie had made about 14 months' progress in the 8 months between his two tests. He had gained 3 points on his standardised score and, more importantly, was able to read for pleasure.

Reading is a skill that requires practice, so the more that children can be encouraged to read the better. New books are expensive but second-hand ones are often extremely cheap. As reading became easier for him, Jamie wanted to read more and more. His foster father made a point of buying him a new book on his way home from work every week, sometimes helping him to choose for himself and sometimes making it a surprise. Carers in learning placements need to talk about the books their young people are reading and introduce them to new authors from time to time.

Another example of promoting reading, specifically in residential care, was the Edinburgh Reading Champion. Beginning in 2008, and funded by Edinburgh City Council, this project used a variety of ways of bringing reading into residential care. Artists and authors were invited to read in residential care homes and young people visited the Edinburgh Book Festival and theatre productions. Within residential homes, care staff became 'reading partners' to particular children, which proved an effective way to overcome lack of confidence with reading. The staff and young people visited bookshops together and developed collections of books for the residential homes. Writing about the scheme, Linnane (2008, p.26) said: 'Sharing books and stories is infectious and generates excitement and togetherness.'

A further example of charities promoting reading is The Reader Organisation, which promotes the practice of shared reading and enjoyment of literature for everyone, including young people who are looked after, and, through bringing people together to read, building stronger communities. This extract is taken from a longer account which appears on The Reader website:

> I started reading [*Skellig* by David Almond] to W, and almost immediately he was hanging off every word. He was just soaking up the story, and watching my face – I wondered if he had ever been read to before. As he mostly looked at me when I was reading, rather than at the book, I made sure I was making as much eye contact as I could with him by raising my eyes from the page when I could – this way, we could communicate through our facial expressions whilst reading, and W certainly had a lot of response in his facial expressions!
>
> When I stopped and asked W open questions like, 'What did you make of the man in the garage? I wonder if he is a man!', W chatted away, showing that he had been following the story completely. I always asked W gently but without any pressure if he would like to have a go at reading, and one day he said yes. He read very, very, very slowly, and haltingly, as the majority of the words he didn't know. But, we got to the end of the page. I praised W a great deal for this, as it had been an admirable effort. I assumed that he had not understood what he was reading because of the way he had read it, and meaning to cover what had happened in the page, I checked first by saying, 'What did you think about what was going on there then?', ready to jump in with an explanation if he shrugged. But, to my surprise, W had understood every word he had read. This was a great lesson for me to learn – that a child's reading ability does not always reflect their level of comprehension.

Bedtime stories

Regular bedtimes support children's behaviour and learning. Kelly *et al.* (2013) found that introducing more regular bedtime routines can improve behaviour, boost academic performance as bedtime stories help nurture a love of reading, as well as enabling a time of togetherness that helps create a calm atmosphere for sleep. However, a survey of 1000 parents in 2013 found that only two-thirds read bedtime stories to their child regularly, and nearly half of children aged seven are rarely or never read to at home (OUP 2013). Many children are losing out on bedtime stories but they can be an important part of the day, especially for children in care.

Henry Maier, the founding father of child and youth care in the USA, believed that group care homes had to foster the all-round development of young people. One of the ways of doing this was to make sure that the everyday rhythms and rituals of the setting support children's development rather than enforce arbitrary or organisationally driven rules. Following this, Vander Ven (2003) argued that bedtimes are a good example of daily rhythm. She said:

> As bedtime approaches, activities might become quieter. Rather than 'totting up the points' for the day and packing the kids off to an inappropriately timed bedtime, think about mixing up a cup of cocoa together, sitting down to discuss the plans for the next day, and using the time together to help newcomers be welcomed into the group. Then, read the kids a bedtime story. I've heard it over and over from those who've tried it. The biggest, toughest acting youths might bluster, but they are all ears when an adult reads them a story. It's all about what they missed out on in their earlier years and the meta-message of caring and nurturance that is conveyed.

Simpson (2013) asked residential care practitioners and young people who were residents about their experience of bedtime stories. The young people thought bedtime reading together with staff was an enjoyable activity, which made them feel closer to staff, safe and relaxed. The staff thought reading stories at bedtime enhanced their relationship with young people, supported their development and provided time to reconnect with a young person after a dispute or a difficult incident. One of the staff members said:

> 'We can interact through the story. It means he can lie down and listen to my voice and it is about the story that we can share and both enjoy and he can just get a bit of my emotion through how I read the story…you've got this pure trusting space…I love it. It's storytelling and it's just great.'

Reading stories also helped create a 'reading culture' in the residential home. A house coordinator said: 'As much as possible we will try to complement the curriculum they're having in school... teaching them through play and fun activities and...it's the same for bedtime reading...stories can mirror what needs to be happening developmentally within the child and we can support that to happen in a very indirect way...'

Bedtime stories are a good example of a common third activity, through which staff–child relationships can prosper.

Reading takes very little planning, other than having suitable reading material to read to children. In fact, some studies with children in care have found that informal situations appear to be advantageous for encouraging reading (Finn 2008; Poulton 2012). The Reading Rich project in Scotland highlighted four ingredients for success in encouraging reading (Finn 2008):

+ Informal settings to encourage participation in reading.

+ Activities that are short and achievable and take place in an informal atmosphere.

+ Making links with popular leisure activities and venues enjoyed by young people.

+ Activities that are seen by children to have a sense of purpose.

Paired reading is another method of improving literacy among looked after children. In one evaluation of carers and primary school age children reading together, each child made one year's progress in reading over just four months (Osborne et al. 2013).

Putting learning at the centre of everyday life

There are implications of learning placements for the everyday experts who care for children and for the recruitment of foster carers and residential workers. Learning placements imply that the carers are academically capable and that they are interested in ongoing learning for themselves as well as for the children they look after. Writing about her childhood in the African bush in the 1920s, the acclaimed author Doris Lessing said of her mother, a nurse by training: 'After breakfast I might go back into my room to read.

Or go with my mother to learn – well, something or other. For if her wonderful lessons stopped when we went to school she never ever lost an opportunity for instruction, and now I am grateful and wish I could tell her so' (Lessing 1994, p.73). This quotation underlines the long-remembered impact of everyday 'instruction' embedded in a relationship of warmth.

In England, recruitment of foster carers and residential care workers gives priority to work and life experience rather than formal qualifications. The National Careers Service states that 'the ability to relate to people of all ages and backgrounds will be important [for those wanting to work in residential care]. You'll also need to gain [children's] trust and have a non-judgemental attitude.' This is all very well, but how can we expect looked after children to do well in education if they are looked after by people with a very low level of education themselves? We cannot at present look to entry qualifications to assess whether residential care workers and foster carers can support young people they look after with their academic work.

However, within preparation training and expected standards there are some glimpses of an educational role. The revised edition of *Skills to Foster* (Fostering Network 2014), the leading resource pack for initial training to become a foster carer, includes a topic called 'encouraging ongoing learning and development'. Within residential care, there is reference in the National Minimum Standards to children having a 'home which promotes a learning environment and supports their development…access to a range of educational resources to support their learning and have opportunities beyond the school day to engage in activities which promote learning' (DfE 2011, p.19). In both cases the intention is there to support learning within the placement but in neither case is the worker's or carer's own educational competence identified as crucial to children's educational success. This is in contrast with the findings on parental support for education, where, as noted earlier, educational level was found to be significant. One factor that would appear to be important in putting learning at the centre of everyday life is the *educational competence* of everyday experts.

In the YiPPEE study, participants were asked to nominate an adult who had made a difference to their education, and who was then interviewed. In England, the 'nominated adults' were foster carers and professionals, whose own educational paths were varied. Three of the five foster carers interviewed had no school leaving qualifications, and two had diplomas and degrees. Among the other professionals, most had a degree and/or a professional qualification, often achieved much later in life. The common thread was a 'belief in lifelong learning'. One foster carer said:

> 'I think life is about learning. I would have liked to have been a marine biologist. I have ambition for my own children; I know they can do better than they think they can. I want them to have the best, to make the best for themselves. They don't get the chance again. But kids in care are too busy fighting the system. You don't ever stop learning or finding out who you are.'

Another foster carer said he'd 'always had to learn, in my job you don't survive without it. I have to do things that before I wouldn't have thought of. Where I failed [in education], for these children I say you must learn, take exams, and have greater opportunities than I had.' One of the professionals, a teacher located within a leaving care team, said he believed strongly in 'education in its broadest sense'. He continued:

> 'I'm peeved by the notion that all learning has to lead to work. I've never met a child who didn't want to learn. How do we turn a six-year-old who wants to know about everything into a 16-year-old who can't be bothered with anything? I did GCSE French last year and next year I'm going to do Spanish, setting an example.' (Cameron *et al.* 2010, p.117)

All these examples were from adults who had promoted learning through example and self-belief in education and passing on the value of education, and many of the young people they had supported had achieved entry to higher education. This is what we mean by educational competence, and it is also what Mollenhauer referred to as upbringing (see Chapter 1).

One way to improve the effectiveness of placements would be to put academic capability or educational competence centre stage in the recruitment and training of foster carers and residential care workers. This would imply raising the entry qualifications required; but perhaps as important would be to require evidence of ongoing learning, and putting learning into practice, whether in relation to creative and practical skills to share with young people or more directly focused on theories and knowledge about children's life circumstances, or a combination of both.

Concluding thoughts

This chapter has introduced the idea of 'learning placements'. We focused on two tools for promoting learning placements: the common third and reflection on practice. We gave a lot of attention to reading as a key skill and source of enjoyment for children in care. There are of course many other skills and sources of enjoyment: building go-karts, doing experiments, climbing mountains and practising maths to name a few. More examples will be given in subsequent chapters. We argued that practitioners' 'educational competence' was necessary for children in care to achieve their potential. Such competence could be seen in part through academic qualifications but also in commitment to their own lifelong learning.

Practice points

+ All placements should offer a culture of learning. Talk with them about the ways in which they do this.

+ All everyday experts should see themselves as continually learning, with and alongside the children they look after.

+ Identify examples of 'common third' activities and how they have supported mutual learning or co-construction of meaning.

+ Being critically reflective is a very important part of learning placements. Examine how this is done and could be done.

+ Reading to children is a key method of supporting learning for young people of all ages. Benefits of bedtime stories are clear. Identify any barriers to reading with looked after children and find ways of surmounting them.

- Identify ways in which everyday experts could engage with further learning to support young people placed with them.

Useful resources

- The Letterbox Club (www.letterboxclub.org.uk) is an award-winning programme managed by Booktrust, in partnership with the University of Leicester, which aims to provide enjoyable educational support for looked after children aged 5–13. The website states that the 'programme has achieved significant improvements in reading and numeracy for many of the children who have been members, and has had considerable success in encouraging children and their families to read and play games together at home.' The website has resources for foster carers, adopters, local authorities and schools.

- Child and Youth Care Online (www.cyc-net.org/profession/pro-history.html) has a wealth of resources, including a section on the history of the child and youth care profession. An article by Thom Garfat outlines the contribution made by Henry Maier over many years to thinking about the components of good quality care, called 'From Yesterday and Today into Tomorrow – or Henry, Fritz and Friends'.

- The Reader Organisation (www.thereader.org.uk/who-we-are.aspx) aims to bring about a reading revolution. Its website has a host of resources, including a section on education and young people, news about reading-related events and connecting readers to reading groups across the country.

CHAPTER 5

Informal Education

The aim of this chapter is to suggest that there is much more to education than school attendance and attainment, though these are important in instrumental terms for easier progression within the education system.

KEY POINTS

▸ A learning placement helps the child or young person to come to know their boundaries and to be able to learn through taking risks.

▸ Learning opportunities in informal settings are important because they are associated with enjoyment, can impact positively on school learning, allow children to learn in different ways and play to strengths, and because they can mitigate the effects of placement moves.

▸ There are many different opportunities for learning at home, outdoors and through spare-time activities, with parents and carers acting as partners in learning, .

Introduction

This chapter begins with an anecdote. The story is real but some details have been changed to protect the identities of those involved.

A new residential worker was appointed to a children's home. A keen gardener, he suggested building a raised bed in the yard. The home's manager supported the idea and provided a small budget. Before long the bed was built and some of the young people had become involved in growing vegetables. One day, the home had a visit from an environmental health officer making a routine inspection. He noticed the vegetable plot and included it in his review. The plot met safety standards, but the officer insisted that the vegetables could not be eaten by any of the children or staff. The explanation was that vegetables grown at home could not be linked to a recognised 'source'. In other words, there was not a supplier who could be held legally responsible should consumption of the vegetables cause food poisoning.

The point of this story is not to demonise the environmental health profession or to minimise the importance of food safety and hygiene. The deaths of elderly people in residential care as a result of food poisoning from bacteria in contaminated meat have led to the environmental health profession being understandably cautious about food hygiene in local authority homes, schools and centres. However, even when raw vegetables are sourced from an approved supplier, they still have to be washed and prepared according to proper food hygiene guidelines. The real point of the story, though, is that there are many informal learning opportunities in everyday living, including how vegetables get from garden to kitchen, and to stomach. Informal learning involves taking varying degrees of risk, but looked after children can often miss out on even simple opportunities because of risk-averse attitudes and practices. Informal learning 'is often undervalued and seldom recognized' (Schugerensky 2006).

This chapter continues with a discussion of the role of informal learning opportunities for looked after children, and the important contributions that parents and carers can make in supporting learning, building on the material in Chapter 4. Following the discussion, we consider three specific examples of informal learning opportunities: harnessing new technologies; play and creative activity; and activities outdoors.

The importance of informal learning for children in care settings

If children are to be successful academically, 'doing well' at school, it is vital that they are actively engaged in the learning process. Engagement is dependent on factors which are external to the child and observable, and also on factors which are part of the child's own internal world or psychology. Important external factors include participation in the academic work of the school, being focused on learning and grades, and the more behavioural aspects of school life, such as attendance and adherence to the school's values and rules of conduct however unreasonable they might seem. Key factors internal to the child include both cognitive (thinking) and emotional (feelings) dimensions. Schools are naturally focused on developing the academic, behavioural and cognitive aspects of children's engagement with education through the curriculum, classroom and school discipline, tests and homework tasks. While schools can also provide opportunities for developing the more emotional and social aspects associated with effective learning, such as interaction with others and taking part in extra-curricular activities, providing opportunities for out-of-school learning is also vital, and therefore a very important consideration for those responsible for the upbringing of looked after children.

Learning opportunities afforded by more informal settings outside the classroom are important for at least four reasons. First, learning in informal settings is typically associated with enjoyment. The association between learning and fun is a very powerful motivator. Second, learning in informal settings can be transformative, in the sense that positive experiences outside school can impact positively on engagement within school. This is because informal learning can provide opportunities for relationship building and for children to develop a sense of self-efficacy, both of which appear to be important determinants of success in more formal educational settings (Jackson and Martin 1998). Third, because children learn in different ways, it is important to have opportunities for learning in different settings and to be exposed to different methods. Finally, and more specifically in relation to children in care, out-of-school learning may help to mitigate the impact on learning of a change of placement or school. For example, where a change of school is inevitable, it is important to try to maintain a child's involvement in clubs or sports activities, and for this to form part of the planning for a looked after child's placement and education.

While opportunities for informal learning can be provided through a school's extra-curricular activities programme, the importance of continuity, as argued above, implies that opportunities afforded by the home, and by involvement with clubs and other 'spare-time' activities, are also important for children in care settings.

Learning opportunities in the home

The most common example of informal learning occurs in the home from a baby's earliest interactions with a caregiver. Informal learning opportunities are present in a parent's or carer's everyday involvement with the child, talking with and listening to them, providing routines, creating opportunities for enquiry and safe risk-taking, and modelling problem-solving strategies. Even when the child starts formal schooling the impact of the parent's or carer's involvement in learning remains high.

As noted in Chapter 1, in a review of the literature on the impact of parent involvement in children's attainment, Desforges and Abouchaar concluded that studies:

> …established that parental involvement in the form of interest in the child and manifest in the home as parent–child discussions can have a significant positive effect on children's behaviour and achievement even when the influence of background factors such as social class or family size have been factored out. (Desforges with Abouchaar 2003, p.28)

The authors also note that while the effects diminish in the case of older children, they remain strong and may be less related to attainment and more influential in encouraging staying on at school and educational aspirations generally. Another revealing finding in their review is that what the authors call 'in-school' parental involvement confers little direct benefit to the child, compared with 'at-home' involvement. In-school involvement includes contact with teachers at parents' meetings and volunteering in the school. At-home involvement includes helping children with reading, providing opportunities for solving problems, and being more generally encouraging and helping to build their confidence as learners.

These research findings have important implications for residential and foster carers concerned with supporting the education of children looked after in the care system.

First, while it is important that carers engage effectively with schools (e.g. in helping teachers to understand the implications of being looked after for the individual child, and to get essential information about the curriculum, courses, assessment and homework), the most significant impact for the child results from doing things together and arranging activities which support the development of good attitudes to learning and acquisition of skills outside of school. This could include encouraging a child to attend a youth organisation, or a sport, music or drama club, as well as engaging the child in learning opportunities at home such as digging allotments, going swimming or learning to knit or sew.

Second, while everyday experts such as parents and carers who themselves have higher levels of educational attainment are likely to be well placed to help children to learn outside school, practical help and enthusiasm for learning are probably more important influences on attainment. The nature of adult involvement in support of learning varies with the age of the child: younger children need more direct help to reinforce fundamental skills in reading and mathematics, while older children benefit from encouragement to learn independently and to internalise a view of being capable and likely to succeed.

Encouraging learning through spare-time activities

The relationship between participation in extra-curricular activities and academic achievement has been the focus of a number of research studies. For example, Nancy Darling carried out a longitudinal study of 3761 students in six Californian high schools between 1987 and 1990 to examine whether taking part in school-based extra-curricular activities was associated with low substance use and depression, higher grades and academic aspiration and more positive attitudes to school (Darling 2005). The findings showed no association between participation in activities and alcohol use or depression; however, there were modest positive associations with academic factors, the strongest being in relation to academic aspiration. The study was not able to examine any differences associated with different kinds of activities or patterns of engagement, for example comparisons between the commitment to regular practice in playing a sport or learning a musical instrument, and more intense but short-lived activities, such as attending a camp or visiting a museum. But the finding in relation to aspiration is interesting and if significant would support the value of participation in a general psychological sense of contributing to an achieving identity or, more practically, to presenting evidence of being a 'well-rounded' individual in the context of a college or job application.

Some authors emphasise the protective merits of participation in activities. These include avoiding harm by minimising the availability to participate in offending or behaviours likely to be damaging to health, as well as accruing benefits such as extending a support network of adult friends and peers. For example, Joseph Mahoney studied 364 boys and 331 girls recruited from seven high schools in the south-eastern United States (Mahoney 2000). The children were initially assessed in either fourth grade (age 10) or seventh grade (age 12) and were assessed annually until twelfth grade (age 17). They were followed up when they were either 20 or 24 years old, with an impressive retention rate of over 90 per cent. The study used a range of measures of social and academic competence, as well as recording involvement in school extra-curricular activities, and reports of criminal activity. Mahoney found that children who participated in school extra-curricular activities were less likely to drop out of school as adolescents or to be arrested as young adults than were similar children who did not engage in activities. The latter finding is particularly important because it suggests that the benefits of participation can last beyond adolescence. This finding was observed primarily among young people at highest risk for antisocial behaviour, and it was additionally found that decline in antisocial behaviour associated with participation was dependent on the young people's social network also being engaged in extra-curricular activities.

The value of participation in extra-curricular and leisure-time interests for developing skills, gaining friendships and acquiring social competence has also been highlighted by authors specifically concerned with the application of research findings to children in care.

Reporting results of the YiPPEE study, Katie Hollingworth (2012) noted that 13 out of the 32 young people interviewed in depth in England said they regularly took part in sport, a proportion much lower than the close to 75 per cent of 16–24 year olds in England reported to take part in physical activity, defined as taking part in at least 30 minutes of active sport in the four weeks prior to interview Seddon (2011). But for those who were involved, the social value was apparent:

> The integrationist meaning of sport to these young people was highly significant; these were activities through which many had been able to develop friendships and widen their social network, mixing and socializing in mainstream activities with young people who are not in the care system. In many cases, young people had been participating in sports activities or clubs for many years and this had provided an important source of stability and consistency in their lives. (Hollingworth 2012, p.440)

Robbie Gilligan concludes that the research evidence suggests there are things carers, social workers and teachers can do 'which can harness the potential benefits of spare-time activities in relation to educational progress' (Gilligan 2013, p.86). Among the nine potential benefits he lists are those which emphasise the value of engagement in activities for stimulating interest in more general learning, those about the importance of offering new experiences, and those which highlight the significance of supportive relationships and developing social networks. Gilligan also notes the research evidence underlining the importance of not having all participation in activities being linked to school so that the benefits of involvement are lost as a result of a change of placement.

So, how is the theory of informal learning to be applied in practice? The following three examples offer some suggestions.

Example 1: Harnessing interest in new technologies

> Despite what you may hear, or even observe, today's students don't have short attention spans or the inability to concentrate that they are often accused of having. Many of the same students who don't concentrate in school will sit for hours, for example, totally focused on movies or video games. (Prensky 2010, p.2)

Marc Prensky is addressing teachers principally, but his advice could equally apply to other important educators, including parents, foster and kinship carers, and residential workers. He makes the point that young people know that when they learn something out of school, they can apply it instantly to something real. When they learn to play a computer game they can collaborate with others close by or in another country; when they send a tweet or post a status update on social media they are writing about ideas and feelings, or influencing policies.

The key idea Prensky advocates is what he calls 'partnering pedagogy'. This concept envisages learning as a partnership – often between an adult and young person, but it could equally refer to peer-to-peer learning. In partnering pedagogy, being a learner involves: finding and following a passion; using whatever technology is available; researching and finding information; answering questions and sharing thoughts and opinions; practising (e.g. through games and other activities); and creating presentations in text and multimedia. Being an educator (or pedagogue) means: creating and asking the right questions; giving young people guidance; putting information in context; and explaining.

Carers often express fears about their lack of knowledge of the curriculum, or subject content: 'I don't understand how maths is taught now.' They worry that a lack of subject knowledge or specialist teaching expertise will make them incapable of having a useful educator role, and as a result they may gladly defer to a liaison teacher, if one is available. The beauty of partnering pedagogy is that the concept works just as well with carers as partners in learning. Using the key roles listed above, the carer can ask children regularly about what they are learning, in or out of school, encourage the use of technology, even when adults are not particularly comfortable with computers and the software they use, and praise young people's creative achievements.

One practical illustration of the value of informal learning in the context of new technology is the concept of 'digital badges', which borrows from the approach familiar to youth organisations that award badges to signify skills in accomplishments as diverse as first aid skills and cycling proficiency. The concept of the proficiency badge is updated to encompass experience, and evidence of performance, in a digital environment. Examples include massive open online courses (MOOCs) and the Mozilla Foundation's 'Open Badges' scheme (Mozilla Foundation, n.d.) which uses the principle of displaying a badge as recognition of skill – from a patch worn on the arm to a digital symbol on a website or social networking platform to 'celebrate skills and passions'.

A very real, and understandable, fear among carers is their own lack of knowledge of new technologies, accompanied by concerns about the risks to young people from, for example, cyber-bullying, cyber-stalking and sexual predation. These risks are real. And even advantages of new technologies can be potentially damaging in the case of children who may be particularly vulnerable. For example, while social networking brings advantages in extending a personal network, the experience of being 'unfriended' in social media can be devastating for young people 'who are learning how to deal with rejection and acceptance, affirmation and exploitation, beauty and truth' (La Mendola 2011, p.4).

In the recent past, risks could be controlled by limiting the access of children in care to internet-enabled devices, and by providing guidance for professionals that often emphasised risks over the advantages for learning. The arrival of 3G and 4G technology means that many older children have unrestricted access to the internet on their mobile phones and so control by restriction is rendered ineffective anyway. Better, then, to embrace technology and face up to the fears and risks, and mitigate them. One approach to mitigating fear is Prensky's use of the metaphor 'verbs' and 'nouns', where verbs refer to the transferable skills good students need to acquire and which are prized by employers, such as thinking critically, making decisions, communicating and persuading; and where nouns are the tools children use to practise the verbs, such as computers, Wikipedia, Skype and YouTube. In encouraging both formal and informal learning, carers can concentrate on the verbs and let children master the nouns. Sources for mitigating risk and protecting carers include advice provided by an agency or a professional body.

It is worth emphasising that the concept of partnership pedagogy applies to learning that is not dependent on new technology, and that it is the pedagogical principles of using the context, being active, creating something and applying newly acquired knowledge that are important. This is demonstrated in a more low-tech way in *An alphabet of learning from the real world*, a resource which offers ideas for learning together, based on the letters of the alphabet (Rich *et al.* 2005). For example, the letter 's' suggests 'surfaces', such as tarmac, paper, textiles, gravel, bark, and so on. The book suggests ways to investigate surfaces (e.g. icing a cake or mulching a flower bed), questions worth asking (e.g. Have clouds got a surface?) and even reading material, for example *Snail Trail* (Brown 2010).

Example 2: Play and creative activity

It is hard to overestimate the learning value of play. Research studies have emphasised both the lone scientist 'discovery' role of play and the social construction of meaning involved in play, as well as sheer fun to be gained through play. For child developmentalist Piaget, for example, play was a means by which children could develop and refine concepts before they had the ability to think in the abstract; it was age and stage related. Another highly influential developmentalist, Vygotsky, emphasised the social and cultural aspects of play. He argued that during play children were able to think in more complex ways than in their everyday lives, and could make up rules, use symbols and create narratives. Froebel, a nineteenth-century German educationalist, argued that play is both a creative activity and a social activity and, through it, children become aware of their place in the world and so their understanding of the world emerges. Play is a fundamental educational process of learning that should take place in whatever setting a child grows up in (Smith 1997). Play, whether characterised by lone discovery, active exploration, creating something, or making music in a social milieu, does not necessarily come 'naturally'; the skills for play are learned through opportunity, interaction and freedom to explore, which are structured, very often, by the adults in children's lives. For looked after children, learning through play has often been a neglected part of upbringing, and skills for play are under-developed.

Helen Chambers has been an advocate for play and creativity in looked after children's lives for some time. Through *Carers Can!*, a magazine for foster carers, social workers and residential care workers, Chambers provides ideas for play and creative activities 'that are fun, and that help children and adults get to know each other better' (Chambers 2005, p.2). She states: 'Children all over the world play. Adults play too – having a laugh with friends, following a hobby or interest. Children need some time every day to play – doing something they have chosen to do and doing it their way' (Chambers 2005, p.6). *Carers Can!* suggests that through play activities, such as making things together, playing with words or getting active together, children can learn much about themselves and being with other people, including greater self-discipline and enhanced self-esteem. Chambers (2005, p.5) relates the story of Geoff, as told by his foster carers:

> 'Geoff came to us when he was 15. At 16 he started a horticultural training scheme, but didn't finish it. Geoff was usually polite and well-behaved, but sometimes problems just built up inside him, until there was an angry outburst and occasionally property got damaged. That's why he didn't finish his training course. But Geoff had many good friends, and he had a good relationship with us. When he heard we were thinking about making a wildlife pond in our garden, Geoff offered to do it for us. He had never done anything like it before, but we thought it was important to let him take control and make it his own project. Geoff was not the kind of person to get involved in activities outside the home. He preferred to be at home where he felt safe and secure. We thought creating a wildlife pond would be an excellent opportunity for him – the project would give him responsibility and a real feeling of self-worth. Geoff got his friends to help with the labour. He chose the plants and rocks himself. Geoff chose wisely, judging by texture, colour, shape and growing conditions. When he found there weren't enough rocks to surround the pond, he used some old logs to give the pond a natural look. We were all delighted with the result. Geoff lit candles around the water at night and stared in admiration at his achievement. Geoff has created a space that is a tranquil area away from the house – where problems can be quietly talked through or just pondered over in solitude. Geoff has given us a part of him that we will always remember, even long after he has left us.'

Playing music and singing has also been shown to be a very successful creative activity for looked after children. Sing Up was a national project to encourage children and carers to sing that ran in seven areas of England. The evaluation of the project found that foster carers were enthusiastic about the benefits they noticed for the children they cared for: they made friends more easily, had greater self-confidence, and talked about thoughts and feelings more easily (Ryan 2011). Foster carers in the project listed some ways of incorporating singing into everyday life when caring for babies and toddlers that have rhythm, repetition, momentum and excitement:

- Get a CD of nursery rhymes and sing along to it in the kitchen or the car.

- Sing action songs together.

- Make up new verses to songs that are old favourites with objects they are interested in.

- Create your own rhymes and songs where you and the child take turns to sing to each other.

- Match the song to the time of day; calming songs at bedtime help reinforce a sense of security and rest at the end of the day. (Ryan 2011)

Chambers stated: 'Singing, music and storytelling are part of childhood all over the world; and bring much joy and satisfaction to children and adults. It is another way of communicating and sharing that is uniquely human – it touches our hearts and minds and connects with our feelings. Music can make us laugh and cry, and create a memory where the feeling stays with us' (cited in Ryan 2011, p.4).

Example 3: Activities outdoors

'I remember my guidance teacher when I was 16 saying, "Right, what are you going to do with your life?" And I said I'm going to be a polar explorer and she just laughed and said, "People like you don't do stuff like that." But even at 16, I knew that was wrong.' (McQuillan 2014, p.14)[1]

---

1   From an interview with polar explorer Craig Mathieson about plans for a Polar Academy for young people from disadvantaged backgrounds (www.thepolaracademy.org).

It is often said that the UK and Ireland are essentially indoor cultures, at least when compared with the Scandinavian countries. In this example, all the activity takes place outdoors, irrespective of weather, providing opportunities to develop respect for and understanding of the natural world. The Nature Nurture Project is run by Camphill,[2] a Rudolph Steiner school in Aberdeen, Scotland, at which all work with children and families is strongly influenced by the principles of social pedagogy. The programme is for children from families affected by alcohol and substance misuse, domestic violence, abusive relationships, neglect and poverty. There are groups for different ages from toddlers to adolescents, and the theory underpinning the programme is that free play in a natural environment provides restorative benefits when supported by 'closely attuned nurturing interactions' with trained staff.

The activities include adventurous play, physical challenge, craft work, social skill building and collaboration. There is a structured framework which allows children to develop a sense of security and to learn to keep themselves safe, but there is also space for child-initiated learning and play:

> The children respond well to this and are encouraged to explore more, to try new things – to climb onto logs and jump off tree stumps, gather new treasures. For children as young as 16 months, who are still learning to walk, small hurdles are major milestones.
>
> There is an atmosphere of happy calm on these excursions and the woodland is dotted with playthings. There are musical instruments like bells and drums, suspended on wooden frames, and a canvas windbreak is strung between the trees, creating a sheltered picnic spot where they sit on moss-covered tree stumps for their snack. (McLeish 2009)

There are two particularly interesting features of the programme. One is that parents and carers are offered places at sessions so they can learn strategies for 'promoting positive development towards resilience', and they are invited to take part in evaluations at the end of sessions. The project also acts as a training programme for social

---

2   www.camphillschool.org.uk.

services professionals and Camphill provides a postgraduate level course in partnership with the University of Aberdeen.[3]

In this example, outdoor play is structured and organised by specialists, but taking part in fun and exploratory activities outdoor should be recognised as one of the many ways in which foster carers and residential workers encourage children to engage in informal learning. There are, of course, many barriers to carers taking children outdoors, as reports such as *Playing it Safe?* (McGuinness *et al.* 2007) and *Go Outdoors!* (Scottish Institute for Residential Child Care 2010) have highlighted. Barriers include overly-bureaucratic approaches to risk-assessment and fears about things going wrong. While it would be wrong to take children on hazardous or wilderness activities in the absence of experience and without specialist qualifications, it is equally wrong to avoid encouraging children to play, explore or camp outdoors. The *Go Outdoors!* report highlights several myths which have led to carers avoiding taking children outdoors or limiting children's experience of everyday activities such as cycling, and making incorrect assumptions about health and safety restrictions:

> Risk-averse practices not only breach children's rights, but also rob looked after children of opportunities to learn how to manage risk themselves. Learning to manage risk contributes to healthy physical, psychological and social development, as well as providing opportunities for learning and enjoyment. A risk-averse and bureaucratic living environment undermines good outcomes for children. (Scottish Institute for Residential Child Care 2010, p.1)

Concluding thoughts

In this chapter we have tried to make two fundamental points: first, helping children to learn and sustaining their engagement in learning is central to the caring role; and, second, learning is too important to be left to schools. The research about the importance of out-of-school learning for success in formal education is compelling. But keeping young people involved in informal learning requires much support from foster carers and other everyday experts who

---

3   Promoting Resilience through Nurturing Interactions and Free Play in Natural Environments (www.abdn.ac.uk).

subordinate their own convenience and leisure time to that of the young person. The importance of relationships and encouragement in developing a secure learning identity suggests there is value in considering partnering pedagogy as a useful concept to support practice.

Practice points

+ Spend time playing and singing together; this is both learning and enjoyable.

+ Actively encourage children's participation in out-of-school activities and sports.

+ Value children's expertise in their interests, such as digital technologies, as a way to build reciprocity between adult and child.

+ Make connections between informal learning and formal learning.

+ Go outdoors and take manageable physical risks together.

Useful resources

+ Marc Prensky's book, *Teaching Digital Natives* (2010), is a good source of practical advice, strategies and examples for carers about how they can be partners in learning with children and young people of all ages. The book uses examples from the new technologies but the principles advocated apply equally to learning opportunities that are not dependent on computers.

+ For an account of the conceptual underpinnings of informal learning, D.W. Livingstone's chapter in *Learning in Places* (Livingstone 2006) is a good source (see References). Katie Hollingworth's 2012 paper, 'Participation in social, leisure and informal learning activities among care leavers in England: positive outcomes for educational participation' in the journal *Child & Family Social Work*, uses case study examples to highlight the valuable influence of participation in different kinds of informal learning opportunities.

- Useful sources of informal learning activities which can be adapted to indoor and outdoor settings include *First Hand Experiences: What Matters to Children* (available from www. richlearningopportunities.co.uk).

- The Spring 2011 issue of the online journal, *CW 360°*, is a special issue dedicated to child welfare and technology. The articles will be helpful to practitioners interested in learning more about the use of new technology and social networking in the particular context of working with children in the care context. The journal is hosted by the University of Minnesota Center for Advanced Studies in Child Welfare (http://cascw. umn.edu).

- Sources of advice on the safe use of the internet include Childnet International (www.childnet.com). Sources of advice for innovative approaches to learning include the Institute for Research and Innovation in Social Services (www.iriss.org. uk).

- For sources related to outdoor learning see the Institute for Outdoor Learning (www.outdoor-learning.org).

- For sources of advice on reading aloud to children see the National Literacy Trust website: www.literacytrust.org.uk. Education Scotland's 'Parentzone' website also has advice about supporting literacy at home: www.educationscotland. gov.uk/Parentzone.

CHAPTER 6

Supporting Education in the Care Environment

The aim of this chapter is to document a range of ways in which school education can be supported and encouraged in care settings, and to show how good quality care placements can provide a bridge to learning in school environments.

KEY POINTS

▸ It is important that care settings promote children's educational development.

▸ Thinking about schooling needs to take place early on in planning for a child's care.

▸ Demonstrating a belief that young people can succeed is very powerful, even when the effects of this influence may only become apparent in future.

▸ Carers and professionals need to harness aspiration and provide support, for example by mentoring relationships that are tailored to the specific needs of children and their families.

▸ There is particular value of participation in expressive arts for supporting social and academic achievement.

Introduction

The life histories of young adults who have been looked after typically feature many years of failure to engage successfully within the formal education system. An examination of case files may reveal behavioural difficulties, conflict with teachers and other pupils, leading eventually to exclusion from school, increasingly poor attendance, and ever more significant gaps in formational subject knowledge. For many, the early childhood trauma associated with neglect and abuse will result in underdevelopment of the brain, with significant consequences for the formation of attachments to teachers, the development of peer relationships, and the capacity to attend to learning.

The kinds of difficulties with education which can be experienced by looked after children are illustrated in this extract from an interview one of the authors conducted with a young man serving a prison sentence in Scotland. The interview ranged over several topics, including an invitation to reflect on his experience of life at school:

> 'From a young age I wasn't really in school. I used to get kicked out a lot. I used to cause too much trouble for the teachers and stuff like that. The only place I've actually been is nursery. I managed nursery fine. Then it got to, like, P1 and P2 [Primary 1 and Primary 2, i.e. age 5–6] I ended up in secure [care] at eight years old. And that was my life from there to be honest, just in and out of secure. And that's when I done schooling. So I've not really had a lot of schooling… I've not done exams 'cos I've missed that much schooling. I used to only enjoy sports and stuff like that. It used to be the only thing I could concentrate on. I couldn't sit in a classroom and do maths or something like that. I just couldn't concentrate properly.'

This brief extract from the interview illustrates several features typical of the early experiences in education of many children in the care system. More informal education which emphasises relationships with caregivers and exploratory learning (in this case, nursery school) is recalled as having been 'fine', while in the more formal setting of the primary school classroom difficulties in attending to task led inevitably to behavioural problems and conflict with teachers. Typically, incidents caused by behavioural difficulties escalate in number and severity. The work of other children is often disrupted and their parents may complain to the head teacher. Another pupil or the teacher is threatened or abused, and exclusion from school follows. After a succession of exclusions, the patience of teachers is exhausted and local authority managers may decide that an alternative to mainstream education is necessary. There are likely to be few options and often these are associated with time spent out of education while a placement is found. Alternative education often means part-time schooling, and a much-reduced curriculum.

Further reading in the case file might have uncovered a story of family stress, and mental health and addiction problems. There might also be references to domestic violence, home moves and a lack of capacity to put the child's needs, and those of any siblings, first. When social services become involved – and the file inspection might show evidence of a sequence of interventions over time – the child's physical safety will be a priority. An important question we might ask is whether anyone was also looking out for the child's educational development and seeking to ensure that difficulties in learning were considered and adequately addressed, and perhaps even made a priority.

Providing support for education in the care system

The relationship between being in or having been in care and low attainment in education is well known, and has been reported in many countries (see Welbourne and Leeson 2013). The relationship is, however, rather complex. First, it is important not to assume causality, that is, that the impact of being in care is itself necessarily damaging to education, even though this may be true if educational difficulties are not adequately assessed with proper supports put in place. While it is crucial to raise concerns about the unacceptably low levels of qualifications gained by looked after children on average by school leaving age, compared with the general school population, and to promote much higher aspirations for attainment among children and adults, it is also important to understand the long-term consequences of damaging pre-care experiences and not undervalue the positive effects of being in care. For example, a review of 13 studies of children in care over time concluded that no research study found that children's welfare got worse while they were in care (Forrester 2008). Carers and professionals often express frustration that softer indicators of developing skills and wider achievements are unrecognised, particularly where educational outcomes are expressed in the rather narrow terms of statistics comparing the examination results of looked after children with those of the non-looked after school population. Viewed over a longer timeframe the academic attainment of care leavers may look better, for example, as a result of improved pathways from further education courses to higher education, but even these positive opportunities are characterised by barriers. The five-country YiPPEE study discussed elsewhere in this book identified several typical pathways in post-school education, including a 'yo-yo' type, featuring enrolment and dropping out of courses and frequent changes of direction (Jackson and Cameron 2013).

The studies reviewed by Forrester were concerned with children's welfare more generally, rather than educational development specifically. There is, however, evidence to support the contention that being in care can promote educational development. For example, researchers in England studied 149 'maltreated' children, who were aged 0–12 on admission to care. While 68 of the children returned home, 81 remained continuously looked after. Information from social workers and teachers allowed the researchers to follow the children for up to four years. The outcomes of the 'in-care' group, including school adjustment, emotional and behavioural development and overall progress, were superior to those of the 'returned' children, even when compared with those whose reunification had remained stable during the follow-up period (Wade *et al.* 2010).

Care placements are very different, in type (e.g. residential, foster, kinship), and in quality, and the resilience of young people in care varies with individual psychology and environmental circumstances. In the research interview referred to earlier in this chapter, the young man talked about his enthusiasm for taking part in education classes in the prison, a positive attitude towards learning which perhaps surprisingly had not been extinguished, despite his lost school years:

> 'It was maths, English, the big subjects I missed out on. I loved it. I used to go every day. I put my name down for Italian… I put my name down for that as well to try and learn new things, and to just try to do something different with my life, something that I never managed to do when I was younger.'

Another young man interviewed in prison described to the author his behavioural difficulties in primary school which had led to him almost being excluded on several occasions. He was aware that the head teacher had nevertheless done everything she could to help him to remain in school. Eventually he was excluded, establishing a pattern of leaving and joining schools which characterised his secondary school years. Nevertheless, it seemed to the interviewer that the efforts of that first head teacher not to give up on the child had contributed to a resilient self-belief and determination to make up for lost education when he eventually completed his prison sentence.

The literature on the education of looked after children and the reflections on their school experience of young care leavers raise many questions. One of these is whether the low attainment of young people in care is related to low aspirations. Another is whether it is possible to influence or overcome a history of low attainment. In respect of the first question, it seems that, leaving aside the inevitable effects on behaviour, concentration and readiness to learn of damaging pre-care experiences and limited opportunities, the educational aspirations of looked after children and their parents and carers are probably not very different from those of children and families not in the care system. For example, in a US survey of 19-year-olds in foster care, researchers reported that more than 86 per cent aspired to attend college or enrol in a post-secondary school training programme (Courtney *et al.* 2007). While we know very little, except anecdotally, about the educational aspirations for their children of the parents of looked after children, there has been research on the relationship between aspiration and education among very-low-income families. Given that children in care come primarily from low-income backgrounds, that line of research potentially has several important messages which are relevant for practitioners working with the parents and carers of looked after children.

First, it is highly likely that children in low-income families attach great importance to school and are no different to children living in more affluent circumstances in that respect, and also that their parents do what they can to support them. But it may be that children in disadvantaged circumstances face more difficulties in knowing how to realise their ambitions, and that children, parents and carers need support in relation to learning about educational and career options so they can make informed decisions (Kintrea *et al.* 2011). Second, what could be mistaken for low aspirations might be higher aspirations eroded by negative experiences; and what could be assumed to be a lack of parental engagement with school might actually be a high commitment to a child's education that is not matched by the capacity of the parent or carer to provide effective support for learning or the ability or willingness of schools to work effectively with parents (Goodman and Gregg 2010).

Case study: School-based mentoring

An example of support tailored to the specific needs of children and their families is school-based mentoring by volunteer adults.

The recruitment of adult volunteers to befriend and give direction to young people in social welfare or youth justice contexts has grown significantly in recent years. The case example is a mentoring project aimed at young people in care which, at the time of writing, had been running for about 12 months in a partnership between Glasgow City Council, the University of Strathclyde, and a charitable trust, the MCR Foundation.

The children involved were aged 13–14 years and enrolled at three schools. They were living in kinship care, foster care, or with families, the last of these either because they had previously been in care or because they were receiving social work intervention. Mentors were recruited by advertising among the university's alumni community and by word of mouth. Schools provide group or individual information sessions for parents and carers, and a mentoring co-ordinator in each school acts as a bridge between school, home and the mentoring programme office, supporting the initial stages of developing mentor–mentee relationships, and liaising with the child's family and teachers.

Mentoring begins with school-based, fortnightly (or more frequent) sessions. The focus of meetings is explicitly educational, and topics covered can include identifying academic strengths and areas of difficulty, helping with organisational skills, and encouraging participation in school cultural and sporting life.

One of the mentors, Noreen, a university administrator, has provided an account with the permission and contribution of her mentee, Pauline. They found writing it a useful means of reflecting together on the development of their relationship. Names have been changed to protect identities.

Pauline has lived in a stable kinship care placement for a number of years. She has been doing well in school, though she faced difficulties in the past, as a result of a disrupted home life. She would like a career in a legal setting, motivated by an interest in law stemming from her need to understand the legal aspects of her own care circumstances. The school felt that support from a mentor would help Pauline to stay focused and avoid the ever-present peer pressure not to value school work. Noreen realised that in volunteering she was making a commitment to a relationship which could last a number of years in order to support Pauline well beyond the minimum school leaving age:

'It has always been my ambition to work with children and young people but the opportunity never presented itself until I was introduced to the inter-generational mentoring programme advertised through the University of Strathclyde.

I was introduced to my mentee as she was ending her second year at high school and we agreed to meet on a weekly basis. This was important to allow my mentee time to get to know who I was and what my role was going to be... I am confident we now have a strong, healthy relationship and that Pauline knows I only have her best interests at heart, as she grows and progresses through her schooling.

My perception of a mentor is someone who listens to, nurtures, supports and encourages a young person to enable them to strive and be the best they can be both academically and personally. A mentor can help to break down invisible barriers, source and create introductions to the right people, both personally and academically, ask the questions that need to be asked or give the young person encouragement and support to ask the questions themselves. A mentor can also minimise any fear and let the young person know they have rights. A mentor should be someone who opens the door, holds the mentee's hand and guides them through to the other side.

A mentor must also work in partnership with the school to ensure they are enhancing the hard work they already do. It is crucial that the parent or carer is also included and informed of what the mentor is working on and how they have the young person's interest at heart.

Along with my personal experience of looked after children and the role of a kinship carer within my own family circle, I believe my experience as a parent and manager, and my counselling skills, have assisted me in my role as a mentor. My role within the university and the many talented, knowledgeable people I am in contact with have also assisted me through the process.

Pauline is focused on her career path as a lawyer and together we have researched the grades required from secondary education, and looked at both the further and higher education routes to reaching her goal, along with relevant funding and scholarships available. I was able to assist Pauline in the final aspect of subject choice for her third and fourth years of high school by sourcing advice from the law school in relation to access requirements and clarifying the selection process.

Along with organising visits to see my workplace in the university, and some of our partner organisations, we will arrange a visit to the law school for Pauline to gain a sense of how courses are run, and to meet some key staff and students. I will also be continuing to assist Pauline by widening her options and looking at a number of other career paths.

Pauline has attended the university's residential summer school programme and is taking part in activities for third year pupils run by a local widening access organisation.

I realise how vulnerable these young people are and also how complex and challenging their lives can be at times. I won't accept second best for my child, so why should Pauline or any other child be different? These are *our* children and we only want the best for them, and I see a mentor's role as that one-to-one support to help this to happen.

I feel honoured that Pauline has accepted me into her life and it is a privilege to know I could potentially be part of the core group around her who can make things happen and help her realise her full potential.'

Research findings are cautious about the effectiveness of mentoring and warn that they may offer only modest benefits (Spencer *et al.* 2010). One review of 73 mentoring programmes concluded that, overall, mentoring was able to support positive development for children and young people (DuBois *et al.* 2011). Mentoring appeared to be associated with improved outcomes in different domains of wellbeing, including behavioural, social, emotional and educational development. An analysis of 19 evaluations of US mentoring programmes found that those which supported children and young people in areas such as education, social skills and relationships were more effective than those focused on behaviour problems, such as aggression and bullying (Lawner and Beltz 2013). A UK-based study of 181 mentoring relationships among young people leaving care found that the relationships generally had 'instrumental' task-focused and 'expressive' befriending roles (Clayden and Stein 2005). The research found that mentoring was valued by young people, supporting them with relationships and confidence building and impacting on their wellbeing. The researchers observed that it was difficult to evaluate long-term benefits because of the multitude of factors impacting on young people's lives, although some young people were able to identify that mentoring had been helpful to them.

Research also indicates characteristics of mentoring programmes which help to improve their capacity for success. First is a sustained relationship between mentor and mentee. In one study, most benefit was found where the relationship lasted at least one year: longer-lasting relationships had 'significant increases in their self-worth, perceived social acceptance, perceived scholastic competence, parental relationship quality, school value, and decreases in both drug and alcohol use' (Grossman and Rhodes 2002, p.206). Second, regular and frequent contact provides more opportunities for practical and meaningful help and this is linked to improved outcomes (Herrera *et al.* 2000). The stable presence of an adult may also help with attachment-related processes. Understanding attachment theory may therefore be important for the quality and effectiveness of mentor relationships (Miles 2011). Third, strong emotional connection appears to be associated with improved outcomes, and it may be that relationship closeness is more important than the amount of contact and the types of activities engaged in (Spencer *et al.* 2010). Furthermore, it is likely that young people who are able to form supportive relationships with multiple adults and social networks will have the most successful outcomes (Collins *et al.* 2010).

Case study: Using drama in a residential school

Another approach to supporting academic achievement is participation in the arts, including drama, which can be a powerful tool for developing confidence in expressing emotion and giving voice to feelings about distressing and frustrating experiences. In our second example in this chapter, Gavin Sinclair (2014) describes working with young people attending Kibble, a residential school in Paisley, Scotland[1] in order to devise a ten-minute play about life in care. The play is called *Please Listen* and is a powerful expression of feelings about being in care[2]. Names have not been changed, in accordance with the young people's own wishes, but only first names have been used.

'We had three weeks to prepare. I approached two boys, Daryl and Jonny, aged 16, who had worked with me for a number of years. We spent two hours just blasting their thoughts about being in care and examples of their experiences. They decided to call the play *Please Listen*. It was an intense two hours and it was getting quite emotional. I noticed Jonny was starting to withdraw and I thought I had bitten off more than I could chew. Still being new to this kind of work, I was worried that I had opened a can of worms. I called a break to give them and me a bit of breathing space and think time. I considered pulling the plug. I thought about my lack of understanding about the psychological effects of these kids talking about the past and their memories. I didn't know what to do, but I have never been one for giving up.

After 15 minutes we met up again and things hadn't improved. Jonny looked really upset and just as I was about to say that we shouldn't continue, out of somewhere an inspirational thought came to my mind. Jonny loves playing characters. He loves taking on a different persona and, as difficult as this might be to understand, he is happier playing a character than he is being himself. I asked, "Jonny, would it be easier if we just gave you a character name, so when we are writing this play and performing it, you will just be playing a character? It's still your thoughts, your opinions, your ideas, but it will be a character." His face lit up instantly and without thought he said, "Call me Bush." I laughed at such a ridiculous name. We all did. Within another hour we had our play complete.

There was a character called Gavin (me), a character called Daryl, a character called Dan and a character called Bush. As long as Jonny was playing Bush and not Jonny, he was relaxed and comfortable. Dan was Daniel Portman, a well-known actor who is a former student of mine. Dan volunteered to help out with the play and his involvement at the early stages was a great help to Daryl and Jonny who were about to embark on an adventure that would take

---

1   www.kibble.org.

2   Adapted, with permission of the editors, from an article in the *Scottish Journal of Residential Child Care*.

them all over Scotland and overseas. None of us had any idea that *Please Listen* would be such a life-changing experience.

We rehearsed the play in total only for about 12 hours. We would be performing to 400 international care professionals. The boys were terrified, but, at the same time, excited about being heard. I focused my energy on their confidence, reinforcing how brave they were to perform their own feelings and opinions to strangers. The boys idolised Dan and were so proud to be performing with a star. He was brilliant with the boys and made them feel like the stars. We performed. At the end of the play there was a silence. It was probably only a couple of seconds, but you could feel a sense of stunned astonishment and awe. We bowed and the entire room stood up. We had done it. We had taken Daryl's and Jonny's ideas and performed their play, their words, their speeches, their experiences, their opinions, their tears and their own creation. They were so full of confidence, they were walking on air. Nothing could stop them now. The next day, they performed it at Kibble in front of their peers. The kids from the audience came onto the stage at the end of the show with tears streaming down their faces. They hugged Jonny and Daryl, congratulating them and praising them. Bravery personified. The end. Well done everyone. Pat on the back to all involved. What will we do tomorrow?

We were inundated with invitations. Daryl's and Jonny's confidence was growing with every performance. We started doing a Q&A session after the performance and we began to realise that this was not about a play, it was not about being an actor, but it was about being heard. They performed in mainstream schools for teachers and pupils, talking to them about growing up in care. We teamed up with Who Cares? Scotland and started performing the play as part of corporate parenting presentations for local authorities. Dan was busy filming and was replaced by Jamielee, aged 14. We changed parts of the script to suit and Jamielee wrote a section for herself, giving her the same feelings of pride and ownership that Jonny and Daryl had enjoyed. They were filmed performing the play and interviewed as part of a BBC Alba documentary.

Well done, you say. It's good they got to do that. That's nice they got to perform their play lots of times and got a holiday out of it... but what? What difference did it make to them? I'll try to explain.

Jonny has spent a lifetime trying to hide his childhood memories from himself and everyone else. He used to clam up and refuse to talk about his childhood, because it was too upsetting. He lived a life of people calling him names like "stupid" and "weird". He lacked confidence in himself and didn't believe that he would ever achieve anything in life. He was ashamed of his childhood and still believed that somehow it was his fault. He is now at college studying acting full time, he is dealing with his learning difficulties and trying to improve his literacy skills, and he has started writing a book about his life. Jonny now tells people about his life in care and before. Jonny has a five-year plan and intends to become an actor or drama teacher. He has ambition.

Daryl grew in confidence. His performances got stronger and stronger as he delved deeper into the emotions of the play. At the first few Q&A sessions Daryl sat with his head down looking at the floor, embarrassed to answer questions and talk to the professionals. He didn't want to offer opinions and talk about the content of the play. After some gentle persuasion and time, he started talking. Within a few sessions he was articulating his feelings and really opening up to strangers. He was confident discussing the care system and offering sensible solutions. These are real life skills. Presenting, discussing and communicating in a relaxed, professional manner about a difficult and challenging subject will stand him in good stead for the rest of his life and career.

Jamielee joined the team as a very angry young girl who was resistant to discussing her feelings. She asked me to attend a childcare review, which was a disaster. She got angry with her social worker, swore quite a bit, shouted lots, and stormed out. Six months later, having performed and presented over 40 times, enjoyed her first experience in an aeroplane, and with confidence rising with every Q&A session, she asked me to attend another review. This time she handed the group a written statement and started the meeting by saying, "This is my review and this is how I'd like it to go. We are not going to talk about my childhood as it's in the past and we can't change that. We are going to talk about the last six months, about my behaviour in school, my work with Gavin, and we are going to talk about the next six months where I want to go home and live with my dad." I nearly cried. This angry 14-year-old was now calmly and assertively taking control of her destiny. She was running the meeting. With every *Please Listen* performance she was learning how to talk to professionals and she was finding that her views were being valued. They were also telling her that meetings, reviews and panels were opportunities for her to express how she felt. Jamielee had learned to control her emotions, talk about her needs and discuss how she felt. She was regularly sitting in a room with 200 adults talking about the care system and her experiences.

Going to a review and talking to seven people was easy. The social work team was impressed. Three months later she was living at home with her dad.'

There is limited but growing evaluative literature on the use of the arts with looked after children. In a systematic review of the literature published between 1994 and 2004 reporting studies of the use of the performing arts in health contexts with young people aged 11–18, reviewers selected 14 reports which met their inclusion criteria (Daykin *et al.* 2008). All of the studies reviewed focused on drama interventions, indicating that there is little reporting of the evaluation of the use of other arts interventions in non-clinical contexts. The reviewers concluded that there is evidence of positive outcomes following performing arts interventions, with the strongest evidence being on the outcomes on peer interactions and social skills. The Office for Public Management (OPM 2013) evaluated three expressive arts projects with looked after children and foster carers and concluded that, post-participation, young people had marked improvement in self-efficacy, had a sense of pride in their creative achievements and greater willingness to try new creative endeavours, take on leadership roles and contribute their ideas and opinions. Artists in all three sites had 'created a participatory learning environment and an informal and non-hierarchical space where the children felt empowered', which had helped the young people focus and learn new skills (OPM 2013, p.40).

A report of a musical theatre production called *City of One* (Salmon and Rickaby 2014) that involved 35 young people, from both care and non-care backgrounds, in acting and support roles found positive benefits for the young people involved. Interviews with ten young people in and leaving care, and with foster carers, residential care workers and theatre professionals were carried out and reported that the mix of young people from care and non-care backgrounds was helpfully non-stigmatising; it broke down barriers and extended friendship networks. Young people said participation had developed a heightened self-awareness and this helped them to co-operate and be tolerant of others. The play was about a teenager whose foster carer was taken ill and the teenager had to move, documenting the upheaval this caused, and young people said they identified with the characters. The performance allowed them to understand how their behaviour may have impacted others.

As well as developing social and expressive artistic skills, participation in educational drama offers the potential to support 'educational resilience' in terms of reading, writing, and speaking and listening. The opportunity to 'learn through doing' provided by drama and other expressive arts is important in instrumental terms. The young people at Kibble, for example, can gain qualifications, since drama is part of the wider curriculum of the school.

Concluding thoughts

We said at the start of this chapter that the aim was to document a range of ways in which education can be supported and encouraged in care settings, and also to show how good care placements can provide a bridge to learning in school environments. The case studies illustrate different ways in which adults are encouraging young people's learning and supporting them to achieve in both a personal and an instrumental sense; and show that those who work with and support looked after children and young people have significant opportunities to integrate education with care in their daily practice, whether this is by demonstrating that they value education in its broadest sense, or by providing practical help with particular learning activities. What connects the case studies is that each involves providing a supportive environment in which children and young people can develop the social skills needed for becoming confident learners. In the example of mentoring, apart from the value of the supportive relationship, there is a connection with the idea of having a champion to help provide encouragement and practical help with school and career decision making. The experience of the mentor, Noreen, in working in a university brought a valuable additional dimension to the relationship because of her specialist knowledge of post-school education. In the example of drama we can draw attention to the link between social skills and self-efficacy learned through performance and confidence in learning academic skills. Gavin, the drama specialist in the residential school, combined high-level relationship skills with specialist expertise in drama.

Practice points

+ Look for ways to value the experience and expertise of young people in care in arts, music and other 'performance' activities.

+ Recruit artist pedagogues and expressive arts trained care workers to residential care, foster care and allied practice.

+ Consider the importance of long-lasting, trusting relationships between teachers and looked after children.

+ Integrate young people in care into mentoring projects which can help to champion their progression in school.

+ Think about learning in a broad sense – where social skills of listening and team work can be gained, self-esteem and academic focus can follow.

Useful resources

+ The paper by Penelope Welbourne and Caroline Leeson (2013) considers the literature on social policy and the practice of caring, identifying placement stability and support at school as significant factors that contribute to better achievement, with therapeutic help and specialist assessments being necessary for improving the outcomes of some children.

+ Several organisations such as the Who Cares? Trust (www. thewhocarestrust.org.uk), the British Association for Adoption and Fostering (www.baaf.org.uk), Centre for Excellence for Looked After Children in Scotland (www.celcis.org), The Fostering Network (www.fostering.net) and In Care, In School (www.incareinschool.com) provide information and resources aimed at teachers and carers supporting looked after children in education.

+ Further information about mentoring programmes can be found on the websites of mentoring organisations such as Big Brothers Big Sisters of America (www. bbbs.org), the Australian Youth Mentoring Network (www.youthmentoring.org.au), the Scottish Mentoring Network (http://scottishmentoringnetwork.co.uk) and Reach Out (www.reachoutuk.org).

• The *City of One* study referred to in the chapter (see Salmon and Rickaby 2014) is a compelling account of the social benefits of active participation in a musical theatre production. Will Barlow (2011) makes the case for drama in helping to engage looked after children with education because of the opportunities it provides for active learning.

CHAPTER 7

Early Years Education in Foster Care

This chapter introduces a rarely discussed aspect of the education of children in care, that of early education. Almost a quarter of children in care are under five yet we know very little about their educational experiences.

KEY POINTS

▸ Many young children spend months or years in foster care before being placed for adoption or some other placement intended to be permanent.

▸ Forming attachments and learning are complementary aspects of children's development.

▸ The first two years are a period of rapid brain development which provides the basis for later learning.

▸ Foster carers are not required to deliver the Early Years Foundation Stage, unlike childminders.

▸ Looked after children from age two are entitled to 15–16 hours' ECEC in high quality settings. Foster carers should be encouraged to take advantage of this entitlement once the child is settled in the care placement.

Introduction

Children are learning from the moment of birth, if not before, but little attention has been paid to the experience of very young children in foster placements. There is a feeling that it doesn't really matter because most of these placements are intended to be temporary. Either the child will go back to his or her parents or will be placed for adoption. But across the UK and Europe, the vast majority of young children are accessing early childhood education and care, and the United Nations Convention on the Rights of the Child (1989) embeds the right to pre-school education within Article 18.

The strong drive to increase the numbers of children adopted from care is beginning to have some effect, with just over 1000 more children adopted in England in 2014 than in the previous year, but there will probably always be many children who come into the care system at an early age and remain for long periods. The numbers are very volatile, but according to the latest available statistics about a quarter of the care population is under compulsory school age. In England, 3880 of those in care on 31 March 2014 were babies under one year old and 11,440 were aged one to four years, making up 23 per cent of all those in care. Of these only 150 were recorded as formally freed for adoption. The comparable figures for Scotland were 700 babies and 1037 children under five – 39 per cent of the total care population.

In the UK, very young children (those under three years of age) who are looked after are in foster care; institutionalised care is not used apart from some residential services that include mothers and babies. This is unlike some other European countries (Browne 2005). However, the average age at adoption in England is 3 years 5 months, so even the minority of young children who are eventually adopted may have spent a long time in one or more foster homes.

Characteristics of young children in care

The majority of these babies and very young children have either been removed from their mother at birth, because she has proved unable to look after previous children at an acceptable standard, or, if later, because they have suffered serious abuse or neglect. Most cases of child homicide involve babies (Munro 2011).

In these circumstances the most important task of the foster carer is to establish basic trust between herself and the baby, so it is not surprising that the priorities of both the carer and social worker are physical care and nurturing. It is unlikely that the child will have experienced any kind of consistency in early upbringing. She may have spent many hours crying for attention without any response, or only an angry one. The foster carer will be trying to give the child some sense of security, so that she can relax, sleep peacefully, feed, play and generally thrive. The task may be complicated by access visits if a parent or relative is entitled to see the child and, especially in that case, social work concerns will be more to the fore than educational ones (Borthwick and Donnelly 2013).

However, we have to remember that, although six months or a year may be a short period in adult terms, it is the child's whole life, and learning opportunities lost then may never be recovered. How else can we account for the wide gap in developmental progress that is already opening up between looked after children and others by the age of two? This is not only a time of extraordinarily rapid learning but may also be the time when the child's learning identity is being formed, the beginnings of self-efficacy, the intense urge to explore and find out (Geary and Bjorklund 2000; Feinstein 2003; Cairns 2013).

Case study: Two babies

Aisha and Kevin both came into care at a very early age and were fostered by experienced carers, mainly offering short-term placements for babies.

Aisha's parents were aged 16 and 17 when the baby was born, and separated a few months after the birth. Aisha's mother, Sally, was depressed at this time and had to be reminded by her partner to feed and change the baby. Otherwise he did little to help and would rather go out with his friends than stay in the house with Sally and the baby. His parents, originally from Pakistan, strongly disapproved of his relationship with Sally, and encouraged him to move back home. After he left, Sally spent most of her time sitting on the sofa smoking and watching television. When the health visitor came round she found the house in a dirty and neglected state. Aisha was crying to be fed; her nappy had not been changed for two days and she had a severe nappy rash. Sally said she had run out of disposables and had no money to buy more.

Aisha was placed under a care order with Pat Green, who had looked after a succession of babies in similar circumstances. The plan was for intensive work with Sally to enable the child to return home, but 18 months later Aisha was still in the same placement. Sally visited from time to time and her social worker continued to hope that she would eventually grow up enough to be trusted to look after Aisha safely.

Kevin's father had served a prison sentence for a violent attack on his previous partner, leaving her with a broken jaw and severe bruising. Kevin's mother, Karen, was a heavy drinker and had had four children removed as a result of neglect or injury by one of a series of abusive partners. The decision was taken to remove the fifth baby at birth (which was four weeks early) and place him with foster carers prior to adoption. Two prospective adopters withdrew after hearing more about Kevin's background. A third placement broke down when the adoptive father suffered a heart attack. So the foster placement with Eileen Richards, when Kevin was nearly six months old, was already his fourth change of carer. Research evidence suggests that this is quite typical (Ward et al. 2012).

Eileen was a divorced woman with grown-up children. Before Kevin she had looked after several young children who had returned to their birth families. She had read books and articles about the effects of ill-treatment on children and was determined to try and make up to Kevin for his poor start in life even if he only stayed with her for a short time. At first he was very unresponsive, resistant to cuddles, and did not attempt to sit up by himself until the late age of eight months. When sat down next to a Treasure Basket (see below), which Eileen had painstakingly assembled for him, he appeared to take no interest in it. The third time, he stretched out a tentative hand and grasped a metal whisk, which he then mouthed and turned over in his hands for almost twenty minutes. Within a few days he had started to wave his arms and legs and make excited noises when he saw Eileen bring out the basket.

Books took a little longer. Eileen thought Kevin had never seen or handled one before. She started to read him a story every day, sometimes several times, and as soon as he could crawl he would go to the book pile and try to pull out the one he wanted. Before long the pile had grown to twenty books and Kevin had clear favourites among them. Later, when they went to the library, he liked to spend a long time choosing his books, examining them closely and sometimes going back to one he had discarded. By the time he was a year old he had grasped the idea of turning over pages without tearing them and often liked to look at books by himself.

Kevin was not an easy child to care for. He would resist being put down for a sleep even when clearly exhausted and would often scream in protest at having his nappy changed or for no apparent reason. For the first few months he woke repeatedly in the night and refused to go back to sleep. Eileen was sometimes very tired. However, eventually things settled down and she was able to establish a routine. This included taking him out every day, whatever the weather. She decided to change her standard buggy for one that enabled her to face the baby and chat to him as they went along. As soon as he could walk himself she encouraged him to do so, even though it meant everything took longer.

Eileen's social worker noticed that she was unobtrusively 'teaching' Kevin all the time, quietly talking to him, naming objects and colours, commenting on his actions and their surroundings and waiting for him to respond, what Trevarthen (2004) refers to as 'proto-conversations'. Eileen said she tried to do things that an ordinary mother would do, counting steps when they climbed the stairs, singing nursery rhymes, taking Kevin to 'baby music', swimming (for which social services reluctantly agreed to pay) and a weekly parent and toddler group in the local book shop.

The family situation of Pat Green, Aisha's foster carer, was very different. She had one daughter at secondary school and two boys of seven and five. Keeping up with the washing and cooking meals for the children and her husband took up most of the time when she wasn't busy looking after Aisha. She bought the local newspaper once a week but otherwise had little time for reading. Once the children were home from school the house became very noisy and busy. Aisha was too young to be a playmate for the older children, although they sometimes incorporated her into their games and she would sit with them watching the television, which was rarely turned off. There were few books in the house apart from school books and Pat thought the library, suggested by her social worker, 'a bit too far to go'. The small back garden was full of footballs and bicycles and Pat did not encourage Aisha to play there, especially after the day when she pulled off all the flower heads.

By the time the two children were 18 months old clear differences were apparent between them. Kevin no longer flinched when an adult approached him. He was sleeping much better, feeding himself with fingers and a spoon and was always willing to try something new. He was walking and climbing confidently, enjoyed exploring indoors and out and taking small risks such as walking along a wall or tackling the bigger slide in the playpark, often giving a running commentary on his activities, including recognisable words. Eileen had started a book to write down his new words every day, and the list soon added up to over a hundred. He could name many objects, correctly identify three colours, say numbers up to five, not necessarily in the right order, and enjoyed scribbling with wax crayons on large pieces of paper. He would demand at least three stories before he went to sleep at night and protest if Eileen changed or abridged them. His favourite toy was a drum containing a large number of differently shaped wooden building blocks but he still liked to play with the objects in the Treasure Basket from when he was younger.

Aisha's social worker was also pleased with her progress. The child was clearly attached to her foster carer, reaching her physical milestones at the expected time, beginning to say a few words, and seemed happy and settled in her placement. She was still mainly spoon-fed from jars of baby and toddler food, and reluctant to try anything unfamiliar. She could ask for what she wanted by pointing, but otherwise her ability to express herself and make choices was rather limited. She had a few favourite soft animals, which she would play with quietly on her own, and was allowed some toys that had belonged to the older children, though not books, as she might spoil them. She had only two board books, given by her social worker. She had not had much chance to hear songs or nursery rhymes – singing did not come naturally to Pat – and conversation between them may have been inhibited by background noise from the radio or television.

Both these placements were assessed as 'good' and were clearly helping the two children to recover from their very adverse beginnings, but only one of them could be described as a learning placement. Already, before the age of two, their developmental trajectories were diverging markedly.

Educating babies

Until the 1990s early child development was exclusively the property of child psychologists and health professionals, with educationists taking little interest in children under the age of three. The field of early years care and education in the UK has expanded enormously over the past 20 years (Maynard and Powell 2014), but the focus of most of the literature is still on the 3–5 age range, the traditional period of nursery schooling. By that time there are already big differences between children of educated middle class parents and those from low income and socially disadvantaged families with few or no educational qualifications (Feinstein 2003). The two-year-old check introduced by the coalition government (2010–15) is designed to identify children who are making less progress and introduce compensatory measures but there is no evidence yet of how successful these are likely to be, and indeed some would argue that the whole enterprise is misconceived because testing such young children produces unreliable results and leads to premature emphasis on formal teaching and learning. The argument is well set by Dahlberg and Moss (2005) and Featherstone *et al.* (2014).

While there is still an almost complete absence of research evidence on the early developmental progress of young children in foster care, there are more and more self-help books addressed to parents of babies and young children, which are equally relevant to foster and adoptive parents. As a result of the rapid expansion of private childcare provision for very young children, more is being written about the group care of babies and toddlers in day care settings away from home, although most of it tends not to be research-based (Jackson and Forbes 2014). It does, however, take a broadly educational perspective, in the sense that we use education in Chapter 1. In the present chapter we suggest that education has been a missing element in the care provided for young children away from home, and may be at least partly responsible for the fact that even good quality foster care seems unable to provide an adequate foundation for educational attainment in the conventional sense. In this chapter we do not discuss the more general aspects of satisfactory foster care, assuming that the placement has been chosen in accordance with the minimum requirements (see Chapter 2) and, we would hope, with attention to the principal carer's ability to look after the child in a loving, sensitive and responsive way.

Educational care in the first year

Susan Hallam (2010) suggests that in acquiring any skill the key requirements are motivation, time and practice, to which we would add appropriate physical conditions and encouragement. We can see this in one of the first physical skills a baby acquires, turning over from front to back. To begin with, this is an immense struggle, and the baby often finds herself stranded on her back, depending on another person to help her roll back again. But once this is achieved she will repeat the action again and again until it comes easily. Of course, all babies eventually learn to turn over, but how quickly they do so depends on the opportunity to practise by having plenty of time lying on the floor, or outside on the grass, as opposed to being confined to a reclining chair or buggy. It is interesting to note that 'tummy time' has been found to build connections in the brain (Goddard Blythe 2009). Some carers have misinterpreted the advice to put babies to sleep on their backs as a protection against SIDS (Sudden Infant Death Syndrome) so that infants are given too little time lying on their front during the day, which they need to enable them to lift their heads and observe what is going on around them.

The next stage in physical development is sitting up, at first propped up by cushions and later independently. This phase, when the child is immobile but actively interested in her surroundings, can be very frustrating for babies and they often complain; this is usually attributed to teething but is just as likely to be an expression of boredom with the often limited and uninteresting playthings available to them (Goldschmied and Jackson 2004; Forbes 2004). Most early years settings where babies are looked after have taken up Goldschmied's idea of the 'Treasure Basket' (Froebel Trust 2013). This is not simply a random collection of playthings in a container but a basket of a particular design containing very carefully selected objects designed to stimulate each of the baby's senses.

The Treasure Basket is a straight-sided basket without a handle, filled with objects from both the natural and the made world. The items it contains are not generally regarded as toys, and might come from the kitchen drawer or anywhere else in the house or outside it, but are all specifically chosen to engage the baby's senses of touch, taste, sight, smell and hearing (Forbes 2004). Elinor Goldschmied, who originated the idea of the Treasure Basket, was insistent that none of the objects should be plastic, as babies are exposed to so much plastic in their daily lives. Babies seated at a well-stocked Treasure Basket will often play with great concentration for as much as an hour at a time (Jackson and Forbes 2014). The theory underlying the Treasure Basket has been verified scientifically by advances in research on brain development (Thomas and Johnson 2008; Geary and Bjorklund 2000; Giedd et al. 1999). We suggest that use of treasure baskets should form part of training for foster carers who look after babies.[1]

Promoting curiosity and independence

The Treasure Basket offers babies an early opportunity to make choices. By allowing them to do this without adult interference,

---

1   The Institute of Education, University College London, runs one-day courses in the use of treasure baskets and heuristic play.

they are learning to make their own decisions, a first step towards autonomy and self-efficacy. At the next stage, once they become mobile, usually early in their second year, they seem to be saying at themselves, 'What can I do with this object?' This is what they will discover for themselves if they are given a chance, not always at the convenience of their carers. Taking things out of containers and cupboards and sometimes putting them back in again is an absorbing occupation for toddlers (Jackson and Forbes 2014). Many early years settings, such as the Thomas Coram Early Childhood Centre described below, offer sessions of 'heuristic play' to encourage this kind of activity. Large numbers of similar items such as hair curlers, cotton reels, corks, ribbons and chains, and natural objects such as pine cones or shells, are set out in heaps in a space defined by a carpet or other floor covering, together with a variety of containers, such as tins, boxes and cardboard tubes, with which the children play freely, exploring the properties of the objects in the process. Gopnik *et al.* (1999) suggest that when children engaged in this kind of play repeat the same action over and over again, they are testing and revising theories in the same way that scientists do. Clearing up is an integral part of the session, providing a first step towards the understanding of sorting and the mathematical concept of sets.

Feeding

Feeding is the primary learning experience for babies. Sadly, most of those in foster care will have been breast-fed only for a very short time, if at all. However, for those who have been neglected or maltreated, bottle feeding by their foster carer can be a form of healing, when they have the full attention of their caring adult and can begin to feel safe again. There is a temptation, as with other forms of bodily care, to treat feeding as a routine matter, to be combined with watching television or looking at a magazine. Close observation of feeding babies has shown that they are very aware when their carer's attention is elsewhere and she is failing to respond to the subtle clues by which they convey their wishes (Murray and Andrews 2000). Eye contact and soft talking to the baby are a message that she is important to the person in whose arms she is lying, and thus one of the thousand tiny building blocks of self-esteem.

But feeding is also an opportunity to show respect for children's right to make choices and express preferences. A baby who is being spoon-fed from a jar of baby food only has one choice, to accept or reject it. The increasingly common practice of baby-led weaning allows her to eat with her fingers and choose from a variety of different foods that might be offered to her (Rapley and Murkett 2008). Research has shown that babies given this opportunity make healthier choices than adults sometimes make for them. They are more likely to choose savoury rather than sweet things and prefer fruit and vegetables to biscuits. Babies allowed to choose for themselves are much less likely to be overweight. Later they learn to manage their own spoon, acquiring manipulative skills in the process.

Communication and language development

There is clear evidence that language development at the age of two predicts children's performance on entry to primary school. Vocabulary and spoken language are the basis for reading and are more important for comprehension than technical aspects such as phonics. Evaluation of a scheme in a London borough to encourage foster carers to support reading found that many children were held back by their very limited vocabulary measured by standardised tests (Hill 2014, personal communication). Wide gaps have already opened up by the age of two. Roulstone and colleagues (2011) estimated the range in words understood at this age to be 200 to 500, closely related to deprivation or social advantage . At 25 months in a sample of 1127 children, 55 per cent of children were using sentences of three to four words, 27 per cent were using two-word phrases, but the rest were still at or below the single-word level.

Although there appears to be no quantitative evidence on the language development of looked after children, it is clear that foster carers play a crucial role. Children acquire language by listening and talking with their parents or other persons they love and trust and also through their play, which enables them to develop and use symbols and the early sounds linked to meaning. Those first 'words' used consistently and repeatedly with a familiar object or person supply the connection between pretend play and early symbolic development (Whitebread 2011). Vygotsky (1978) observed that it is often in their pretend play that we hear self-directed or private speech, a running commentary on what they are doing, which can provide valuable insights into the child's inner experience. Foster carers do not need to teach children directly to speak, but to provide a communication-rich environment in which they have the opportunity to share ideas and thoughts and ask questions that are carefully listened to and receive a thoughtful response. Bruner's concept of scaffolding is helpful here, where the adult is supporting the learning through unobtrusive intervention to enable the child to be successful in a task and thus internalise the understanding and be able to re-use it in the same or a different situation at a later point (Bruner 1977).

The difficulty that looked after children experience in mathematics is much less discussed than their backwardness in reading, but research by Rose Griffiths, founder of the Letterbox Club, found that it has similar roots, in that their early home life, or foster placement, did not provide the foundation for understanding basic mathematical concepts. In our case study, Eileen showed that she was fully aware of this as an important aspect of her role. Maths is much more resistant than literacy to improvement by one-to-one tutoring (Alexander 2010). Griffiths shows how children will use their energies on trying to cover up their ignorance or guess what answer the teacher might want rather than engaging with a task which may seem completely baffling (Griffiths 2013).

Language development and television

Dr Linda Pagani and colleagues (2010) in Montreal conducted a study to determine the impact of TV exposure at age two on future academic success, lifestyle choices and general wellbeing. She found that every additional hour of television the child watched predicted a future decrease in classroom engagement, poorer achievement in maths, and poorer language development at school entry. Advice is generally that children under two should not watch any TV at all, and it is important to limit exposure for the 2–5 age group. Now, not only television but the almost universal tablets and smart phones mean that toddlers are constantly exposed to images on screen (Arnold 2014). Limiting screen time is difficult for foster carers and has to be a matter of deliberate policy agreed by the whole family if it is to be successful. Pagani's finding echoes that of Pecora (2012), who found that school attainment in adolescence was inversely related to time spent playing video games.

Music, singing and rhymes

Our case study foster carer, Pat Green, was inhibited from singing to Aisha, which meant that her foster child did not enjoy this very basic and enjoyable experience. Social workers, and other professionals who support foster carers, need to make it clear that the carer does not need to have 'a good voice' to give pleasure to a child. Songs and rhymes are important in developing listening skills, and understanding of poetic structures, vocabulary and rhythm. Children love familiar nursery songs and want them repeated over and over again. They are also important building blocks in the development of language and music education.

Learning to love books

Rudolf Steiner, one of the pioneers of early childhood education, believed that up to the age of seven children should be interacting with people and objects in the world around them, especially the natural world, and spend as much time as possible in the open air (Nutbrown *et al.* 2012). Book learning should come later. Steiner Schools were exempted from the Key Stages framework which sets rigid targets for children's attainment in English primary schools. While we strongly concur with the first part of this proposition, early reading and a love of books have often been noted as crucial assets for looked after children and can sometimes help to make up for deficits in their care (Jackson and Martin 1998). We therefore take the opposite view to Steiner on this subject, and suggest that it is good for babies and young children to become familiar with books and stories from an early age, besides being a source of obvious enjoyment as they were to Kevin in the case example.

Every time a foster carer reads with a baby or toddler on her lap she is showing him how books should be held. Letting him turn the pages encourages him to show care and respect for them. Talking about the pictures provides an opportunity for discussion and conversation and learning to follow a narrative. There is now an enormous wealth of children's literature suitable for children from a few months old up to school age on which librarians are happy to advise. The foster carer's role is not to teach reading but to instil the idea that books are a source of interest and pleasure, along with all the other things a child of this age might be doing (Bruce and Spratt 2008).

Using outside resources

Fostering a baby or young child can be quite a solitary occupation, and the carer may need encouragement and support from a social worker to make full use of the resources of the local community (Jackson and Forbes 2014). There are now more chances for parents of young children to share play and learning in groups while their babies and toddlers are still mainly looked after at home. Examples are book and music groups, baby yoga and massage, baby swimming, painting and modelling, dance and movement, and many other activities offered in children's centres (although sadly diminished in some areas as a result of local authority budget cuts). These are important not only for social interaction and first steps in acquiring particular skills but also because they promote closer attachment between carer and child. Privately provided groups and facilities often charge quite high fees and foster carers may have to argue strongly for the children they look after to have the same learning opportunities as those with their own parents. Foster carers may also feel some awkwardness about having to explain their relationship to the child (or making the decision not to do so), and it may be helpful for them to talk this through with their social worker.

Childcare and early education settings

In England, two-year-old children in care are entitled to additional resources under the government-funded Pupil Premium Plus and to 15 hours a week early education in a formal setting. In Scotland, a similar entitlement exists for children who are looked after in public care or are under a kinship care order or living with a Parent Appointed Guardian; they are entitled to almost 16 hours a week ECEC, along with all those children aged three and four in both countries. But, as noted above, we do not know how many children in care attend early childhood education services, or how well they do, compared with other children from similar backgrounds.

In fact, we know almost nothing about the attendance of children in foster care in early childhood education and care (ECEC) settings. There is little research on the subject, but some evidence that children in care are less likely than others to receive any formal early childhood education; this is also true in other European countries (European Commission 2012). Moreover, the European Union Report on youth and social inclusion comments that disadvantaged or marginalised children, for reasons of ethnicity or disability, may sometimes be physically present in ECEC facilities but psychologically absent. Evans (2000) found that some foster carers felt that, since they were being paid to look after the child, it would not be legitimate to use other services. There is a further argument that a child who may already have experienced several changes of carer in her short life needs above all to form a secure attachment with her foster carer, not to have to cope with yet more new people.

This is a very valid point, but we would argue that forming attachments and learning are complementary aspects of children's development, and that, once a child is settled in a foster placement, a high quality ECEC setting with well-trained staff can offer, for a few hours a week, many facilities, learning opportunities and social experiences which may not be available in the foster home. Moreover, the Early Years Foundation Stage requires all group settings to operate a key person system, by which a specific staff member has responsibility for looking after the wellbeing and progress of each child in attendance (Elfer *et al.* 2012). When the system is working effectively, this person provides most of the day-to-day care and tending required by a baby or toddler, such as feeding, changing, dressing, and recognising the child's need for a sleep or a cuddle. The key person develops a close relationship not only with the child but also with her family, and becomes an important addition to their support network (Jackson and Forbes 2014). There is no reason why this should not equally apply to a foster family.

For a fostered child it may be desirable to extend the normal settling-in period so that the carer is present in the nursery until the child feels entirely happy and safe with her key person and has no sense of rejection or abandonment. Children are able to form attachments to more than one person, and there is no reason why close and warm relationships in an ECEC setting should diminish their ability to become attached to their foster carer. Another objection sometimes advanced is that these relationships are liable to be short-lived as the child may be moved to another placement and both the child and the adult will suffer pain from the separation. We stress throughout this book the enormous importance of stability and the preservation of affectional bonds, but have to recognise that placement changes are sometimes unavoidable. That does not devalue the experience. As the great Italian poet, Primo Levi, expressed it:

> ...remember the time
> Before the wax hardened
> When everyone was like a seal
> Each of us bears the imprint
> Of a friend met along the way.

Social development

Attending a good quality early years setting is important for social learning as well as cognitive and emotional development. All studies of the school experience of looked after children find that their progress is likely to be delayed by behavioural problems and difficulty in social relationships (Jackson 2000; Jackson and Cameron 2014). They are far more likely to be subjected to suspensions and exclusions, both temporary and permanent, than other children (see Chapter 9), resulting in at best missed schooling, and in the worst case referral to some form of special provision such as a pupil referral unit (Blyth and Milner 1996; Poyser 2013). Children who begin to be looked after at the age of two or three may already have been exposed to very poor models of social interaction, in households where disagreements are common, and more often resolved by shouting or violence than by reasoned discussion.

One of the most important skills that children learn by attending good ECEC settings is negotiation: how to take turns, share, be aware of other people's right to have their wishes taken into account, and sometimes accept that they cannot have what they want at the precise moment they want it (Jackson and Forbes 2014). Early years educators are helping to resolve these small disputes all the time.

If they are reflective practitioners they will also observe carefully how they arise and consider how they can be avoided, for example by ensuring that there are always plentiful supplies of the most popular playthings and arranging the space to avoid overcrowding. They will also model how to express differences without acrimony, how to speak to other people in a calm tone of voice, and not to use negative or discriminatory language. These are all valuable lessons for the child to take into school and may make it less likely that they will come into conflict with other children when they get there.

Choosing an ECEC setting

Free childcare places are supposed to be taken up only in settings assessed as good or outstanding by Ofsted, but not all local authorities are able to provide them in sufficient numbers. Very few places for two- and three-year-olds are now provided directly by local authorities; nearly all are with approved childminders or in private nurseries or childcare centres. The numbers of these have grown exponentially – in fact childcare is one of the fastest growing small business sectors in the economy. This means that, at least in urban areas, there may be a choice of settings. Ofsted ratings are no more than an indication: inspections are on a four-year cycle, and quality is not a fixed attribute but can change quickly depending on who is in charge of a centre and the staff employed (Jackson and Forbes 2014). Children who begin to be looked after when they are already in their third or fourth years are very likely to be behind in development so it is important that they attend the very best early education setting available.

Children's centres, considered to be one of the great successes of the 1997–2010 Labour Government (Eisenstadt 2011), were set up as a universal service, available to everyone in a local area. Although they were located in areas of social need they provided a holistic service crossing traditional boundaries of care, health, education and leisure, and originally they had to provide childcare in order to access government funding. Unfortunately they have been a soft target for local authority cuts: 400 closed in the first two years of the coalition government and by 2014 many of the remainder had drastically reduced the services on offer, and most had abandoned full day care as unaffordable.

One exception is the Thomas Coram Centre, which was designated as one of the Early Excellence Centres under a programme which ran from 1997–2006 and continues to provide an example of outstanding practice.

Case study: Thomas Coram Centre

Thomas Coram Centre offers high quality, fully integrated education, care and family support in partnership with parents and carers and runs all year round. The children come from all sections of the local community and reflect the cultural, religious and linguistic diversity of the Kings Cross area – with children speaking 23 different languages. A proportion of places are reserved for children with special educational needs or those deemed to be in need for family-related reasons, which would include children in care. The Centre is led by senior staff with backgrounds in education and social work so there is a good understanding of family problems and there are support groups for parents. The ethos and practices of the Centre mean that staff work in partnership with foster carers as well as birth parents and can manage transitions for children when they move between the two. There is a comfortable and attractively decorated parents' room, and activities for fathers as well as mothers.

The Centre is designated as a school and has a strong educational ethos. There is a core programme for the majority of children who attend in the morning, and extended hours for a smaller number whose parents need childcare. The head teacher is the author of several books on ECEC (e.g. Duffy 1998). Of her two deputies, one is a teacher and the other has a social work background. The building is very well designed to provide an attractive and ordered environment with maximum freedom for the children to explore and plan their own activities from an early age. The 'home rooms' open onto a wide corridor with sitting areas and doors leading out to the garden. The 17 early years educators operate a free-flow system so that children are able to explore as soon as they can move by themselves. There is a three-weekly planning cycle known as the 'Avenue of Exploration', building on events in the children's lives. The garden is a genuine outdoor learning area with allotment spaces to enable staff to grow things with their key children.

The curriculum and approach to learning of both children and staff make use of a range of theoretical ideas, with a strong emphasis on staff reflection and discussion, for which time is built in during the working day. Elinor Goldschmied's influence is discernible, with treasure baskets stacked on the shelves in the baby room and regular sessions of heuristic play. There is a well-developed key persons system (Elfer et al. 2012). Another major influence is the early childhood service in the Italian city of Reggio Emilia (Abbott and Nutbrown 2001) and this can be seen in the creative use of space, attention to the visual and sensory environment, the wide range of activities offered to the children and the democratic ethos of the Centre.

There is no substitute for first-hand observation. It is a good idea for the foster carers and social worker to do a joint visit to any setting that might be considered – convenience and accessibility obviously have to be taken into account, but a key consideration is how far the setting adds value to the care provided in the foster home and contributes to making it a learning placement. Carers should be encouraged to look round several nurseries before making their choice. Organisations such as the Family and Childcare Trust, Pre-school Learning Alliance and National Day Nurseries Association all produce guides for parents about what to look for and what questions to ask.

Donna, whose journey through care is related in Chapter 3, did not attend any pre-school setting and this is probably typical for looked after children. Few of the YiPPEE young people in England mentioned going to nurseries or any other form of ECEC, although one interviewee did remember enjoying pre-school, in contrast to his unhappy school experiences later. We know that children of lower socio-economic status families (of which Donna was one) fall behind their peers in terms of acquisition of cognitive competence very early on in life. High quality early education can offer some compensation in terms of promoting resilience, supporting disadvantaged children, and accelerating the process of learning (Sammons et al. 2007; Wood and Caulier-Grice 2006; Cassen and Kingdon 2007).

In the influential EPPE study, a 'high quality' ECEC setting was defined as one where staff possessed good qualifications and the manager was a trained teacher. Other characteristics were:

• having a good proportion of trained teachers or staff who understood how children learn and had a knowledge and understanding of the curriculum

- a behaviour policy which focused on staff managing children's behaviour through reasoning and talk – negotiation rather than coercion

- activities that included interaction traditionally associated with the term 'teaching' and instructive learning environments

- education and social development seen as complementary and equal in importance, including a focus on literacy, maths and science/environment as well as 'diversity'

- warm, interactive relationships with children, who were encouraged to initiate activities and be involved in shared thinking with adults

- parents engaged in their children's learning and parents of vulnerable children supported to improve the home learning environment.

(Sammons *et al.* 2007)

So it would appear to be an early educational disadvantage not to attend ECEC and one which could be overcome by making it clear to foster carers that attendance is not only legitimate but expected. It also gives the carers some breathing space, which may be much needed if they are looking after a child with multiple difficulties.

The role of foster carers

Important as ECEC can be, by far the largest single influence on children's early learning is parents playing with, talking and reading to children, and although there is no direct evidence relating to foster parents there seems no reason why this should not be equally true for them. Specific programmes mostly focus on children over three, by which time there is already evidence of delayed development. However, some targeted programmes have demonstrated that it is still possible at that age to address the impact of social disadvantage on early learning.

For example, the Peers Early Education Partnership (PEEP) is a two-year programme of focused intervention on building self-esteem and literacy development and it benefits disadvantaged three-year-old children and families, when compared with non-participants. Evangelou and Sylva (2007) evaluated the PEEP programme and found substantial progress in children's verbal comprehension, vocabulary, concepts about print, numeracy, and cognitive and social competence. The PEEP programme was a partnership with parents, and worked to a specific curriculum that included use of music and rhythm, story times, sharing of books, home activities and opportunities to borrow playthings and equipment. It involved intensive staff training in preparation for implementation of the programme. One of the statements from the curriculum underlines the significance given to self-esteem: 'How children feel about themselves is important for learning. Children who feel good about themselves do so for a variety of reasons. One reason is when other people enjoy being with them. Children who feel good about themselves are more likely to want to learn' (quoted in Evangelou and Sylva 2007, Table 1). This view of learning underlines the broad perspective on education discussed in Chapter 1 and the important role of foster care in helping children to develop a secure learning identity.

Concluding thoughts

In this chapter we have argued that much more attention should be given to the learning environment provided by foster care for the youngest children, those under four, who make up nearly a quarter of the care population at that age. Halvorsen (2014) comments that educational methodologies which are part of the standard curriculum in early years and teacher training are seldom mentioned in the social work literature, and education is a subject that hardly appears at all in foster parent training programmes, either in the UK or in the author's native Norway. Just because the placement is intended to be short-term or temporary is no reason to regard the experience of these very young children as unimportant. This is a time of extraordinarily rapid learning of which we should take full advantage. Warm and responsive care attuned to the individual child is essential but not sufficient. Foster carers need to be constantly aware of the occasions for learning offered by everyday life and ordinary care routines. However, foster carers cannot be expected to provide all the learning opportunities offered by a high quality ECEC setting, especially if the child they look after has special needs. Social workers should give the same attention to arranging enrolment in an early education setting as they would do in choosing a school placement for an older child, and ensure that all foster carers take advantage of the part-time free entitlement.

Practice points

+ Create an educationally rich environment, a learning placement. Babies and toddlers need this as much as older children.

+ Make use of a Treasure Basket. This is a valuable resource for foster carers, offering babies the chance to use all their developing senses and make choices before they can move independently.

+ Remember that very young children enjoy looking at books and hearing stories, songs and rhymes long before they can talk themselves.

+ Talk and listen – speech develops from conversational exchanges with close adults.

+ Once the child has formed a secure relationship with the carer, enrol him or her in part-time attendance at a high quality ECEC setting. This can enhance the educational value of the foster placement.

Useful resources

+ The Early Years Foundation Stage Framework is the English curriculum for young children outlining the standards that early childhood education and care settings should reach (www.foundationyears.org.uk/eyfs-statutory-framework).

+ www.communityplaythings.co.uk: examples of excellent environments for children aged 0–3.

DVDs

+ *Discovered Treasure, The Life and Work of Elinor Goldschmied 1910–2009.* (The Froebel Trust 2013). Footage taken at Eastwood Nursery School Centre for Children and Families in 2013, rated outstanding by Ofsted, shows Goldschmied's continuing influence in current childcare and education practice (www.tvroehampton.com; www.froebeltrust.org.uk).

+ *Baby It's You: Inside the Baby's World* 1994, a Channel 4 series showing the world from the viewpoint of babies and toddlers under three, produced by Dr A. Karmiloff-Smith (www.beckmanndirect.com).

+ *The Wonder Year*, a series of DVDs about the first year of development distributed by Siren Films Ltd with accompanying notes (www.pengreen.org).

Early years organisations

There are many early years organisations providing support to professionals and with good resources on their websites. The following represent just a few of those available:

+ The Family and Childcare Trust (created from the merging of the Daycare Trust and Family and Parenting Institute) campaigns for increase in affordable day care provision and promotion of equal opportunities. It provides research, consultancy and useful publications (www.familyandchildcaretrust.org).

+ I CAN is the children's communication charity. Many children have language delays or other communication difficulties, including children in care. I CAN helps children develop speech, language and communication skills through providing information, supporting research and toolkits for practitioners. Examples include Early Talk and Early Talk

0–3, which are evidenced-based oral language intervention programmes (www.ican.org.uk).

• Professional Association for Child Care and Early Years (PACEY, formerly National Childminding Association) aims to support childminders, nannies and nursery workers to gain recognition for their 'vital role in helping children get the best start in life' through setting high standards, providing information and guidance and requiring members to commit to continuous professional development each year (www. pacey.org.uk).

CHAPTER 8

Caring Schools

The aim of this chapter is to explain what we mean by 'caring schools', drawing on a model of practice developed in the USA, experiences of practitioners in the UK, as well as the duties of schools and ideas for promoting awareness of looked after children within schools.

KEY POINTS

‣ In caring schools pupils feel valued for their contribution and believe the school cares about their wellbeing.

‣ Children in caring schools make very good academic progress, especially those from disadvantaged backgrounds.

‣ Looked after children are more likely to thrive in school where they are able to develop supportive relationships with teachers.

‣ Attendance at school is vital for success in education, and it is important that schools follow up absence and promote good attendance of their looked after children.

‣ Schools are enormously diverse and getting more so, especially in the secondary phase.

Introduction

James Wetz, an experienced head teacher writing about the importance of relationships in secondary schools, makes the point that teachers typically learn only part of a child's story, and that: 'the fuller story, including the family story, is seldom heard by the school; and the school story becomes a series of events to which the school is compelled to respond rather than a narrative of information which might help to enable the young person to engage' (Wetz 2009, p.38).

A local authority decided to improve the support provided for looked after children in the transition from primary to secondary school. In order to inform their plans, managers commissioned narrative accounts of young people who had recently left care, using schools' and social work records. One example from the narrative account of a young woman illustrates the problem associated with having only part of the picture. The social work records showed that at age eight her life was highly disrupted, characterised by several changes of home, as she moved between her birth mother, grandmother and temporary foster care placements. The school records completed at the same time show that she was falling behind in reading and the class teacher noted that 'she needs to consolidate reading at home'. There was no evidence of recognition in the school records of a home life that was not conducive to reading or how this might be impacting on her life at school. Similarly, the social services' records made no mention of the effect of the disruption at home on her education or gave any indication that the school had been actively involved in plans for support.

In this chapter we consider ways in which teachers can become better involved in the 'narrative of information' so that schools can become more caring environments for looked after children.

What is a caring school?

A caring school is one underpinned by an ethic of care, in which all members, children and staff feel they belong and that they have a voice. From the perspective of care theory, Noddings (1998) argues that education (in its widest sense) is central to the cultivation of caring in society. She states that as fundamental education happens in loving parental homes, teachers should look to see how parents educate children as a starting point for educational methods in schools. She suggests that there are four ways teachers and other school staff should demonstrate caring:

♦ *Modelling:* demonstrating warmth of care in staff relations with children.

+ *Dialogue:* fundamental to caring is talking about it and discussing practice.

+ *Practice:* children in school should have opportunities to practise caring, for example for a pet, and to reflect on that practice.

+ *Confirmation:* recognising admirable qualities in others and encouraging their very best.

A school improvement programme in the USA found that helping schools become a 'caring community of learners' was a central plank in enhancing students' progress. The Child Development Project (Schaps *et al.* 2004) introduced programmes in a range of schools that deliberately built up the sense of connectedness between children and staff and engagement in learning. Called the Caring School Community (CSC) programme, evaluations showed that children made very good progress academically and socially when their sense of community within a school was the prime focus of attention, especially those children who came from disadvantaged backgrounds.

A sense of community or 'caring community of learners' exists when school students feel valued, contributing and influential members of a classroom or school and when they perceive the school as dedicated to the wellbeing of all its members (Schaps *et al.* 2004).

Building a sense of community in school, they suggest, has four key components:

+ Actively cultivating respectful, supportive relationships among and between students, teachers and parents.

+ Promoting a shared understanding of the school's goals and values, such as fairness, concern for others and personal responsibility.

+ Providing regular opportunities to help and collaborate with others, and to reflect on interactions with others, so building up collaborative working skills and richer networks of relationships as well as a sense of reward from helping others.

♦ Providing opportunities for autonomy and influence. Having a voice in establishing the agenda and climate for the classroom is intrinsically satisfying. It also helps to prepare students for the complexities of citizenship in a democracy.

To accelerate academic progress, the authors first recommended that, in addition to building a sense of community, schools establish high expectations of every student's continuing progress; and, second, noted that there are important, challenging and engaging opportunities for learning that build skills and knowledge in a range of academic, practical, creative and social capacities (Schaps *et al.* 2004).

The CSC programme is aimed at primary school age children and is implemented in every class in a school, building communities within and across the school. This whole-school approach gives staff a common language so they can discuss issues that arise in implementation. The programme introduces four elements, each designed to build children's sense of responsibility for their own learning and to value others as well as themselves.

The four elements are:

♦ *Class Meetings.* Regular opportunities to set group norms, build the team, problem solve or make decisions about issues in common, and to reflect on/appreciate the class community.

♦ *Cross-Age Buddies Programme.* This pairs whole classes of older and younger children for language, maths, art and other activities to help build caring cross-age relationships. Teachers plan together, support the buddy pairs during the activity, and reflect on the experience with their class afterwards.

♦ *Homeside Activities.* These are mini-projects that start in school, include tasks for parents/carers, and then finish in school with group interaction and sharing. One example was talking about being 'old enough' to take on new responsibilities and privileges.

♦ *Schoolwide Activities.* These are non-competitive school-wide projects that link children, parents, teachers and other adults in the school; they help foster new school traditions, and promote helpfulness, inclusiveness and responsibility.

An example was creating a whole-school collage of everyone who works in the school, as depicted through children's interviews with and drawings of members of staff and volunteers.[1]

These four elements, implemented over a year, develop children's sense of belonging to a school community, autonomy and voice, and competence, so that they feel valued. These are the foundations for academic learning that schools can foster for all children, not just children in care.

A caring school is also one where attention is paid to the physical environment. Wetz (2009) argues that the size, design and organisation of large secondary schools increase the difficulties experienced by pupils already disengaged from school and learning. If a school cannot easily bring together its entire community in a single space to address a crisis together, he contends, it is hard to provide the social and emotional support needed to avoid institutional exclusion. Wetz's thesis is that many children who fail to thrive in school are affected by the consequences of poor attachment experiences at critical times in childhood. These negative experiences impact on the child's capacity to develop a secure identity as a successful learner and his or her ability to cope with school.

Wetz advocates what he calls 'human scale' relationships as the key to helping young people who are disengaged feel accepted by school to the extent that they are willing to invest their own time, emotion and intellect in the learning activities on offer. He identifies three conditions for such relationships: (i) consistent contact between teachers and pupils; (ii) teachers and pupils seeing a lot of each other during each school day; and (iii) unhelpful change being kept to a minimum. In a situation where carers and social workers have opportunities to select a school for a looked after child, these conditions could serve as important touchstones in considering whether the school is likely to meet the child's needs.

A caring school for looked after children

Looked after children will benefit from a school environment where the characteristics of a caring school are in place. However, there

---

1   www.devstu.org/caring-school-community.

are some more specific features of a caring school for looked after children. Foster carers interviewed for this book emphasised the need for school teachers to know about children in care from an early stage in their training. One foster carer, from Scotland, thought it very important that 'trainee teachers should know about young people who are misbehaving, [they] are often not trying to upset a lesson, that they are often expressing a need. Teachers need a more general understanding about the lives of children in care, and then they need to know about attachment and attachment disorders.'

Another foster carer, also from Scotland, described her child in school and her worries about moving up to the next school phase. She said, 'He is in primary school. I wish he could have had more years in the current school, his life chances would have been so much better. I worry about him in high school. He has sexualised behaviour, possibly Asperger's, and is violent. He can't count or tell the time. He needs factual information, delivered in a succinct way. Even getting around school will be a problem.' She went on to say that there needed to be much more support during the transition phase to the next school.

A third foster carer, this time from England, had a child with 'very extreme behaviours, very demanding... [who was] aggressive in class'. When a three-day residential trip was planned, the initial assessment from the company leading the trip was that the boy could not attend due to his behaviour. But the school staff protested at this, saying it was not fair on the child and, the foster carer continued:

'What can we do to allow him to go, and to make sure that it's not dangerous and also that everyone enjoys it..? So what they did was work out a plan where they had a teaching assistant from the school go with him. He would be picked up from home, early in the morning, taken to the place, have breakfast with everyone there, stay till early evening, when they had hot chocolate. He did not stay there overnight but he had everything everyone else had, went canoeing, rock climbing...all the things social workers don't like them to do. But the school went out of their way to find a way for him to be able to do something that was unusual and different, not normal school life but really exciting for everyone; he got to do that as well, despite all the issues.'

The impact on the boy was:

> 'tremendous. He loved it. The report back was that there were some occasions when he had to come down a level but overall it was the best they had seen him. For example, his ability to say "please" and "thank you"; sounds really simple, but he never said "please" and "thank you", he was always one for taking – but when back at school he was saying "can I have" and "can I sharpen my pencil". It triggered something for him, almost as if he was thanking them in his way, for letting him. At home, he was not one for hugging or high fives, but when he came home he gave me a hug and said, "Thank you for letting me go." I am fairly sure he knew there were conversations about whether they would let him go or not. He was aware. It had an impact emotionally on him.'

In the experience of this small group of foster carers, the ways in which schools care about and for looked after children varies a good deal. One question that repeatedly arises is that of how much information teachers need, or should have, about a looked after child's particular circumstances. A fourth foster carer took a young person to talk to a group of trainee teachers at a Scottish university. She said that her foster daughter was able to tell these trainees that:

> 'it is important not to single out someone as a fostered child but that the teachers should know what is happening […] to know that she liked a particular scarf…to read emails. To know it wasn't easy for her. Not to go out of the class because of misbehaving, but to have more understanding that if kids are looked after it is really difficult for them in the class.'

School support for looked after children: designated teachers

All UK countries provide guidance to schools about how to support looked after children. In England and Wales guidance has the backing of statute. The Children and Young Persons Act 2008, s.20, specifies that the governing body of a maintained school must designate a member of the staff at the school as having responsibility for promoting the educational achievement of registered pupils at the school who are looked after.[2]

Maintained schools in England, including academies and free schools, are required to designate a teacher who has a specific responsibility to promote the educational achievement of children who are looked after. The role of the designated teacher is to:

+ promote a culture of high expectations and aspirations

+ ensure young people have a voice in setting learning targets

+ advise staff about differentiated teaching strategies

+ prioritise looked after children in one-to-one tuition arrangements

+ make sure carers understand the importance of supporting learning at home

+ lead on the development and implementation of the child's Personal Education Plan (PEP) within the school.

In Scotland the term 'designated manager' is used, indicative of the expectation that the role should be undertaken by a promoted member of school staff who is in a position to negotiate arrangements within the school and liaise appropriately with social services and other agencies. The 'core tasks' to be performed by designated managers are listed under the four headings of communication, meeting the needs of looked after children and young people, advocacy, and learning and development (Scottish Government 2008a).

A cross-party parliamentary committee in England also recommended that the designated teacher should be a senior member of staff who is also committed to the educational progress of looked after children (APPG 2012). A senior teacher appointment can 'ensure [the role] has gravitas and teeth…help raise awareness amongst staff, governors, carers and young people themselves' (APPG 2012, p.25).

---

2   Their work is supported by that of a local authority officer, a Virtual School Head, whose role is to promote the educational achievement of looked after children (Children and Families Act 2014, s.99). See Chapter 2.

In primary schools, the designated teacher was often the head teacher, but in secondary schools this was, in the evidence presented to the APPG, far more variable, with consequent effects on the extent to which they could provide leadership, information and advice to others.

Designated teachers have a particular role in tracking the progress of individual children. According to the APPG, designated teachers need to act as a 'pushy parent' and be in a 'constant conversation' with members of teaching staff, carers, learning mentors and others with an educational role with a looked after child. With this kind of approach a true picture will emerge of progress and the impact of interventions, and 'the right decisions [will] be made in a timely manner'. Designated teachers may be involved in identifying particular talents of a looked after child and finding ways to promote them.

Information about children is held in a Personal Education Plan (PEP) (or Personal Learning Plan in Scotland), a document that records, in one place, everything about a child that is required to support the delivery of their education. The designated teacher is responsible for ensuring that PEPs are completed, updated and that progress in relation to education targets is monitored.

Designated teachers have a specific role in relation to helping looked after children make the transition to the next phase of education, often a difficult time. The APPG recommended that the designated teacher role should be extended to the post-compulsory sector in order to make these transitions easier, at least from the perspective of transferring paperwork.

While it is clear that having someone who knows them and can advocate on their behalf is helpful for looked after children, particularly in meetings, the designated teacher is not with them every day and in every lesson. Just as the foster carers noted above, the APPG recommended that subject and class teachers have training to know how best to recognise and address the particular learning issues of children in care.

The Scottish Government's guidance to local authorities on corporate parenting, *These Are Our Bairns*, provides a set of self-assessment questions for schools with the general question: 'How will we know when we have made a difference?' and proposes seven measures (Scottish Government 2008b, p.40):

+ When pre-five centres, schools or other educational establishments are places where looked after children and young people and care leavers feel happy, safe and valued, through teaching and learning approaches which are sensitive to their needs.

+ When young people who are, or have been, looked after make the transition from school into sustained placements in further or higher education, employment or training.

+ When you can give a positive answer to the question 'Would this be good enough for my child?'

+ When there is no difference in the rate of attendance or exclusion of looked after children and young people as compared with their peers who are not looked after.

+ When looked after children and young people and care leavers are just as likely as their peers to participate in out-of-school activities and wider school community activities such as sporting competitions.

+ When looked after children and young people and care leavers receive the additional support they require to participate in mainstream education, regardless of whether they are placed out of authority.

+ When the educational outcomes for looked after children and young people and care leavers, in terms of attainment and achievement, are the same as those for their peers who are not looked after.

Case study: In Care, In School

Education Scotland, the executive agency responsible for improving education provision in Scotland, has created a website, The Journey to Excellence (www.journeytoexcellence.org.uk), which aims to showcase examples of innovative practice in education and other children's services. In one of the video clips provided, teachers at Mearns Academy in Aberdeenshire, Scotland, and a young woman who had been out of formal education for two years explain the support which has allowed her to get to the point where, in her own words: 'Now I see the value in school.' The strategies adopted included:

+ reviewing the school's protocol and procedures for supporting looked after children

+ gathering information needed for planning a good school experience by consulting with teachers and other agencies

+ having regular meetings which involved the child 'so they know what's happening, because it is about them and we want them to feel they have ownership as well'

+ tailoring the curriculum to suit individual needs

+ finding the pupils' strengths and using these to build up their confidence and self-esteem

+ one-to-one support in a 'safe haven'.

The young woman interviewed explained that her return to school had been managed 'at a pace I could handle and where I was ready for it and it wasn't rushed or forced'. She began attending for two hours per day, which increased to half-day attendance and finally to full days. Working with primary school pupils and with younger secondary pupils on paired reading has been important in developing confidence and a desire to stay on in school.

In England, the In Care, In School project (Parker and Gorman 2013) aimed to introduce awareness about children in care to teachers and pupils in schools via teacher trainees. The project was a collaboration with young people who were members of the In Care Council (ICC). Originally, the intention was to generate materials that could be used as part of personal, social and health education in secondary school, although, as the project progressed, it became clear that the target audience should be teachers working with children in primary schools, and teachers working across all curriculum topics. The main educational method was to produce filmed scenarios, based on the real-life experiences of ICC members, that each pose open questions about how to support young people in practice. Films are short, only 1–2 minutes in length, and are supported with suggested activities for teachers for each film. Films cover topics such as being asked to write an autobiography, being asked to step out of a class to speak to a social worker, taking photographs of class members for websites and newsletters, and asking about what children did at the weekend. The scenarios open up for discussion issues about protecting the anonymity of children in care, being visible and invisible in school, and knowing how to manage the responses of a peer group when someone is 'different'. Supporting activities invite questioning assumptions about how teachers interpret the behaviour of school children, and how assumptions guide reactions to behaviour.

For example, teacher trainees were asked the following questions when faced with a film clip showing a child's behaviour:

> 'What assumptions do we bring to bear when interpreting children's behaviours? How do these assumptions inform our subsequent actions? Think about the situations described at the start of the session. In what circumstances might these behaviours be appropriate and make sense to the child? How can schools balance the need for consistently maintained high standards of behaviour on the one hand yet be flexible and resilient enough to recognise that all behaviour requires empathetic interpretation and – at times – different responses?' (Bath Spa University 2012, p.9)

Throughout the project the important role of the ICC in directing the content, helping develop the scripts and having oversight of the materials developed carried on through the ethos of the teacher training. Young people who were in care were seen as 'experts in their own lives' and gained considerable kudos from this expert status (Parker and Gorman 2013). Teacher trainees used the materials when on placement, with the same ethos, with positive results, as this trainee explained:

> 'I asked the child in care if he minded me teaching this lesson or if he would rather go and do some other work whilst I delivered it (I did this after school the day before on a 1 to 1 basis). He was happy to remain in class. In fact he actively participated. This was really amazing, I thought he was really brave and what he said came over to the class a lot more powerfully than anything I did. I must confess that I was worried that this could have gone the other way and he and others could have become very emotional.' (Bath Spa University 2012 p.20)

Some teachers who were approached to take part in the project were concerned about whether showing the films in class and raising the issues in them might be too distressing for children in care themselves. Overall, however, the authors believe that the model has wider applicability, including the potential to be extended into foster care training, and as the basis for a national quality standard for attachment-aware schools. An initial evaluation found that the use of the materials led to improved relationships between children in schools, had enabled some children in care to be experts and lead lessons, and had raised awareness of the educational issues for children in care among student teachers and others (Streeter 2012). What was apparent in implementation was that support from school managers was crucial to success. Some were resistant to raising potent and sensitive issues, while others were much more confident of the potential benefits of doing so.[3]

Schools and the whole looked after child

One of the enduring difficulties for looked after children in school is the passage of information before, during and after school between professionals and carers. It is almost as if, despite the attention in recent years to integrated working, each professional group is only concerned with one 'part' of the child – the school child, the foster child, the child of birth parents, the legal status of the child, and so on.

One of the recurring recommendations for social work practice is that a child's schooling is considered at the same time as their care placement. Guidance in England is that children should not be moved to a new school when a care placement begins.[4] If and when a school is selected for a looked after child, this should be one judged by Ofsted to be 'good' or 'outstanding' and never one considered 'inadequate', and it should be on the basis of being able to meet children's needs, taking into account their wishes and feelings (DfE 2014c).

Assuming there is no change of school at the point of a care placement, it is so important that the child's school is informed. It helps the school to understand implications for schooling and it reinforces the value of school for stability in the lives of children undergoing considerable change, who may have developed attachments to particular teachers, and who, in turn, can be understanding but maintain expectations of them. For many children in care, the school may be a 'haven' of continuity, where they can feel relatively 'normal'.

The trick is to maintain the child's sense of being 'normal' while at the same time attending to the differences for children in care in school. Most noticeably, all children in care in England must

---

3   Further information from www.incareinschool.com.

4   The Care Planning, Placement and Case Review (England) Regulations 2010 – Regulation 10, avoidance of disruption in education.

have a Personal Education Plan, which may, if they have special educational needs, be incorporated into an Education, Health and Care (EHC) plan.

Applicable to children of all ages, the PEP is a multi-agency record of the resources required for children to progress and fulfil their potential. The PEP should 'raise aspirations and build life chances' (DfE 2014c, p.14). The EHC plan covers the same ground, but may involve information from a wider range of professionals, such as health and care. Both the PEP and the EHC plan are subject to regular review to ensure the targets and resources to meet them are appropriate and relevant. When a young person reaches the age of 16 or 17 and preparation for leaving care begins, the information in the PEP should feed into the leaving care 'Pathway Plan' (DfE 2014c, p.17). The aim is to reduce duplication of effort in the information recorded about young people in care and create a jointly held understanding of each individual's needs, wishes and potential, and how these will be met. Such a joint understanding is often missing.

A foster carer in England, contributing to a recent dissertation about education and looked after children, described her experience of working with schools over 20 years:

> 'We have had a really huge range of experiences… [almost all the children] have had really significant educational needs because their lives have been so disrupted. In some cases the schools have been absolutely wonderful – they've really worked with us to try to help the children. They've given us resources to use with them, they've given us computer programs…all sorts of things. They organise regular meetings. And in other cases we've had to almost kill ourselves persuading the school that the child has any special needs at all. We've had huge battles…some have been very, very supportive and others not.' (From Spector 2014)

Concluding thoughts

Caring schools, along with learning placements, form a central plank in the education of looked after children. Schools that put caring at the centre of their ethos and placements that put learning at their core are two halves of thriving and wellbeing for children in care.

However, much needs to be in place for schools to adopt this position. First, school leadership and policy must recognise the importance of an overall ethos of welcoming children in care, and vulnerable children of all backgrounds. In fact there is much to recommend in cultivating a sense of belonging to a caring school community for all children in order to build wellbeing and learning.

Second, for children in care, school policy and practice has to be sensitive to their wishes to feel 'normal' and to 'fit in'. While full information is clearly critical to enable adaptations to be made to the curriculum, and to the way teaching addresses home life, for example, or expectations of homework, or how young people are singled out in the public environment of classrooms, getting the balance between sufficient information to be aware of these sensitivities and too much information, or information that is handled without due regard to young people's complex histories, requires careful thought and skilful interpersonal practice from all school staff.

Third, it seems clear that young people have to be considered in some respects 'experts in their own lives'. They need to be fully involved in their schooling, recognising what they find difficult, what they do well and what they can contribute to school life. Likewise, full engagement with foster carers and others who have the most direct knowledge of young people in care, and often have the clearest idea of their strengths, limitations and idiosyncrasies, is important. Regular dialogue from a position of mutual respect and partnership where roles and responsibilities are clear underpins successful schooling.

Fourth, teachers can benefit from additional training that raises their awareness of the particular circumstances of looked after children and how to address them. Video-based materials delivered in conjunction with care-experienced young people can be very powerful tools.

Fifth, there needs to be an influential driver of children's progress – the equivalent of the pushy parent – and enjoyment in school. In school this is the designated teacher or manager who is committed to following through on plans made to address particular or special needs and takes action if a child falls behind or needs an advocate.

Finally, and perhaps most important, school needs to be a place where looked after children feel happy and safe, where enjoyment of extra-curricular activities, sports and the arts, as well as more general skills for life, take equal place alongside academic achievement.

Practice points

♦ In assessing how welcoming the school is likely to be for children in care, assess the degree to which every child feels valued and that they belong to the school community.

♦ Include in teacher training, opportunities for trainees to learn about children in care and what it is like to go to school from a care placement from the care leavers themselves.

♦ Prepare carefully for school admissions of looked after children, including involving pupils in planning their own school attendance.

♦ Critically reflect on assumptions held about the behaviour of 'children in care' as a group.

♦ Plan placements with school attendance to the fore, closely followed by out-of-school activities and enjoyment.

♦ Be aware that empathy and flexibility of approach are necessary ingredients for young people's success in school.

Useful resources

♦ Education Scotland's 'Journey to Excellence' website (www. journeytoexcellence.org.uk) is a treasure trove of resources, including video clips about school improvement. The section on Culture and Ethos is particularly useful. The Nurture Group Network website (www.nurturegroups.org) provides information on using nurture groups in nurseries and schools. The Child Trauma Academy website (http://childtrauma.org) has a library of articles of interest to educators and carers.

♦ Enquire (The Scottish Advice Service for Additional Support for Learning) (http://enquire.org.uk) has excellent resources, including the guide *Extra Help at School When You Are Looked After*.

+ *Settling to Learn* Bombèr and Hughes (2013) is an extended dialogue between a teacher and therapist and a clinical psychologist which uses numerous case examples to show how past trauma and abuse affect everyday behaviour in school, even for children in good quality foster care. It is full of practical advice for teachers and shows how empathetic understanding based on attachment theory and building relationships is the most effective way of promoting learning for troubled children.

+ In Care, In School. DVD and written learning resources to help schools understand what it means to be in care and in school (www.incareinschool.com).

+ Produced by the Who Cares? Trust, *Teachers in the Know* is an interactive CD-ROM that aims to provide teachers and other professionals concerned with looked after children access to first-hand experience of navigating the educational system through film clips from children in care, care leavers, teachers and children's services professionals. Further information from www.thewhocarestrust.org.

CHAPTER 9

What Happens when Mainstream School Isn't Right

This chapter examines the problem of school exclusion and what the alternatives might be.

KEY POINTS

‣ Children who are already disadvantaged, for example by low income and special educational needs, have much more risk than more advantaged children of being excluded from school.

‣ Exclusion from school can end a young person's chances of acquiring useful qualifications.

‣ Foster carers and residential workers have an important role in helping schools to support children, for example by telling them about strategies that are successful in the home.

‣ Proportionately more looked after children attend alternatives to mainstream schools, such as pupil referral units (PRUs), than their age cohort as a whole. Three-quarters of students attending PRUs are boys.

‣ Factors which are likely to lead to better educational outcomes in alternative provision and a pathway back into mainstream school or college include trusting relationships, a strong learning ethos, high expectations and a school-like environment.

Introduction

There are different views about the purpose of an education and, consequently, what schools are for. Some may regard schools in individualistic and instrumental terms, a means to an end, such as gaining qualifications to get a place at university or an apprenticeship. Others will see schools as having a more social role in, for example, making good citizens or helping to overcome the disadvantages caused by poverty. These different perspectives also have a part to play in the assumptions that determine educational services for particular groups of children, such as those with disabilities or those in state care. The underlying issues include whether the default position is 'inclusion for all' compared with specialist provision for some, and whether schools and educators should have a role in changing society.

In this chapter we will examine the mainstream–specialist dimension in the particular context of provision for looked after children, exploring such issues as attending to individuality, and the meanings and use of terms such as 'special needs', 'behavioural difficulties' and 'exclusion'. We will consider placement dilemmas, such as deciding whether a particular school is right for a child and advocating and managing a proposed change of school. We will also examine alternatives to mainstream settings, such as pupil referral units, and on-site schools, as well as specialist services operating within mainstream schools.

The problem of exclusion from school

Government statistical reports published in the nations of the UK show a consistent picture of looked after children experiencing exclusion from school at significantly higher rates than the average for all children. They also appear to show a change in recent years, with falling rates, presumably in response to challenges by individuals and organisations advocating for improvements in the educational outcomes of looked after children. The governments in England, Wales and Northern Ireland distinguish between permanent and fixed-term exclusions, while permanent exclusions are not permitted in local authority schools in Scotland. The rate of fixed-term exclusions of looked after children in England in 2011/12 was 11.36 per cent (down from 13.32% in 2008/09), compared with

4.05 per cent for all children. The Welsh government found that while permanent exclusions of looked after children had fallen to very low levels as a result of 'managed moves', the number of fixed-term exclusions increased from 232 in 2007/08 to 304 in 2010/11.

Concerns have, however, been raised about the accuracy of these statistics amid suggestions of such practices as 'informal' exclusions which do not follow government guidance or local authority protocols, and delays in making school placements amounting to exclusion from education that is unrecorded. An investigation by the Children's Commissioner for England found that while many schools try to hold on to children who are troubled, there were also '…situations when a school requires a young person to leave the premises but does not record it as a formal exclusion', effectively 'illegal' exclusion (Children's Commissioner for England 2012, p.16). In calling for reform in the system, the Commissioner noted that in order to be compliant with the UNCRC, statutory guidance should specify that the interests of the child must be paramount in any decision to exclude, and that a child's views should be taken into account. A report of a series of seminars held in Scotland to consider the effect of new guidance on 'inclusion' noted that:

> Seminar participants expressed some concerns that exclusion can be used as, and perceived to be, punishment. This becomes clear when children and young people are not only excluded from classes but also from the other aspects of school that might be protective; breakfast clubs, school lunch, after school or sports clubs or even voluntary sector programmes that the young person has been referred to by the school because of concerns or vulnerability. (Morrison 2012, p.5)

The report by the Children's Commissioner for England described examples of unrecorded short-term exclusions to allow children to 'cool off', pupils being 'sent home' and not allowed back into school until after a meeting has taken place with their parents, and pupils being 'coerced' by head teachers into moving to different schools. One year later, the Commissioner published a further report which focused solely on 'illegal' exclusion. In her findings, Maggie Atkinson listed three types of illegal activity presented in evidence to her committee:

+ 'Schools failing to follow proper procedures in excluding children, either for a short period or permanently.

+ Schools following formal exclusion processes, but failing to take account of other elements of law in doing so. This is most common in cases where schools have failed to have due regard to their legal obligations under the Equality Act 2010 and predecessor legislation.

+ Schools and local authorities failing to fulfil their legal responsibility to provide alternative education for those excluded for more than five days.'

(Children's Commissioner for England 2013a, p.23)

Various school practices were identified, including the use of part-time timetables, extended study leave, encouraging parents to home-educate their children and sending children home if their carer or teaching assistant is unavailable. Although there is no systematic evidence of the extent of these practices, they appeared from the investigation to be known in large numbers of schools. The report highlights a lack of awareness of the law on exclusion by teachers and school leaders, and children and their families being unaware of their legal rights.

In a second report in 2013, the Commissioner considered exclusion from the perspective of equality (Children's Commissioner for England 2013b). In her findings, she noted that in England in 2010/11 the two per cent of pupils with statements of special educational needs were six times more likely to be formally and legally excluded than pupils with no level of special need, and the 18 per cent of pupils regarded as having special needs but without statements were nine times more likely to be excluded than pupils with no special need. Child-related factors which appear to be related to the risk of exclusion from school were reported to be ethnicity, gender and income: black Caribbean pupils were four times more likely than children from other ethnic groups to be excluded; males were three times more likely than females; and children in receipt of free school meals (a proxy for low income) were four times more likely to be excluded than pupils not eligible for free meals.

Case study: A carer's experience of exclusion

Margaret is a kinship carer looking after her daughter's two children, a boy and a girl, both now in secondary school. She talked to one of the authors about her experiences of school exclusion. While her granddaughter had always coped well with school, and was progressing in her studies, her grandson, John, had great difficulty settling in a classroom setting, problems that were apparent from the earliest years in primary school. He had a diagnosis of attention deficit hyperactivity disorder (ADHD) and his behaviour could be challenging for teachers. Despite this, the school's head was supportive of Margaret and was willing to listen to her ideas, based on her experience of strategies that worked at home. If John became distressed and the staff could not calm him, the head would call Margaret and ask her to come to the school to help. This was very disruptive to Margaret's life, particularly as she had a part-time job, and it was not always easy for her to drop everything and rush to school. But she was prepared to do this since it allowed John to maintain his place in mainstream school. On one occasion she was called to the school to coax John down from the top of a cupboard, something the class teacher had not managed to achieve. John then spent time with the head in her office before returning to class.

Unfortunately the head teacher was moved to take charge of a bigger school. The new head was unwilling to work with Margaret and said that teachers could not be expected to deal with such disruptive behaviour. John experienced the first of a series of exclusions, a pattern that continued when he transferred to high school. Margaret had been told that John would be better placed in a special school, something she was intent on fighting. She said she had felt supported by the fact that the previous primary head was willing to listen to her, showed understanding of her circumstances and would even take her advice about strategies for managing John's behaviour that worked well at home. She had not found her personal expertise valued in this way by staff in the secondary school. She felt they just wanted John moved on.

The significance of exclusion

Teachers face a difficult task. They usually work with children in groups of a significant size. They understand that learning is best facilitated when it is structured, children have a clear idea of what is expected of them, and there is a supportive and happy classroom atmosphere.

The optimum learning environment can be adversely affected for all children when one child's behaviour becomes challenging or unmanageable. Teachers and the parents of other children have been known to put pressure on heads to exclude children perceived to be regularly disruptive. It can help when class teachers have training, for example in attachment theory, to help them understand why some children appear to misbehave. Better understanding, together with support from senior staff and intervention strategies, can help to prevent difficulties escalating.

A social pedagogue interviewed for this book reflected on the critical role schools have in securing continuity in looked after children's education and wellbeing:

> 'Looked after children would really benefit if schools had a different approach to exclusion. They often see young people as a threat to the school. If there could be more options for internal exclusion, if schools could be more flexible and offer mentoring. School staff also need to know enough about trauma to know what might be preventing young people engaging in the curricula. If schools had the flexibility to work together with therapists, that would help. They are often torn between performance, and Ofsted, and the young people not being at expected levels, and young people who have been in care have often missed a lot of school, had neglectful parents, or the care system has caused breaks in schooling, [and] when placements break down, new schools are needed.'

Clearly articulated policy from government is also important in giving a lead. In Scotland, for example, following the publication of the *Learning with Care* report (Her Majesty's Inspectors of Schools and Social Work Services Inspectorate 2001) which highlighted exclusion of children in residential care as a particular problem, official guidance was issued to schools to reduce the use of exclusion as a sanction. Rates of exclusion began to decline but there were protests from teachers' and head-teachers' organisations, and the government appeared to backtrack in the face of the pressure. When exclusion rates increased the then Minister for Education and Young People even welcomed the news as evidence that schools were 'using powers at their disposal to crack down on troublemakers by removing them from their classes' (Denholm 2006).

Perceptions appear to have changed across the UK in recent years. When the Scottish government published revised guidance about exclusion of school pupils in 2011 with the more positive title, *Included, Engaged and Involved*, there were several pages devoted to looked after children, and the negative effect of exclusion for them, including the following advice:

> School staff should consider very carefully the decision to exclude a Looked After Child and if at all possible should avoid taking the decision to exclude them. Staff should discuss any potential decision to exclude a Looked After Child with the designated social worker and lead professional, if different, prior to the exclusion taking place. Staff should refer to the Looked After Child's Plan, assessment, support and provision agreed for that child, and contingency planning in the event of a potential exclusion. (Scottish Government 2011, p.45)

Revised government guidance in England in 2012 specified that head teachers should, as far as possible, avoid permanently excluding any child with a statement of special educational needs or who is looked after by the local authority (DfE 2012c). Schools should also be proactive in working with foster carers, residential care workers and the local authority that looks after the child. Moreover, where there is a risk of exclusion, schools should consider what additional support or alternative placement may be required. This should involve assessing the suitability of provision for a pupil's special educational needs. Where a pupil has a statement of special educational needs, schools should consider requesting an early annual review or interim/emergency review. Fixed-term exclusions were reduced by 25 per cent through the work of home–school support social workers in secondary schools (Webb and Vulliamy 2004) and exclusions were also reduced as a result of preventive health services for young people in need of therapeutic support (Pugh and Statham 2006).

There are several important arguments in support of deploying resources to help schools avoid the exclusion of looked after children, or to plan alternative placements with care and sensitivity. One is that reactive exclusion from school most often means loss of access to education and related social activities. The psychological impact – given that exclusion is another form of rejection by adults – is significant for children who typically have deep-rooted difficulties with attachment associated with previous trauma as a result of abuse or neglect (Furnivall *et al.* 2012). Being excluded reinforces in young people feelings of alienation which inevitably make it hard for teachers and students to reach each other. A second reason relates to the costs associated with exclusion. Schools understandably often focus on the time spent by staff in dealing with unruly behaviour and its aftermath. But there are considerable costs to society in general when children are excluded from school, for example for the police, social services and the criminal justice system (Evans 2010; Parsons and Castle 1998). A third reason is the significance of exclusion from school in predicting offending and substance misuse behaviours which are destructive to the individuals who receive convictions, and to society. The Edinburgh study of youth transitions and crime found: 'The critical moments for youngsters in terms of conviction trajectory appear to be linked to truancy and school exclusion in the early years following the transition from primary to secondary school' (McAra and McVie 2010, p.197).

Alternatives to mainstream school

Proportionately more looked after children attend alternatives to mainstream schools, such as pupil referral units (PRUs), than their age cohort as a whole. In 2010, of those children who had been looked after continuously for at least 12 months, 1.30 per cent attended PRUs in England as opposed to 0.18 per cent of all children. Pupil referral units are one of several forms of 'alternative provision' (AP) available for children who have been excluded from mainstream school or who need an alternative to mainstream school on a temporary or ongoing basis. The proportion of looked after children in AP is 4.75 per cent, compared with 0.30 per cent for all children (Parnell 2011).

Students attending PRUs tend to share many characteristics with looked after children: they are very likely to have special educational needs (around 80%), to have behavioural issues or anxiety, and to come from highly disadvantaged home backgrounds. Nearly three-quarters of PRU students are boys. In 2011, an estimated 23,000 young people were in full- or part-time alternative provision of which 14,000 were attending PRUs (Gosling 2013). In the same year, a study of Year 11 students attending PRUs in six local authority areas found that half of them did not have a clear post-16 destination (Brown 2011). According to Gosling (2013), 'Just over 1% of AP pupils achieve five or more GCSEs with grades A* to C', clearly a very poor level of achievement, which is likely to reflect a wide range of factors, including the high level of special educational needs as well as health and emotional needs, among the population attending. However, there is some concern that PRUs do not always provide sufficient academic focus for their students (Gosling 2013; Poyser 2013; Brown 2011).

In a study of children's and teachers' views of practice in one pupil referral unit in England, Hart (2013) found four potential protective factors that help achieve more positive outcomes for students. These were:

+ Trusting relationships, in which teachers had time to focus on individual students, get to know them and be fair and kind, were considered very important for learning. This contrasted with students' experiences in larger and more impersonal schools.

+ A strong learning ethos, opportunities to succeed that built self-esteem, and learning that was relevant to developing practical life skills and required active participation.

+ High expectations and consistency of approach between staff, supported by clear guidelines as to behaviour and boundaries, and achievable targets.

+ A school-like environment with classrooms and timetables, that is quiet and orderly, and a small building but one that offers space for children.

Arguably, these are features of schooling that would benefit children in care and, indeed, all children of school age.

An alternative to mainstream schooling which is not a PRU is Red Balloon Learner Centre. Aimed at the recovery of bullied and traumatised children, Red Balloon offers young people aged 9–18 a place to learn that has a timetable and terms and expectations of a school day and that is 'a safe place to be with rooms for different activities, a community room with sofas, a kitchen where good food is cooked daily by the housekeeper. There is no staff room, no playground and children and staff use the same front door, stairs and lavatories. Bullying is not tolerated, nor can it thrive at a Red Balloon.'[1] The philosophy behind Red Balloon is building self-esteem through highly personalised learning. Young people attending Red Balloon can design their own curriculum, and are encouraged to develop their own educational identity, focused on practical and social skills, as well as academic achievements. Nearly all attendees return to mainstream school or other educational settings better equipped to withstand bullying behaviour from others. Around three-quarters of those who have attended have achieved at least five GSCEs graded A*–C.

Case study: Inclusion Plus, an alternative to exclusion from mainstream education

Inclusion Plus was formed from a consortium comprising Apex Scotland, SkillForce and Includem in August 2013, in collaboration with Dundee City Council and supported by grant funding from The Robertson Trust, with the aims of improving the life chances of young people in four Dundee secondary schools and reducing the number of exclusions and progressions to off-campus provision.

The three organisations brought complementary experience of a range of approaches.

Apex Scotland provides a 'school inclusion unit' which is used as an alternative to exclusion from school. Pupils attend the unit within the mainstream school, full-time, for the period they would otherwise have been excluded, up to a maximum of 10 days. They continue with regular school work and engage in social activities and are helped to develop skills in anger management, problem solving, conflict resolution and employability. They can also attend the unit subsequently for two hours per week for seven weeks for additional support and individual counselling.

SkillForce provides an in-school unit aimed at helping to avoid exclusion. Instructors work in pairs with groups of young people on a half-day per week focusing on 'skills for life' with opportunities to gain recognised qualifications and awards, such as the Scottish Qualifications Authority's 'Employability' award, Duke of Edinburgh, ASDAN (Award Scheme Development and Accreditation Network), John Muir Trust 'Environmental Award' and Sports Leaders UK awards.

---

1   www.redballoonlearner.co.uk/about-general.htm.

Includem provides a home-based support programme outside the school day. There is an emphasis on support for young people at weekends to help them keep a focus on progress at school and there is access to a 24-hour helpline. Support is also given to parents and carers to help promote their involvement in their children's education.

Concluding thoughts

'Fear underlies much of the challenging behaviour that characterises the looked after child' (Poyser 2013, p.113). Maria Poyser's observation is important because it is a reminder that understanding the origins of behaviour and changing perceptions can be the first step in breaking the inevitable slide into exclusion from school (Bombèr and Hughes 2013). As this chapter has shown, a significant contributor to the poor educational outcomes of looked after children is the large extent to which they are excluded from school and consequently denied opportunities for learning. The solutions are not easy but the case examples we have quoted suggest at least three important messages. The first of these is the value of foster carers and residential workers who know children well working co-operatively with teachers. The second is early intervention, which ensures that problems are not allowed to escalate and so the child is aware that their difficulties are at least recognised. The third is the use of multi-agency approaches, as demonstrated in the Inclusion Plus example.

Practice points

+ Provide additional support for looked after children at school during transitions, such as placement moves and moving from primary to secondary school.

+ Help teachers to understand the effect of trauma on learning and the value of the school environment for helping children to feel safe and develop confidence.

+ Include specific educational aims within care plans and identify responsibilities for helping children to achieve them.

- Facilitate relationships between mainstream schools and alternative provision so that children do not feel rejected when a change of school becomes inevitable.

- Have high expectations of students. Regardless of setting, students learn best when there are high expectations of them as individuals, coupled with trusting relationships with teachers that they can rely on and feel are worth investing in.

- Find alternatives to school that 'model' school in some respects, such as timetable and subjects, and offer a safe space to be.

Useful resources

- Websites such as the Pupil Inclusion Network Scotland (PINS) (www.pinscotland.org) and the Social Care Institute for Excellence (scie) (www.scie.org.uk/topic/careservices/lookedafterchildren).

- The chapter, 'Is Inclusion Always Best for Young People in Care? A View from the Classroom', by Maria Poyser is a very accessible discussion of the issues involved in planning education that meets the needs of children who experience emotional difficulties and exhibit significant behavioural problems that are challenging in mainstream school classrooms (Poyser 2013).

- The CELCIS/Scottish Attachment in Action report by Furnivall *et al.*, *Attachment Matters for All*, is an accessible guide to the importance of understanding attachment, with examples of how carers and workers are using their knowledge and skills to support their practice (www.celcis.org/media/resources/publications/Attachment-Matters-For-All.pdf). Judy Furnivall also writes about attachment-informed practice with looked after children on the IRISS website at www.iriss.org.uk/resources/attachment-informed-practice-looked-after-children-and-young-people.

CHAPTER 10

Staying in Education

16–19 – The Muddle and the Prospects

This chapter outlines the options for care leavers and those in care after Year 11 (S4 in Scotland) and details six pathways through upper secondary education. It gives an example of a particularly successful leaving care service and identifies the main barriers to educational participation at this age.

KEY POINTS

- Participation in upper secondary education is now the norm for 16–18-year-olds.

- In England, from 2015, legislation will require young people to participate in education or training until the age of 18.

- Upper secondary education is not clearly defined as a phase of education and is characterised by a variety of possible institutional options and a confusing array of possible courses.

- Young people in care are most likely to attend larger and less supportive institutions and should be encouraged to stay on at school or attend smaller and more specialist colleges to gain more personal attention.

- Staying in education should be part of care placement planning from an early age to raise expectations for young people.

> ▸ Local authority services and other relevant stakeholders should be well coordinated, underpinned by common commitment and willing to overcome organisational barriers to educational participation.
>
> ▸ Leaving care teams should include a qualified teacher.

Introduction

Staying in education after the age of compulsory schooling has become the norm for young people. Since the raising of the school leaving age to 16 in 1972, the rate of participation in further education has increased steadily. Now, around 88 per cent of 17-year-olds in England are in education or training (DfE 2013b) and in 2015 the so-called 'participation age' was raised again. All young people must participate in education or training until the age of 18 if they began Year 11 (or years below) in September 2013. Participation means being in full-time education, following an apprenticeship or in full-time employment or volunteering, combined with part-time education or training. In Scotland, the emphasis is different. Rather than raise the compulsory leaving age, there is a policy commitment to provide all 16–19-year-olds with an appropriate place in post-16 education and training, and to extend this offer to those aged 20–24 through 'flexible learning opportunities and skills enhancement to enhance employability' (Liddell and Macpherson 2013, p.6). One of the aims of the Scottish post-16 reform was to bring some coherence to the further education sector by encouraging collaboration among the many different training providers, from universities to schools, and regional colleges to workplace learning.

Although there are plenty of opportunities and choice for young people, lack of coherent pathways through the immediate post-16 phase, an issue certainly not confined to Scotland, often creates particular problems, even a muddle, for those young people in care or in the process of leaving care. In this chapter, we document the experience in upper secondary education of young people who are in or leaving care. Recent policy initiatives to retain young people in education have focused on the role of leaving care services in supporting their education and training. Here, after illustrating young people's experiences, we highlight the role of some particularly innovative services. Given that the raising of the school leaving age is so new, and is not restricted to school attendance, much of the data reported in this chapter refers to post-16 educational options and choice-making.

Post-16 options

At age 16, there are a number of options for young people. They might stay at their secondary school, if there is a specialist 'sixth form' (approximately 36% of 17-year-olds in upper secondary education); attend a dedicated sixth form college (12%); or a regional or subject specialist college (33%). Alternatively, they might take up an apprenticeship (3.2%). The choice of school or college is partly subject-related but is also influenced by GCSE grades and social class. Students from more affluent backgrounds and with higher grades largely attend sixth forms and sixth form colleges, while others go to further education colleges (Payne 2003). Young people from a public care background are likely to be in the latter group unless they are strongly advised otherwise by social workers, carers and/or mentors.

The range of options reflects the complexity of the English upper secondary system. It neither completely separates vocational from academic routes and qualifications nor completely merges them. The system gives young people many different progression routes and 'second chances' but can also be extremely confusing for those lacking informed advice (Hannan *et al.* 1996, Ball *et al.* 2000).

In parallel with the array of institutional options, there are also a range of qualifications available at the upper secondary phase. There is no universally recognised endpoint or certificate of achievement at the completion of upper secondary education as there is in most other countries. The English Qualifications and Credit Framework (QCF) groups qualifications according to their difficulty from Entry Level to Level 8. Upper secondary qualifications, such as A-levels or BTECs, are Level 3. Despite the broad equivalence intended by the QCF, some Level 3 qualifications are valued more highly than others. Entry to higher ranked universities is effectively limited to students who study A-levels (or the increasingly popular International Baccalaureate) at sixth forms in schools and specialist sixth form colleges. Eligibility is further defined by subject choice: 'traditional' and theoretical subjects (such as English, history, mathematics and physics) are more highly valued than vocational studies. There is a strong social class element to subject choice. Young people from low income backgrounds and those in care are much more likely to choose applied subjects, such as IT, media studies, drama, sport, childcare or those involving technical skills. Alternative upper secondary qualifications are available, with a more vocational orientation, such as BTECs, which require students to demonstrate knowledge based on real-life work and study. A Level 3 BTEC Diploma is supposed to be equivalent to between one and three A-levels but is unlikely to be treated as such by the more prestigious universities. In Scotland, the main upper secondary qualifications are Highers and Advanced Highers; the latter are encouraged for entrance to high status universities and may qualify students for direct entry to the second year of a four-year programme.

Figure 10.1 illustrates the different qualifications in the English education system and their associated pathways, mapped onto the QCF. Level 1 (not shown here) covers entry level awards such as literacy and numeracy certificates and GCSEs graded D–G, and the starting point of apprenticeships. Qualifications that provide a passport to higher education begin with Level 2 qualifications, which are primarily GCSEs graded A*–C and vocational awards considered equivalent in terms of demand or difficulty. Levels 3–5, which cover the upper secondary phase, are the most diverse, encapsulating the range of options available for young people.

Many young people in care are delayed in acquiring educational qualifications or have a mixed profile of academic and vocational qualifications at Level 2. For this group, further education colleges play a pivotal role in providing diverse options through the wide range of vocational, practical and academic courses and qualifications that are on offer in flexible study arrangements (Ainley and Bailey 1997; Green and Lucas 1999). Such flexibility can also mean less individual support and guidance than a student might expect if they were to stay on in school. One leaving care manager known to the authors described their local further education college, which has around 30,000 enrolled students, as 'massive and anonymous' and a place where young people were in danger of getting lost or flitting from one course to another.

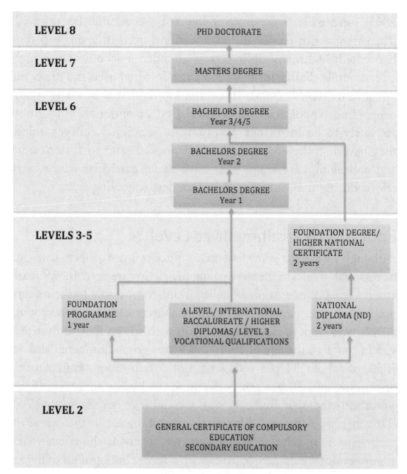

Figure 10.1 English qualifications and academic pathways
Source: Hauari with Cameron (2014)

With high youth unemployment (in 2014 almost 17% of 16–24-year-olds in England were unemployed), there is every incentive for young people to participate in upper secondary education. Few young people leaving secondary school are employed full-time; indeed, they are not expected to be under the new 'participation' legislation.

However, those at greatest risk of finding themselves not in education, employment or training (NEET) at age 16 are from the poorest socio-economic backgrounds, those who are disabled, have special educational needs, are excluded from school, teenage mothers, or are looked after by local authorities (Ainscow and Sandill 2010). Those most likely to be low educational achievers in England, in

2005: were male; were from a low socio-economic background; had parents with few or no qualifications; lived in a single-parent household; had many siblings; and attended a school with a high rate of pupils eligible for free school meals (often used as a proxy for low income) (Babb 2005). This is the profile shared by many young people from a public care background. Post-16 options for this group are likely to be in further education or vocational colleges unless they have had the good fortune to be looked after by foster carers and/or leaving care teams that have made particular educational efforts during the young people's secondary schooling years.

Educational attainment at Level 3

Although we cannot know for sure, as the data is not collected, we can be reasonably certain that few young people in care aged 16–19 years attain a level of educational qualifications comparable to their peers not in care. The English government collects data on those young people who were in care at age 16 and with whom local authorities stay in touch to the age of 19. In 2013, this group numbered almost 7000, of whom 34 per cent were not in education, employment or training and 58 per cent were either in higher education (6%), education other than higher (29%), or training or employment (23%) (DfE 2013b). Although this tells us something about the extent of participation at Level 3, it does not tell us about the educational attainment of young people in, or with a recent background of living in, care placements. A survey of local authorities found that 44 per cent of young people in or formerly in care and known to leaving care teams were in education, and nine per cent were attending universities (Hauari et al. 2010). This is encouraging, but English government data for all 16–18-year-olds in 2011 showed that 93 per cent were in education and/or training (DfE 2013b) while the Wolf Report (Wolf 2011) revealed that among all young people aged 16 and 17, 38 per cent were studying for A-levels, seven per cent were studying for A-levels plus other qualifications, and 21 per cent were taking other Level 3 courses. We do not have this level of detail for children in care.

Experiences of young people in care

In Chapter 1 we introduced the YiPPEE study (2008–10). In England, alongside data collected from relevant professionals, thirty-two young people aged 18–24 were interviewed in depth about their educational participation post-16, as well as their childhoods and their aspirations for their future. Each young person had been in care aged 16, had spent at least a year in care, and had obtained some Level 2 qualifications. These criteria were chosen in order to maximise the chances that they would go on to upper secondary education. Of these 32, 25 had been in some form of sustained education since leaving compulsory schooling. Of the 25, twelve young people were in higher education and 13 were studying in further education institutions. Of the remaining seven, two were in employment and five were not in employment, education or training (NEET). All but two of those studying in further education settings were enrolled on courses that would lead to further study in higher education and the young people undertaking these courses all intended to continue with their education; many had already applied to universities for the following year. This group represent a rich array of experiences of trying to navigate the system of upper secondary education in England. We grouped these into six main educational pathways, summarised below.

Six educational pathways of post-16 'choices'

Table 10.1 summarises the six pathways we found among the young people interviewed for the YiPPEE project in England. As well as some qualification at age 16, all of the young people had had acute difficulties in their home lives as children and had been in and out of local authority care. Here we illustrate some of their stories. Those with most stability in their home lives, with foster carers, were also those with least delay in acquiring qualifications and most support in making post-16 educational choices. One young man interviewed, who we have called Barnaby, was a good example of the *high achievers* group. At the time of interview he had been accepted onto an MA programme at a prestigious university. His mother had died from cancer when he was just ten, but she had already raised funds for him and his sister to go to university. He went to live with foster carers who supported this ambition. He described his mother's role in his education:

'My sister and I were both keen to bring books home and my mother was keen to read with us. Mother was studying part-time at university. We were doing very well at school. In Year 3 we were working with the Year 4 age group. When my mother died she had raised a lot of money. She was adamant that we were going to go to university.'

Those arriving in the UK as unaccompanied asylum seekers usually had experienced family bereavement, war, and severe economic hardships; they had usually arrived too late to complete a two-year GCSE course and were reliant on extra resources, particularly English language teaching, to achieve their goals. Where they had this resource, had come from families that valued education, and had active support from foster carers or leaving care workers, they frequently made very fast progress through the education system.

Jaime came to the UK as an unaccompanied asylum seeker aged 14 and was taking a *roundabout* route to higher education. She was sent to live with two sets of foster carers, neither of whom were very satisfactory. She was treated differently to other fostered children and to the foster carers' own children. She said that what kept her going:

'is the fact that I had a good friend and they were telling me… like for example I met this lady through Social Services because she used to do activities for young people…like dancing and swimming…and she would call me and tell me everything would be okay, just concentrate on your education. And you know she really helped me. She always gave me extra support because she knew that I can't speak and I was frustrated because I couldn't speak English properly. I also had good supporting teachers and a counsellor and they encouraged me to go to university and… you know if you want to be somebody one day, you'd better go to university. Yeah, and then I applied for the course and they accepted me. So that's when I started.'

On the other hand, Marco was 16 when he arrived in the UK, too late for secondary school GCSE courses, and went straight to college to do an online English language course (ESOL), maths, IT and ICT. Initially, his ambition was to 'get a good job to not go looking for a job in a factory or somewhere else'. But without GCSEs he could not progress academically and instead enrolled on a motor vehicle maintenance NVQ course and planned to do GCSE evening courses. At the end of the motor vehicle course he was still without a job. He had nothing to do and spent his days walking to garages asking for work. He could not continue his studies because his technical English was not sufficiently proficient and courses to improve it were not available. He had some support from the leaving care team and some friends with whom he played sport. He was contemplating moving to another city where there might be more opportunities. He was one example of *building a life* in the UK against formidable odds.

Attachment to locality was a factor for two of the groups portrayed here. For some, *family and community* were more important than pursuing individual educational ambition that might lead them to move away from their home locality. Jane was a good example of how multiple commitments structured her post-16 choices. She had five GCSEs and A-levels and had clearly enjoyed school as a young girl, despite disruptions caused both by living in different placements and by being a carer for her mother's younger children. Her mother had developed alcoholic dementia and, when interviewed aged 22, Jane had adopted her youngest brother, who would otherwise have been taken into care, and was caring for her partner's two children as well as working as a childminder. After her GCSEs, she said she was 'trying to…stay in education every year until I went to university, so I was just doing like an evening class to…'cos I like learning as well, I enjoy learning. But I'd come…half past six…so I was finishing work at half past five, getting to college for six o'clock and not getting home till half past nine, twice a week.' Eventually she had to focus on work and caring, and postpone plans for university. This was contrary to the advice of her foster carers, but it is rather typical for young people in care to put family demands and caring responsibilities before their own educational opportunities.

For other *home-based locals*, usually young men with learning and behavioural difficulties, attachment to mothers, despite a clear lack of support from them, and despite a lack of employment opportunities, kept them rooted to a neighbourhood.

One finding from this study was the important role of voluntary work in helping young people, especially those who had had difficulties in secondary school, find out what they enjoyed and were good at, and, from there, a route into formal education and/or employment was sometimes possible. This was often a feature of accounts from those who were *just about surviving* in the face of serious ill health, both physical and emotional.

Louise had been abused and neglected from an early age. She self-harmed as a teenager and was admitted to a psychiatric unit after a suicide attempt and from there went into local authority care. She tried to continue with education and gained a range of qualifications including a diploma in theatrical and media make-up. She partially completed an Access course but health problems prevented her from finishing the course. In parallel, and supported by her leaving care worker, she had taken up volunteering opportunities with a local theatre company and planned to take these further by setting up a theatre project for children in and leaving care. She had been asked to write scripts for a leaving care conference and she had organised young people to write scenes and perform together. The value of drama for young people in care as a means of self-expression was discussed in Chapter 6.

As well as the expressive arts, young people in the study also talked about faith-based volunteering, sports and working with local children's services departments to support work with children in care. Leaving care workers were important in brokering voluntary work.

Sally said her leaving care worker 'got me some volunteer work at a nursery 'cos I was interested in children and that kind of…well I wasn't sure where I wanted to go yet, but I knew it was somewhere in that general area.'

Table 10.1 Six educational pathways for young people in and leaving care aged 18–24 (N = 32)

	Educational participation	Home life context	Support	Ambition
High achieving – delay 10, of which 7 incurred delays (7 female, 3 male)	GCSEs/A-levels/ university.	Delays in acquiring qualifications due to life events such as death of a parent, unplanned pregnancy, accident, illness, making a wrong choice of course, and taking a year off.	Foster carers, teachers, leaving care workers very important in offering continuous and accurate guidance.	'I want to do a PhD in Abnormal and Forensic Psychology.' 'I just always have wanted to, I've always wanted to better myself and if I'm going to do something, I go the whole way.'
Unaccompanied asylum seekers – roundabout route to ambition 6 (5 female, 1 male)	Arriving in England too late to start GCSE courses and with little English language; FE colleges to retake minimum number of GCSEs and vocational courses with potential to enter higher education.	Family background of bereavement and war in home countries. Educational attainment highly prized by birth families. Frequent moving of schools once in England incurring delays, repeating courses and changing subjects.	Lack of informed guidance, prolonged upper secondary phase, reliant on peers and internet for information. Lack of financial security, restrictions on employment, and uncertain immigration status.	Bachelor degrees and financial independence.

cont.

	Educational participation	Home life context	Support	Ambition
Community and family, over ambition 2 (female)	GCSEs/A-levels.	Multiple commitments to children and birth family, voluntary work and local community. Health problems.	Supporting others. Some support from foster carers. Part-time employment.	'I want to do what I really enjoy.'
Surviving – just 6 (4 female, 2 male)	Low-level academic qualifications. Often repeated. Voluntary work related to personal interests.	Serious ill health, bereavement, neglect and abuse. Mental illness, homelessness, childcare responsibilities.	Insufficient support from professionals to address scale of difficulties in home life. Leaving care worker important in negotiating volunteering opportunities.	'I'd like to go to university but I just can't really see it with a kid.'
Home-based locals 4 (male)	Entry-level courses, dropped out, resumed, none, unemployed.	Learning and behavioural difficulties. Locality important. Attached to birth mothers despite neglect. Bullied in schools.	Very limited. Little peer support. Family not resourceful.	'I like it outside of education.' 'There's just no work anywhere.'

Unaccompanied asylum seekers – building a life 4 (male)	Low-level vocational qualifications or none.	Minimal secondary education, arrived in England aged 14+ from politically unstable countries and from uneducated families. Limited English language. Limited involvement in organised leisure activities or voluntary work.	Peer support important. Little or no support for learning technical language necessary for qualifications. Leaving care team important. Lack of financial security, restrictions on employment, and uncertain immigration status.	Clear sense of purpose, and personal responsibility for work, and possibly eventual higher education.

Source: Jackson and Cameron (2014)

Case study: Post-16 support service

Young people in care and leaving care aged 16+ are often highly motivated and discuss their plans in terms of self-determination and self-responsibility. But the YiPPEE study showed that few young people can achieve, and succeed in, further and higher education without a high level of personal and professional support. They need financial, practical and emotional support that is reliable, continuous and committed to them as individuals.

One local authority area in the YiPPEE study employed a teacher within the leaving care team whose specific role was to support continued engagement with education, both formal and informal, as part of a high-level policy commitment, introduced in the mid-2000s, to the education of looked after children. This commitment reflected a long-standing interest held by the Director of Children's Services at the time. In this local authority, all children in local authority care were considered to be pupils of a virtual school. The Virtual School Head (VSH) had direct access to the Strategy Head and was a person of high status within the authority. The remit of the Education of Children Looked After Service (ECLAS) team and the VSH was initially limited to children aged 2–16 years, with a strong focus on improving attendance and performance at Key Stages and GCSEs. But, during stakeholder interviews for the YiPPEE study, they expressed a commitment to promoting post-16 education, working closely with the Leaving Care Team. The Leaving Care Team takes over from the Virtual School Head after Year 11 and is responsible for post-16 Pathway Plans. All members of the team believed in encouraging young people to stay in education and improve their qualifications or go on to higher levels of study. Leaving care was seen as a process in which the pace and timing should be adjusted to the needs and readiness of the young person concerned, rather than being tied to an arbitrary cut-off point. There was the possibility to leave care and return if it did not work out. Discussion of leaving care was delayed until after GCSEs and every effort was made to persuade young people to remain in care up to 18 years, or longer if necessary.

The teacher's role was to focus on educational participation post-16. This teacher was unique in being able to offer direct help and advice on educational matters, such as, for example, revision for GCSEs, or choosing key texts for college courses, or helping to write personal statements. He negotiated educationally valuable work placements for young people. For instance, for one young woman being placed in the local authority IT Department enabled her to go on to a Master's course and a permanent job. Since the teacher's arrival the number of young people from care attending university in the authority had risen from one to 18, and a large majority continued in some form of education or training after 16. When interviewed, the teacher thought there was much unrealised potential among looked after young people; children's services professionals did not hold sufficiently high expectations of what young people could achieve with the right level of support, but there was also a problem of limited horizons and perhaps a lack of careers advice. He thought the main constraint was the low level of support and understanding in the home environment and the care placement. However, he also thought that some educational environments were better than others. In particular, large further educational colleges were probably less supportive than school sixth forms or colleges, and care placement planning needed to bear this in mind. Like many of the stakeholders nominated by young people in the study as having made a difference to their lives, he was dedicated to lifelong learning and education in its broadest sense and disliked the notion that all learning has to lead to work.

This example, the only one of a teacher employed in a leaving care team we came across during the YiPPEE study, shows how promoting the educational engagement and achievement of looked after children is a multifaceted responsibility that spans hierarchical layers within local authorities requiring both high-level policy recognition and operationalisation at all levels. In this example, 'education' and 'care' responsibilities were combined within the same leaving care team in practical ways.

Barriers to achieving ambitions

One of the main barriers to achieving educational ambitions post-16 is what happens to young people well before that age. Support, self-belief and motivation for education conveyed by birth families and care placements was highly influential in making choices, taking up options and staying the course among the young people interviewed.

Nevertheless, not continuing in education beyond 16 is now not an option, as all young people must 'participate' to age 18; indeed, most of the young people we interviewed wanted this to happen. It is now more important than ever that barriers to achieving ambitions for young people in care are dismantled to enable them to fulfil their potential and achieve financial independence. Here, we highlight four features of the organisation of care and education services for young people in and leaving care that are critical ingredients in such an ambition.

Support from managers and Virtual School Heads

Managers from leaving care teams and Virtual School Heads both argued that young people require multifaceted support that starts early in children's lives, in order to most effectively prosper at school and take advantage of further and higher education. Mirroring the parental support role for children not in care but splitting it across everyday experts (foster carers and residential care workers), resources (national and local politicians, children's social work, leaving care teams, schools and Virtual School Heads) and general strategy (managers) requires considerable coordination and, ideally, common educational values. These are not always present. Leaving care managers pointed out that when day-to-day carers do not have sufficient education themselves to help young people with homework, or do not have the willingness and commitment to embody educational aspiration in their everyday lives, it is difficult for them to make an impact on young people's motivation (Griffiths 2013). Virtual School Heads drew attention to the frequency with which social workers change posts, and the discontinuity and disruption this often means for young people's educational lives.

Continuity of care experience

Nearly half (15/32) of the young people interviewed had had more than three placements, changes which often produced other undesired changes such as loss of proximity to friends and leisure facilities, and in some cases, placing young people out of reach of school and extra-curricular activities which did much to support their self-esteem. However, some changes of placement are for the better. Lucy, for example, was placed with a foster carer far away from the school that she attended, and due to transport difficulties she missed out on participating in after-school clubs and activities. Once she moved to a foster placement closer to her school, Lucy resumed extra-curricular activities, particularly drama and singing, which in turn had a positive impact on her attitude toward school.

Using resources imaginatively

The corporate parent role demands imagination, ingenuity and going beyond the minimum requirements. Some local authority managers offered young people who had been in care work placements within the local authority, which enabled them to develop expertise and credentials for university entry. Some areas realised that minimum financing would not support good academic outcomes. One official stated: 'They get a top-up on benefits, free travel, maintenance, course materials and trips as part of the course and the rent is paid' until the end of the course. This authority expected their undergraduates to have a part-time job while at university but others recognised that working during term-time risked undermining academic progress.

Imaginative use of resources often required a good level of coordination and multi-agency working within and across local authority organisations and agencies. Expertise relevant to careers, welfare benefits, legal advice, health and mental health, education and mentoring all had to be pooled. Delivering this level of service required a relational approach. As one manager said: 'It is vital that young people develop a good relationship with their key worker so that they have a constant adult figure in their lives', and, arguably, that the key workers have sufficiently full information to provide individualised support.

Most of all, local authority managers argued that avoiding underachievement and continuing in education after 16 required close attention early on in young people's childhoods, and as soon as they entered the care system. It was often too late by the time young people arrived at the door of the leaving care team as disengagement had set in much earlier. In particular, addressing young people's poor levels of numeracy and literacy needed decisive action early on in their school career, as otherwise their post-16 choice would be severely constrained, in addition to their future life chances. This is not just an issue for young people in care. Around half of all young people do not hold good qualifications in maths and English at age 16, two subjects required for access to many courses and most skilled jobs (Wolf 2011). The Read On, Get On campaign led by Save the Children, the CBI and Teach First estimates that 40 per cent of disadvantaged children (including those in care) are not reading well by age 11, and that this could cost the UK £32bn in growth by 2025.[1]

---

1   www.readongeton.org.uk.

The role of schools and teachers

Post-16 participation for young people is also structured by the experience of schooling and teachers at earlier stages. In one fieldwork area, schools had been excluding young people with a care background, even though this is illegal, and the designated teacher role was seen as having been implemented in a 'tokenistic' way. In another, the attitude of head teachers was seen as critical; if they are willing to accommodate young people in care and actively support them, it can make a vast difference. Frazzle, age 21, said, 'All my teachers were briefed on my situation because you know they needed to be, otherwise they'd just think I was being obnoxious, so they all knew about it.' One teacher was particularly supportive:

> 'He was my head of year...he shouldn't really have been dealing with me in Year 12, but he did because I got on with him. So you know we got on like a house on fire, we'd have a chat... and we'd sit down having a natter...he didn't like me calling him Sir, he preferred me to call him [by his first name]. He said, "The only time I want you to call me Sir is when there's other people around. If it's just us two walking round having a chat then fine..." We'd just go off, sit in his car, have a fag, have a chat...and then I'd go back to my lesson, or go to my next lesson, and I'd be in a better mood. They'd be like, "Well, you've cheered up a bit."'

In summary, most effective post-16 educational participation builds on high-level policy commitment to education embedded in care placement policies, adequate resources, stability of personnel and educated everyday experts, alongside professionals who work together in imaginative ways, underpinned by commonly held values about educational participation for young people, including those whose personal circumstances and histories might suggest that acquisition of formal educational qualifications is but a pipedream. These factors suggest a wide-ranging examination of operationalisation of commonly held educational and care values within every local authority to ensure children and young people in care are getting the range of options and guidance that matches those of children raised in educationally committed birth families.

Concluding thoughts

Staying in education after compulsory schooling is becoming the norm, and the rate is rising among young people in care too. However, the experience of many young people in care and from a public care background is that the upper secondary phase is confusing, with too many qualifications and possible institutions to attend, and too little well-informed guidance. Most effective support comes when the prospect of post-compulsory educational participation is embedded in care planning from an early stage and continues through the leaving care services, ideally with a teacher employed to actively work with young people, paralleling the educational support that many parents give their children. As linear pathways become less common, and as leaving school at 18, rather than 16, becomes the norm, it will be even more important that Virtual School Heads continue to support young people in care for longer, through higher education, and that leaving care teams respond flexibly to the 'yo-yo' patterns of education, employment and unemployment, with implications for financial support and accommodation that are typical for many young people who have been in care.

Practice points

♦ Encourage young people in care in Year 11 or S4 in Scotland to plan to stay on in a school setting if possible, and avoid going to large impersonal further education colleges.

♦ Instil a belief in educational potential in young people from an early age and keep continuity of care placements to enhance possibilities of post-compulsory school study.

♦ Ensure expert and well-informed guidance during upper secondary education, even for those young people with high levels of apparent self-reliance.

♦ For managers in leaving care teams and Virtual School Heads, mirror the commitment to further education that educationally committed parents fulfil with their birth children.

+ Use local authority services as a resource for internships for young people in care to gain experience of different work and skill environments.

+ Allow young people in care to develop constructive relationships with school teachers they can trust and who can act as advocates.

Useful resources

+ The Catch22 National Care Advisory Service (NCAS) is a very useful source of information on young people's transitions from care to adulthood. The website has a section on education, training and employment and includes details of NCAS projects (http://leavingcare.org/home).

+ ANV is A National Voice for young people who are in or have been in care, run by its members. It provides training toolkits for developing policy and practice in respect of young people's representation and participation in local authority structures, such as children in care councils, corporate parenting and recruitment of staff (www.anationalvoice.org/about/about-anv).

+ The Care Leaver's Foundation is a grant-giving organisation for care leavers below the age of 30 who might not otherwise have funds. The organisation has also developed a Charter for Care Leavers which calls for a number of principles to be embedded in all relevant services and policies. These are 'respect us, listen to us, work with us, believe in us and hold aspirations for us, make sure we have somewhere we can call home and don't forget about us' (www.thecareleaversfoundation.org/About_Us).

+ In Scotland the Scottish Throughcare and Aftercare Forum (STAF) (www.scottishthroughcare.org.uk) and Who Cares? Scotland (www.whocaresscotland.org) provide advocacy services and support for young people leaving care.

CHAPTER 11

Going to University from Care

The aim of this chapter is to outline how young people in care can excercise their right to go to university if they have the ability and the desire to do so (see Chapter 2). The critical message is that thinking about university as a possible destination should start from early on in school careers and carers, social workers and teachers need to encourage and support such ambitions if they are to be realised.

KEY POINTS

‣ Going to university from care in the UK is still very unusual and represents an exceptional achievement for the young person concerned, which should be acknowledged and celebrated by the local authority, their corporate parent.

‣ Conversations about university need to start early, preferably when children are still in primary school and long before they are thinking about leaving care.

‣ According to the Who Cares? Trust (2012), 40 per cent of 16-year-olds in care would like to go to university but do not see it as a realistic aspiration. In suitable cases, care plans need to include university as a possible goal from an early age, more specifically from Year 9 (S2 in Scotland) when subject choices are made, and then the Pathway Plan should set out in detail how it might be realised.

‣ Social workers, carers, mentors and young people themselves need to be well informed about study opportunities after GCSE National Qualification and exactly where different choices might lead. The general principle is to keep options open as long as possible.

> ▸ Very few care leavers are ready for university at the age of 18 or 19 because of the many obstacles and delays they have encountered in their earlier education. Higher education should not be ruled out whatever the young person's current level of attainment.

> ▸ Prospective students need to be confident that they will receive adequate financial and personal support, both from their local authority and their chosen higher education institution.

Introduction

Going to university has become a normal expectation for the majority of middle class young people living in their own families but remains a very rare destination for care leavers. Despite all the policy and legislative changes designed to improve educational opportunities for young people in care, the proportion accessing higher education in England and Scotland is very low. Young people in care are estimated to be five times less likely to obtain a university place than those not in care. In this chapter we look at some of the reasons for this discrepancy and how they might be overcome.

Of course, getting a place at university is just the first step. Many other questions then arise, such as where students are going to live, how they will support themselves financially, how well they will cope with the academic demands of their degree course and where they will turn if they run into difficulties. The legal obligations of local authorities towards students formerly in their care were set out in Chapter 2. It is important for care leavers and those supporting them to be aware of their entitlements and insist on receiving them.

The By Degrees study

The evidence base on participation by care leavers in higher education remains very weak. There is only one substantial study in the UK focusing on university students with a care background. This is the study known as 'By Degrees', funded by the Buttle Trust, a long-established children's charity, with a consortium of other charitable bodies and government support and based at the Institute of Education, University of London (Budge 2011). Three successive cohorts of 50 care leavers who had applied and been accepted by UK universities were tracked through their university courses for three years, two years and one year respectively. Including follow-up, the study continued for almost five years and by the end the researchers were still in touch with 129 of the 150 young people (Jackson *et al.* 2003, 2005).

The majority of the research participants had completed their degree courses successfully and had good prospects of building on this achievement in their future lives, in contrast to the outcomes for the majority of care leavers with few or no educational qualifications (Jackson 2007; Stein 2012). However, even for this group, who could be considered outstandingly successful compared with their peers, the pathway had been beset with difficulties and the performance of local authorities in their capacity as corporate parents extremely variable.

The other study on which this chapter draws is the YiPPEE research in England described in Chapter 1. This focuses on the 19–21 age group and only a minority of the respondents had completed their university studies at the time they were interviewed. The findings, however, confirm many of those in the earlier study, such as the priority given by many professionals to encouraging young people to become self-supporting at an early age, in preference to pursuing educational objectives (Jackson and Cameron 2012).

Preparing the ground

In order to overcome all the obstacles that litter their path to university, young people in care have to want to go very much. The relative success of some asylum-seeking young people in accessing higher education against even greater odds than the average care leaver, underlines the key part played by motivation (Jackson *et al.* 2005; and see Chapter 12). What can everyday experts and social workers do to increase it?

First, they need to help young people who may not have experienced much success at school at the point before they come into care to develop a confident learning identity. As we discussed in Chapter 4, this means finding ways to make learning enjoyable and underlining the satisfaction to be gained by learning new things. This need not be only academic knowledge. It could be a physical skill such as roller blading, horse riding or playing the violin; it could be recognising and naming different kinds of trees, stars, birds or a hundred other things. It could be learning to speak or sing in another language. What is important is for the child to have effort and achievement recognised. That is the job of the everyday expert, but maximising learning opportunities also requires resources and it is for the social worker to obtain and justify these.

Whatever the age when a child starts to be looked after, the idea of higher education as an attainable goal should be one that everyday experts bear in mind and talk about in the course of their shared lives. Naturally, it will not be suitable for all young people and there are other ways of continuing in education, but the aim must surely be that all looked after children who have the desire and capacity to go to university should be able to do so.

There are many legitimate reasons for wanting to go to university: ideally to learn more about a subject that fascinates and engages you, but also to have more time to discover what it is that you are really interested in, time to experiment, explore the world and grow up in an environment which still offers a measure of protection, as opposed to having what Mike Stein (2012) describes as an accelerated and compressed transition to independence. University is a place to meet people without a care background, to explore music, art, politics, sport, literature, science and new ideas of all kinds. Perhaps for most young people the idea of 'going to uni' is more important than studying any particular subject. This was certainly true for many of those in the YiPPEE England sample who had arrived as immigrants, and who told the researchers that their parents had impressed on them that education was the only way they could achieve a good life in their new country. Several of those who did well at school and succeeded in going to university said that they had been inspired by thinking how proud their parents (mostly no longer alive) would have been.

In many families frequent discussions take place over the years about 'what I'll do when I grow up', some realistic and some pure fantasy. In this way children gradually clarify their own talents and interests so that when they come to make choices of exam subjects and courses they have some idea where they might be going.

This kind of discussion also needs to happen in foster and residential homes and to inform planning. It must be iterative, not something that can be done in a brief question and answer session.

The problem is that most carers do not have personal experience of higher education so are not able to convey more than a general idea to their foster children, though some independent agencies employ education officers to support them and encourage young people to stay in education (Walker 2001). Of course, all universities and colleges now have their own websites and produce highly polished prospectuses and brochures, but these are a form of advertising. How are first generation university entrants to distinguish between them?

Ball *et al.* (2000), discussing the educational choices of young people from different social and ethnic backgrounds in London, describe this as the difference between 'cold' and 'hot' knowledge. Cold knowledge comes from printed sources and official websites, hot knowledge from people with personal experience and an overview of matters such as the relative prestige and reputation of different institutions or, alternatively, how much importance they give to teaching or student satisfaction and welfare as opposed to promoting high-profile research. Universities that are ranked highly on research measures are not necessarily the best places to take your first degree, although it may help when competing for jobs after graduation.

Increasing participation of care leavers

In England, in order for universities to be allowed to charge tuition fees over £6000 they have to submit an access agreement to the Office for Fair Access (OFFA) setting out their plans to improve access by under-represented groups in each academic year. An analysis of these agreements by the Who Cares? Trust found that three-quarters of them mentioned care leavers but fewer than a third set any kind of target for increasing participation, and these did not include any of the top ten universities. There were also wide discrepancies in the definition of care leavers, some using the same criteria as the CLCA 2000 (see Chapter 2) and others defining them simply as students who were in local authority care at some time before starting their university course (Who Cares? Trust 2012). Since the By Degrees report recommended it, a tick box has been introduced into the UCAS application so those who wish can identify themselves as care leavers, and this enables universities to direct them to sources of additional funding and to alert student support services. The research on which this recommendation was based found that many students with a care background missed out on much-needed grants and bursaries because they applied too late.

The Buttle Trust Quality Mark

An important finding of the By Degrees project (Jackson *et al.* 2005) was that most universities were unaware of the existence of children and young people in care as an especially disadvantaged group and knew almost nothing about the experience of care. The Trust decided to set up a system to identify higher education institutions which recognised the special difficulties of looked after children in accessing and surviving in higher education and took steps to meet their needs. For almost ten years Buttle UK awarded a Quality Mark (BQM) to universities and colleges which had developed a comprehensive policy aimed at increasing the number of applications from care leavers and better meeting the needs of those who obtained places (Starks 2013). The Trust achieved considerable success in encouraging universities to seek accreditation, with over half signing up to the BQM, including all those in Wales, all the Oxford colleges and 17 of the 24 Russell Group universities.

A BQM signifies that the following are in place in universities and colleges which offer degree courses:

+ Outreach activities such as open days and summer schools are accessible to those in care/care leavers and their carers and include them as a specific target group within access schemes.

+ A designated member of staff (a named person) is appointed to act as a key point of contact and advisor to care leavers both before entry and throughout their time at the university.

+ Information on finance, welfare and accommodation is readily available, for example via dedicated website pages.

+ Additional financial support is provided for care leavers, as well as ensuring that they are aware of and know how to apply for bursaries, hardship funds and access to learning grants.

♦ Targeted information is provided on provision for any special needs, such as dyslexia or health problems.

Independent research commissioned by Buttle UK found that only six per cent of students who had been in care were significantly influenced in their choice of university by whether it had the BQM. However, the existence of the award did greatly raise the profile of looked after children and care leavers within the institution, making it more likely that information would be provided about the support to which they might be entitled as students (Starks 2013). The BQM requirement that a care leavers' coordinator be appointed who could work across all the departments of the university was found to be very important in channelling support – financial, accommodation and personal – to students formerly in care and this could be crucial in decisions about continuing to pursue their course or dropping out. Students who did best were those who had good financial and emotional support both from the university and from former foster carers or local authority advisors.

Although the Buttle Trust no longer awards or monitors the Quality Mark it is likely that institutions that previously held the award will continue to be more aware of the needs and potential problems of care leavers. In 2015, the Buttle Trust will introduce a practice guide and a toolkit for colleges and universities to use with the Quality Mark Framework, and at the time of writing replacement schemes were being planned in the different countries of the UK.

Taking the long view

Some of the more successful young people in the YiPPEE study said they knew they would be going to university from the age of seven or eight. Of course they might only have a very vague idea at that stage what it involved, but it meant that they carried in their heads a vision of education stretching into the future and a goal to aim for beyond school examinations at age 16. Social workers sometimes feel that it is no use thinking far ahead because children are not likely to stay in the same placement for long. It is true that the UK out-of-home care system is very unstable compared with other countries (Jackson and Cameron 2014). However, education can be the most stable element in a turbulent childhood. Some young people, such as Donna in

Chapter 3, speak of school as a haven of calm, the only place where everything can be depended on to stay the same.

Official guidance is that young people in care should stay in the same placement and the same school at least during Years 10 and 11, when they are working for their GCSEs (or Standard Grades in Scotland). There are many reasons why this may not happen, but it should not be a reason for failing to think ahead.

Qualifying for university entrance

One obvious reason for the very small proportion of care leavers who go to university is that they do not have the necessary qualifications (see Chapter 10). The choice of secondary school is absolutely crucial. There is far more chance that care leavers will think about aiming for university if they go to a school where this is the norm and all their friends are staying on to do A-levels/Highers. That means that every school must have the opportunity for advanced level study (which many do not, especially in less prosperous areas) or a strong link to a college with advanced level study (such as sixth form colleges in England). In general, examination grades from further education colleges are much lower than from high-performing schools, which puts care leavers at a serious disadvantage in competing for university places. But expectations are probably the most important factor. 'All my friends were going to university so I assumed I would too. I didn't really think about it too much', we were told by a young man in the YiPPEE study. The School Admissions Code in England requires schools to provide places for looked after children and young people even if they are officially full. Although this provision has been eroded by the proliferation of academies and free schools, it can still be used by social workers, carers and the looked after children education service (LACES) and the VSH to argue for admission on behalf of particular individuals.

Applying to university

Deciding which university and course to choose is a complicated matter and a subject of anxious discussion in many households with 17-year-olds. Young people in care should be able to take full advantage of open days and the summer schools offered by many institutions between Years 12 and 13 (senior phase in Scotland) to explore universities with different characteristics and different situations (see below). Some prospective students may be more attracted by those which are part of the life of a city, others will prefer campus universities or those in rural areas. Seeing with your own eyes is very different from reading about it in a library or on the internet. In addition, attendance at open days usually offers a chance to meet current students and hear what it is like to study in that place at first hand.

Local authorities should pay fares and expenses for these visits, both for the prospective student and for an adult to accompany them if they feel apprehensive about going alone, but it is important for young people or their carers to apply in very good time in case there are delays in authorising payments. The lead person in the LACES team or the Virtual School Head should be able to help.

Case study: Proactive recruitment

Sheffield Hallam University took a proactive approach to recruiting students from care backgrounds through its Raising Aspirations project. This offered young people a two-day event called 'A Taste of Uni'. During the visit young people could explore 'what being a student is, their lifestyle and the type of work they would do at university' (Learning and Skills Council 2009, p.18). A physical visit to the university provides an alternative source of inspiration, away from foster carers, who 'themselves may be a barrier to the aspirations of young people in their care…they may not have experienced university themselves or do not know of anyone who has been and therefore may not see it as a viable option' (Learning and Skills Council 2009, p.19). This model is now a familiar one. The Sutton Trust and the University of Cambridge provide five-day Summer Schools for young people in Year 12 (age 17), free to attend, including train travel to get there, for those at a state maintained school or college who have at least five A grades at GCSE or five National 5 qualifications in Scotland and are taking subjects appropriate to their chosen course. Selection criteria include young people who are or have been looked after in public care (www.cam.ac.uk).

The Pathway Plan for a young person aiming for university should include decisions on these matters, and especially who is responsible for helping to complete the UCAS application form and ensuring that it is submitted in good time. If the young person has a mentor, he or she may be the most suitable person. The personal statement which forms part of the application is extremely important and even the most competent and confident candidate will need informed help in writing it. Some young people told us that they were fearful of revealing their care status in case it proved stigmatising, and this issue needs to be discussed with their everyday expert and local authority advisor. Almost always it will be an advantage for admissions tutors to know that the applicant has been in care and has had to overcome difficult circumstances to arrive at the point of applying to university. Some universities automatically offer interviews to care leavers, and make special arrangements such as deferred places to allow them to improve qualifications, as in Louise's case described below. They can also provide information designed specifically for young people in care on finance and accommodation.

Matching qualifications and HEIs

As a general rule it is best to encourage young people to apply to the highest ranking institution where they might get an offer. These universities are likely to have more resources, better student accommodation and more distinguished staff. All universities publish advice and give examples of typical offers, which vary between subjects. Most Russell Group universities require at least two As and a B at A-level or AAAAB in Scottish Highers and would not consider vocational qualifications such as BTEC, even though a Level 3 BTEC Diploma is supposed to be equivalent to between one and three A-levels (see Chapter 1). Other universities may offer places on much lower A-level/Higher grades and are prepared to accept alternative qualifications.

One problem is that offers are made on the basis of A-level/Higher grades predicted by schools and colleges, not actual examination results. This may especially work against those in care whose post-16 school career has been disrupted by placement changes or life events. Carers should be prepared to challenge predictions if they think they underestimate a candidate's ability, and enlist the help of teachers other than the one responsible for the prediction if necessary. For those whose A-level/Higher results are much better than expected there may be scope to switch their choice to a university they would prefer once the results are known, through clearing. It is very important to be on the spot ready to do this immediately, and the young person will probably need help from a teacher or advocate. This is even more vital if the candidate's grades do not meet the conditional offer made by the university. There may well be extenuating circumstances due to the difficulties which care leavers often encounter at this stage in their lives; social workers, or preferably teachers, should be prepared to telephone admissions tutors and advocate strongly on their behalf.

Case study: Louise

Louise, in this example, illustrates how easily an academically able young person can be thrown off course if care arrangements fail to take account of educational matters. In this case her university career was delayed, but not wrecked, thanks to the efforts of the woman who became her everyday expert.

Louise had lived with her foster family for seven years. She had always done well at school, passed 10 GCSEs with all As and Bs and had offers from two universities to read law. On the basis of her AS-level results (Year 12) she expected to meet the lower offer of two Bs and a C with no difficulty. Then her foster father had to give up work through illness and she was told, three weeks before she was due to take her A-levels, that the family was planning to take two more foster children for financial reasons so she would have to find somewhere else to live at once. Her social worker found her temporary lodgings – 'not the ideal place to work for exams' – but much worse was the emotional impact of being thrown out of what she had thought of as her home, which she described as 'like a bereavement'. She found it impossible to concentrate on revision and was disappointed but not surprised by her exam results which were far below her previous expectations.

She might have given up hope of university at that stage had it not been for her social worker, who found her new lodgings with a retired FE teacher. This person was familiar with the universities admission system and keen to act as an advocate. She found out the name of the relevant tutor, telephoned the university, explained the circumstances, and obtained the offer of a deferred place, subject to Louise improving her A-level results. Louise developed a warm relationship with her landlady and stayed with her for three more years, until in her third year she moved to a shared house with other students.

Case study: Darren

Another young person whose placement ended at a bad moment for his educational prospects was Darren, a participant in the YiPPEE study. In his case the move unexpectedly turned out to be for the better, thanks to support from a very active leaving care team.

Darren was placed with foster carers at the age of six in a rural area, far away from any of his family and from his home local authority. At primary school he was always in trouble and was even diagnosed with ADHD. But soon after he moved to secondary school his behaviour problems seemed to disappear. He was outstandingly good at all sports and very frustrated in being unable to compete at the appropriate level because he was dependent on his carers for transport, which they were often unwilling to provide. Although the school considered him highly intelligent, his foster carers, who were farmers and had both left school at 16, took little interest in his education and rarely bothered to attend parents' evenings. This could not in any way be considered a learning placement and Darren complained to his social worker and at his six-monthly reviews but felt no one listened to him.

After obtaining five GCSEs with good grades, Darren went to FE college, where he again did well despite the lack of home support and was on course to pass two A-levels and a BTEC. The farm was not doing so well, however, and his carers began to drink heavily. After a furious row, his foster mother smashed up his laptop with all his work on it. Darren walked out, carrying what he could in a backpack, and never went back. He slept on friends' sofas for a few weeks and then decided to move in with his mother – he had kept in touch with her through the years. He was still technically in care, and fortunately his mother lived in an area with a leaving care team strongly committed to promoting educational participation. With continued support from his after-care worker he decided to enrol for A-level courses at the local college and work part-time to save for his university expenses, pursuing his original aim of studying for a degree in sports psychology at a high-ranking university. Without this support, and the encouragement of his mother, who had always wanted him to go to university, he would probably have given up the idea of higher education altogether.

Case study: Nina

Nina's progress through education was less problematic than that of most young people in care but even she relied heavily on the support of a teacher in the leaving care team.

Nina came to England with her mother and two brothers at the age of 14. She had been attending a selective Catholic girls' school in Jamaica where she was considered an able pupil. Her father, who was supposed to join them, never arrived, and her mother developed severe mental health problems. Nina and her brother were placed with a foster family, who had two older children at university, and provided an educationally rich environment. After passing GCSEs with good grades, she moved on to a Catholic sixth form college 'because that's where all my friends were going'.

Nina could have gone to university anywhere but, like many young people with a care background, she chose a local one in order to stay close to her family. This may have been a mistake as her academic progress was frequently threatened by demands on her time caused by the chaotic lives of her relatives. However, with the support of the leaving care team, Nina managed to stay on track. After a false start studying English, she found that she was really good at computing. Through the leaving care team, the local authority offered her holiday jobs in the council offices and paid for her to stay with her foster family, although this was not yet mandatory for young people in full-time education. Nina went on to take a master's degree, with strong encouragement and continued support from a teacher in her leaving care team. She became unintentionally pregnant during her second year but was well supported by her partner and was awarded her MA three weeks before her baby was born. A year later she was offered a well-paid permanent job in the local authority.

Louise, Darren and Nina were all ambitious young people with above-average academic ability who knew they wanted to go to university. Yet, for very different reasons, each went through a period when they were at high risk of being derailed and would probably have dropped out of education without the support provided by a combination of everyday experts and strong support from their leaving care team. This is very typical of the lives of looked after young people and shows how important it is for the local authority, as their corporate parent, to keep close track of their educational pathways and intervene promptly to help at critical points.

Accommodation

The YiPPEE study found that living conditions can be a great problem for young people in upper secondary education, especially those who are in residential care in England. Most children's homes are uncongenial places for study, despite exhortations from government going back to the Children Act 1989. The Scottish Government has made a determined effort to improve conditions (Her Majesty's Inspectors of Schools and Social Work Services Inspectorate 2001; Scottish Executive 2002; Connelly 2013) but so far they have had little impact on attainment. Many young people have told us how difficult it is to work for exams when there is constant coming and going, noise and disturbance. In addition, most children's homes only cater for residents up to 16, after which almost half (44%) move on to various independent living arrangements, so understandably the emphasis in the homes is on learning skills for daily living rather than remaining in education (House of Commons Education Committee 2014).

That is probably why hardly any young people are able to go to university directly from residential care, though some who have been in children's homes return to education in their twenties or later in life (Mallon 2007; Cherry 2013). It is considerably easier for those in stable long-term foster care, and that is the most common background for university students who have been in care (Jackson et al. 2003). An important finding from the By Degrees study is that even at the age of 14 or 15, a placement with foster carers who give high value to education can lead to unanticipated success in examinations and eventually to university (Jackson and Ajayi 2007; Bentley 2013; Driscoll 2011). It is especially important for social workers in areas with high numbers of asylum seekers to be aware of this evidence, as these young people often do not come into the care system until quite late in adolescence and their ability is likely to be underestimated, especially if English is not their first language.

Many young people see getting the tenancy of their own apartment as a major step forward, but it can prove a trap in terms of their education. They are usually not allowed to sub-let so that they are effectively tied to the area where they live, which may not be the best place to go to university. Alternatively, they may have a long journey to attend the institution where they are enrolled and unreliable public transport can affect their attendance. Hassan, who had survived an abusive childhood to obtain a coveted place on a degree course in aeronautical engineering, was so often late for classes because of buses not turning up that he started to fall behind with his work and eventually gave up and took a job working in a garage (Jackson *et al.* 2003).

The best option is usually for care leavers to live in university halls of residence in their first year. This provides opportunities for them to make friends and learn how to relate to people from different backgrounds. Some universities guarantee places in their own accommodation for applicants who tick the box on the UCAS form to say that they have been in care (or inform student support services). They should also be allowed, if they wish, to stay during vacations, although one ex-care student pointed out that to find yourself the only inhabitant of a student residence on Christmas day is a pretty miserable experience. After the first year they may prefer, like most students, to live in a shared house or flat with a group of other young people. It is a job for the personal advisor to ensure that university students formerly in care have suitable accommodation during vacations, which is an entitlement under the Children (Leaving Care) Act 2000 in England and Wales.

Finance

The By Degrees study concluded that care leavers successfully completing their courses were on average about £2000 more in debt than non-care students. The government responded by requiring local authorities to make a one-off grant of £2000 to young people in England at the start of their university courses. This not only takes no account of inflation over the last ten years but does not begin to meet the cost of attending university, which is closer to £8000 a year, excluding tuition fees (not charged in Scotland) (Universities UK, n.d.). Some young people in care may be put off applying to university by fear of accumulating unmanageable debts or being unable to maintain themselves. They need to be reassured that fees (£6000–9000) do not have to be paid upfront, student loans are not repayable until they are earning at least £21,000 a year, and as already noted there are numerous sources of grants and bursaries for students in need. Young people may need help from their everyday experts and social workers to understand that education is an excellent long-term investment, seen purely in financial terms, leaving aside its quality of life benefits (Jackson 2007). That is not to deny that managing financially can be a problem for students who have been in care and will certainly require careful budgeting and support from their local authority advisor. Local authorities can help by paying realistic allowances and not expecting students to take paid work during term-time, which can seriously undermine their opportunities for participation and academic success.

Concluding thoughts

Going to university, or any kind of tertiary education, from care remains rare. The overall proportion of care leavers going on to university after school has been stuck for many years at less than one in ten. But some local authorities achieve much higher figures, closer to the national average of 40 per cent for all children, which shows how much scope there is for improvement. The first step is starting as early as possible to raise the aspirations and expectations of young people themselves, their carers and social workers. Both the Personal Education Plan and Pathway Planning meetings offer occasions to do this, and may be helped by the legal requirement from 2015 to stay in education or training up to the age of 18 in England.

Young people in care need skilled, personalised advice from knowledgeable people about the processes of choosing and applying to university or college. Foster carers and residential workers will need to seek outside help if they are not equipped to provide this themselves. What they can do, however, is to ensure that their young people are confident of adequate financial and personal support if they are successful in obtaining a university place. In some areas this may require forceful advocacy from social workers, especially on behalf of those already living independently.

At present 'learning placements' for young people in care who would like to go to university seem to happen more by chance than design, but why shouldn't local authorities run an active recruitment programme for carers who see supporting the educational progression of the young people who live with them as one of their primary tasks? Provision for young people to stay in foster care after the age of 18 through 'staying put' (see Chapter 2) may prove very helpful although it is too soon to tell if it will be successful in increasing the proportion who are able to access higher education.

Current guidance means that students with a care background are entitled to accommodation, both in university terms and vacations. Those who can return to a supportive foster family at least during their first year are more likely to complete their university courses successfully (Jackson *et al.* 2005). Going to university is valuable in itself and likely to lead to better employment prospects and a better quality of life, but it also gives care leavers a breathing space, time to move to adulthood and independent living at a pace that is much closer to the experience of their non-care contemporaries. Some see it as a way of leaving behind their care identity to 'become a normal person', others go on to take leading roles in student organisations and become powerful advocates for young people like themselves.

Practice points

+ Integrate thinking about higher education options into Personal Education Plans and pathway planning from Year 9 onwards.

+ Provide individualised support for applications to universities, including visiting open days, attending summer schools and writing personal statements.

+ When selecting universities, look out for Buttle Quality Mark provision or similar schemes which develop after Buttle UK ends its provision.

+ Respond quickly on results day, with strong advocates available to contact universities on young people's behalf.

+ Ensure care leavers are aware of the full range of financial support available and take steps to minimise accumulating debt while at university.

+ Adapt policies on accommodation options for care leavers so that if a university place is available, tenancies are not a barrier to taking it up.

Useful resources

+ The Who Cares? Trust is a voice and a champion for children and young people in the UK living in care. It produces resources to support their belief that every child in care should receive encouragement and opportunities to achieve and enjoy life, such as workshops, publications and participation projects, including a website-based library (www.thewhocarestrust. org.uk).

+ Universities UK is the 'definitive voice' for universities across the UK, committed to exploring and promoting the contribution of universities to all areas of society. It aims to provide high quality leadership and support to its members, and to promote a successful and diverse higher education sector (www.universitiesuk.ac.uk).

+ The Buttle Trust is a children's charity supporting those in poverty through grants, research and partnership organisations. It developed the widely praised BQM in the higher education sector. It has a school fees programme for certain children, including those who have been adopted (www.buttleuk.org).

+ *Supporting Care Leavers into Higher Education*, the HE handbook for care leavers by the Who Cares? Trust (2014), provides useful information about the support that is available at higher education institutions, and further education institutions that offer university and college education courses, in England and Scotland:

  ◊ www.thewhocarestrust.org.uk/data/files/H.E.Hand book_2014_England.pdf

  ◊ www.thewhocarestrust.org.uk/data/files/H.E.Hand book_2014_Scotland.pdf

  ◊ www.thewhocarestrust.org.uk/pages/the-college-hand book.htm

CHAPTER 12

Supporting Recent Migrants

The aim of this chapter is to highlight the experience of children who become looked after as a result of their status as unaccompanied migrants. We provide a summary of the complex legal context and the experience of children, most of whom have fled conflict and repression, as they seek asylum and adjust to an unfamiliar culture. And we also examine their particular needs for support in relation to education.

KEY POINTS

▸ There are lessons for all looked after children and young people from the experiences of supporting migrant children in education – valuing the whole child.

▸ Unaccompanied migrant children constitute a diverse group with very different individual circumstances, including differences in their prior experiences and attainment in education.

▸ Education is valuable in helping children to settle and have a normal life, even when immigration status is uncertain.

▸ Young people who arrive as migrants are often ambitious to go as far as possible in education and this aspiration should be strongly supported.

Introduction

A significant number of children and young people whose immigration status is temporary or uncertain are being supported by care and education services in the UK. Some will have arrived as asylum seekers unaccompanied by adults, and others will have been part of family groups but have been separated for one reason or another. Some of these young people succeed very well in education but others do not. All have to cope with uncertainty about their legal status as well as overcoming language and cultural barriers. The role of early parenting in stimulating a belief in education is an important factor in the resilience of many of these children.

The terms 'migrant' and 'immigrant' are not precisely defined, and are used both interchangeably and differently in everyday speech and even in more formal discourse. Migrant implies temporary settlement and yet the children with which this chapter is concerned have often been cared for and educated in the UK for many years, and some will remain permanently. For the most part, the term migrant is used in this chapter to refer to children who arrive in the UK seeking asylum from war or destitution, and who are subject to immigration controls. But the term migrant could also apply to children whose legal rights to live in the UK are not questioned, for example a child arriving as part of a family from another EU country who later becomes separated or estranged from his or her relatives. Those readers who are interested in the more technical aspects of migration and its implications will find the publications of The Migration Observatory helpful (e.g. Anderson and Blinder 2014).

> The majority of separated and unaccompanied asylum-seeking children arrive from countries experiencing armed conflict or serious repression of minority groups or political opponents. Over the past three years, the top countries of origin of unaccompanied children seeking asylum in the UK included Afghanistan, Iran, Eritrea, Vietnam, Albania, Somalia, Algeria, Iraq and China. (Dorling and Hurrell 2012, p.9)

Very few of these children have been regarded by the UK government as refugees, a status which would provide entitlement to special protection under the 1951 UN Convention relating to the Status of Refugees,[1] and would normally lead to them being granted five years' leave to remain, entitlement to benefits and the right to work. A report by The Children's Society stated that 'most unaccompanied

---

1   See UN Refugee Council at www.unhcr.org.

children who apply for asylum in the UK are refused refugee status or humanitarian protection' while, alternatively, they are granted discretionary leave to remain for 30 months or until they reach the age of 17½ (The Children's Society 2012). The Coram Children's Legal Centre noted that 20 per cent of applications by children for refugee status were granted in 2011(Dorling and Hurrell 2012). It is possible for a young person to request an extension when the discretionary leave period comes to an end, but the number of requests granted appears to be very low, around 290 out of 5280 decisions (5.5%) in the five years prior to 2012, according to information supplied to the Coram Children's Legal Centre by the UK Border Agency (Dorling and Hurrell 2012, p.12).

The UK government's National Statistics agency recorded 1288 asylum applications from unaccompanied asylum-seeking children in the year ending March 2014, accounting for five per cent of total applications for asylum. This figure was an increase of 15 per cent from the previous year and well below the peak of 4060 in 2008.[2] The actual number of unaccompanied migrant children in the UK is likely to be higher than this since some children will not be recorded in official statistics and not all make applications for asylum. A report in 2012 by the House of Lords and House of Commons Joint Committee on Human Rights indicated that there were 2150 unaccompanied migrant children in local authority care in England alone (550 under the age of 16), representing three per cent of the total number of looked after children. The Committee also neatly summed up the legal and psychological contexts within which support for unaccompanied migrant children is provided:

> These children are entitled to protection under domestic legislation and international agreements, the most universally accepted of which is the UN Convention on the Rights of the Child (UNCRC). Providing protection and support effectively is crucial: the asylum and immigration process can be complex, and the stress it can cause can be particularly acute for children. (Joint Committee on Human Rights 2013, p.3)

---

2   *Source:* www.gov.uk/government/collections/migration-statistics.

In the following three sections of this chapter we outline in more detail the legal position, the asylum process and the experience of unaccompanied migrant children seeking asylum in the UK.

The legal context

Migrant children who are separated from their families and country of birth constitute a diverse group, both in terms of individual circumstances and by the particular reasons which have brought them to the UK. These reasons include being the victims of human trafficking, seeking asylum from the effects of war or oppression, and becoming separated from their family once in the UK.

Whatever the reasons that lie behind a child becoming an unaccompanied migrant, the UK government has accepted the principle that all refugee and migrant children are children first and foremost, and are therefore entitled to the same rights and protection as are all other children. In this regard, the UK government accepts the principles of the UN Convention on the Rights of the Child (UNCRC) which require that the rights of all children must be protected, that their best interests must be a primary consideration, and that they must be afforded the right to express their views in all matters affecting them, including in judicial and administrative proceedings. The legal force of this principle was emphasised in a ruling by the UK Supreme Court in which Lord Kerr stated that a child's best interest:

> is not merely one consideration that weighs in the balance alongside other competing factors. Where the best interests of the child clearly favour a certain course, that course should be followed unless countervailing reasons of considerable force displace them [...] the primacy of this consideration needs to be made clear in emphatic terms. (United Kingdom Supreme Court 2011, paragraph 46)[3]

Nevertheless, the House of Lords and House of Commons Joint Committee on Human Rights said they had heard evidence 'from a significant number of organisations' (Joint Committee on Human Rights 2013, paragraph 23) questioning whether immigration

---

3   UKSC 4 (2011, paragraph 46): www.bailii.org/uk/cases/UKSC/2011/4.html.

practice was consistent with this ruling: 'Many of those who gave evidence considered that problems in assessing best interests arose because immigration concerns too often took priority' (Joint Committee on Human Rights 2013, paragraph 24). The Committee recommended that government guidance to those safeguarding and making decisions about the future of unaccompanied migrant children should 'reassert the primary need to uphold the welfare and wellbeing of those children' (Joint Committee on Human Rights 2013, paragraph 31), a recommendation which the UK government accepted in its response.[4]

The UNCRC has not been incorporated in full into UK law – though there are significant nuances in the degree to which the devolved administrations have been prepared to consider the implications in the Convention – and this has sometimes caused tensions between UK governments and the Convention and the devolved administrations and organisations advocating on behalf of children. It is not possible to go into detail about these legal issues and debates here, not least because this is an area where information and decisions are subject to change, and readers interested in conducting further research into this aspect should refer to the sources listed at the end of this chapter.

A contentious area of asylum is the assessment of age to determine whether an applicant is legally a child (under 18) or an adult. This occurs because migrants typically arrive with no or incomplete documentation. Older children may find that their age claims are disputed, leading to examination which can be perceived as intrusive, and it has been suggested by some commentators that the burden of proof is loaded substantially against the child in a climate which seeks to reduce immigration; and where budget pressures mean there is little incentive on local authorities to identify migrants as children, with implications for their financial support, without UK government contribution (Dorling and Hurrell 2012).

Acceptance of the primacy of welfare and wellbeing of migrant children and young people means that, once placed with a local authority, it is the relevant child welfare law and its guidance in the particular country of the UK where they come to live that governs

---

4   CM 8778 (2014): www.parliament.uk/documents/joint-committees/human-rights/ UMC_Report_Govt_Response_Cm_8778.pdf.

their care and education. This complexity has not always made for smooth arrangements in supporting children. For example, the Scottish Refugee Council, in its evidence to the Joint House of Lords and House of Commons inquiry, said that: '...policy formulation by the Department of Education or the Home Office rarely takes the Scottish context into account. This leads to confusion in the course of policy implementation and may prevent young people from benefiting from more generous provisions to which they are entitled in Scotland' (Scottish Refugee Council 2012, p.5).

The asylum process

The arrangements for the reception of an unaccompanied migrant child or young person under 18 arriving in the UK who becomes known to the police, the UK Border Agency or other agencies are different from those used in the case of adults. The local authority in whose area the child arrives or presents as being 'in need' has immediate responsibility for the child's welfare, while the UK Border Agency has the authority to make decisions about the legitimacy of an asylum claim.

Since these matters are not entirely distinct, there can be tensions between these respective legal duties. Also, for these matters to be effectively and sensitively handled, there needs to be good liaison between agencies, something which several reports have alleged has not always happened (Matthews 2012; Scottish Refugee Council 2012; The Children's Society 2012). For example, several reports have been critical of interviewing practice used in determining claims for asylum, suggesting they have not always been conducted in a child-friendly manner, or ensured that the child understood the proceedings sufficiently, or given sufficient opportunities to listen to the child (The Children's Society 2012).

An unaccompanied migrant child first encounters a screening process which means that travel documents are checked, details logged, and a short interview is conducted. If it is accepted that the applicant is a child, the relevant local authority is responsible for providing care, including a suitable placement, financial support and education, while an application for asylum or other leave is being considered. If an applicant's age is disputed, the local authority is responsible for arranging for an assessment to be undertaken. If the outcome of the assessment indicates that the applicant is over 18, he or she is treated as an adult for the purposes of determining a claim for asylum, which can mean being liable to fast-track detention. We do not consider the circumstances of adult migrants claiming asylum here, other than to point out that applicants subsequently discovered to be children can experience adult detention in the meantime, adding to their frightening and stressful experiences, as is illustrated by the following case study.

Case study of 'A': The experience of a migrant child initially treated as an adult[5]

The child we will call A left Afghanistan after being forcibly recruited to the Taliban. He had no documents and did not know his date of birth. He thinks he was 14 when he left Afghanistan. His journey was arranged by agents and he travelled in cars, lorries and on foot. He was apprehended by the police and was arrested and handcuffed. At his Screening Interview there were problems with the Home Office interpreter and A did not feel that what he said was being interpreted accurately. In September 2009 A's application for asylum was refused by the UK Border Agency. He was granted neither refugee status nor humanitarian protection, but was given discretionary leave to remain. The age he claimed to be was disputed by the local authority, who said he was an adult, and the UK Border Agency accepted the local authority's assessment of A's age. A was moved and placed in a house with four men much older than him. He felt very isolated and spent a great deal of time on his own in his room. The local authority said they would get him an advocate but this never happened. They cited practical problems, saying that it was not possible to provide an advocate for 'an adult', even though his age was in dispute.

With the assistance of a legal aid immigration solicitor, A appealed against the UK Border Agency's refusal to grant international protection. His asylum appeal was allowed in April 2010. A's age was a relevant factor in the determination of his asylum appeal and the judge considered A to be 'under 17'. The judge assessed the local authority age assessment as well as evidence submitted in support of A's case by his solicitor, including an independent paediatric assessment, and the appeal was allowed.

However, A has still not received his refugee status papers because the local authority still insisted that A was older than he said he was and

---

5   Reproduced by permission of the Coram Children's Legal Centre.

the immigration judge found him to be. With the help of his solicitor he is continuing to challenge the assessment of his age. Until there is an outcome to this challenge he continues to live in limbo, and the legal complications have affected the support he has received (Dorling and Hurrell 2012, p.17). If a young person is assessed as over 18 years of age, he or she no longer comes within the orbit of mandatory educational participation and so their educational rights are denied if the assessment is wrong.

The experience of migrant children

'They come to us seeking safety, only to find a bewildering, suspicious and damaging system they are expected to negotiate alone. In short, they are denied a childhood' (Nandy 2007, p.7).

A report by the UN High Commissioner for Refugees (UNHRC) on Afghan children who have migrated to Europe says that all migratory movements have two elements: a context and a trigger (Mougne 2010). Contexts are country- and situation-specific, but generally involve several of the following: poverty and economic hardship; political instability; physical insecurity and fear for life; risk of forced labour and kidnapping; poor educational prospects and lack of hope for a brighter future. Specific triggers for departure reported by boys interviewed for the UNHCR study included family conflict, violent incidents such as kidnapping, the death of a parent, or threats made against the family or individual family members.

The actual mechanism of travel for most of the young people typically involves a parent or relative entering into a costly contract to pay a smuggling gang involved in transporting goods, weapons, drugs and human beings for profit. Given the costs involved, it is not unusual for payment to be made in instalments – perhaps following the sale of goods, possessions or property, or obtaining a loan – and if a payment is delayed the young person's travel to the agreed destination will be held up. In such circumstances, children are forced to seek illegal employment in the country where they are held up, or to work for the smuggling gang, in either case under exploitative conditions. As a result, journeys can take many months or years and are hazardous, with children experiencing frightening and traumatic events, injuries and abusive treatment:

Several boys told of terrifying experiences [crossing from Turkey to Greece in a small boat] as they struggled desperately to keep afloat, while seeing fellow travellers drown before their eyes. Two boys (interviewed in different countries) broke down when recalling how they were forcibly separated from an accompanying brother prior to the crossing to Greece as the smugglers placed them in separate craft, never to see each other again. (Mougne 2010, p.19)

The trauma experienced by unaccompanied child migrants is the result of prolonged and sustained exposure to repeated stressors, similar to that occurring in psychological or sexual abuse (Derluyn and Broekaert 2008). This is the accumulated effect of the events which occurred before leaving the home country, the terrifying and abusive experiences during the flight, and the experiences associated with being a refugee, including immigration procedures, worrying about the future, and facing racist hostility. A particular issue is that these children and young people are required to provide proof of the persecution they might face if returned to their home country, and that the likelihood of being successful in an asylum claim is contingent on having this proof (Wright 2012). Uncertainty about asylum status is associated with depression, and psychological problems have been found to be more prevalent among unaccompanied than accompanied children (The Children's Society 2012).

The personal histories and continuing challenges faced by these young people indicate the importance of access to specialist services and effective multi-agency support. Evidence given to the Joint House of Lords and House of Commons Committee drew attention to a lack of access to specialist therapeutic support for children.

The implications for education

'Schools and colleges are places where the lives of unaccompanied young people can regain an ordinary rhythm' (Wade *et al.* 2012, p.6).

Jim Wade and colleagues carried out research between 2009 and 2011 in four local authorities in England, using methods which included a survey of foster carers looking after an unaccompanied young person, and interviews with foster carers, young people, workers and managers (Sirriyeh and Wade 2013). The young people were typically male (88%) and aged 15–17 years (80%). All were in foster care, mostly (88%) in the independent sector. Most (82%) were awaiting a final decision on their application for asylum. The researchers found that the young people varied considerably in their prior experience of education, with some having had no schooling, while others had been in school for several years. Most had not previously studied English and some had no experience of using technology, such as computers. A third of the young people experienced delays in accessing education in the UK, related to disputes about age, or because they arrived near to the end of a school year, or because of difficulties in co-operation between social work and education teams.

Despite these considerable barriers, refugee and asylum-seeking young people have often been described in academic studies and by practitioners as being highly motivated to achieve in education (Stevenson and Willott 2007). Such motivation may be driven by long-held ambition to achieve professional qualifications, or to overcome loneliness and make friends, and a belief that doing well in education will have a positive effect on a claim for asylum or to remain in the country. For some, their aspirations will mirror those held by their parents. The authors of one study observed that education provided the young people they studied 'with something to aim for and focus on, and many of those who did not access a school place immediately spent the time in libraries instead' (Brownlees and Finch 2010, p.94). Sirriyeh and Wade (2013) found that few of the young people in their study had attendance problems and, according to their foster carers, most were enjoying and receiving an appropriate education. Indeed, foster carers were important mediators of education, particularly in helping with the learning of English, crucial for progress in education and for social interactions at school, 'through everyday routines within the home; initially, for example, by using dictionaries, flash cards and resources on the internet' (Sirriyeh and Wade 2013, p.198).

But the experience of education is not so positive for some unaccompanied migrant children. The Joint House of Lords and House of Commons inquiry heard evidence about inequalities in access to early years education, 'especially for young people whose legal status was insecure' (Joint Committee on Human Rights 2013, p.58). The Committee also heard that uncertainty about immigration status restricted access at all levels of education by, for example, introducing delays in confirming a school or college place. This can lead to feelings of pressure, since 'the time in which young people can achieve and progress in education is often compressed both by their experiences and by future possibilities. Many felt the pressure of the clock ticking…' (Sirriyeh and Wade 2013, p.198). Some young people have experienced bullying and instances of racism, adding to feelings of isolation.

There are significant barriers for asylum-seeking young people in accessing college and university education, particularly in relation to financial support, and inconsistencies in approaches to admission between institutions. The Coram Children's Legal Centre noted that it had 'on several occasions offered legal advice and clarified with student finance that a young person with leave to remain is in fact eligible for support' (Dorling and Hurrell 2012, p.20).

Case study of 'B': 'I want to make something of myself'

B is a young man aged 17 when interviewed. He had arrived in the UK from an African country, aged seven, with his parents and siblings. He was removed from the family aged 11 when social workers intervened after a teacher raised a concern about one of his siblings on child protection grounds. In fact, B said that he had on two occasions previously disclosed his own fears about his physical safety to a teacher without protective action resulting. On the first occasion, he said he was not believed and the matter was apparently not escalated through child protection procedures. On the second occasion, school child protection procedures appear to have been followed but B said he had recanted his claims for fear of being beaten. In care, B experienced foster and residential care placements, which were not particularly happy experiences. In the children's home, he experienced hostility directed towards the colour of his skin and because he was studious. He said, 'This was one of my worst experiences. I never bonded. I had no friends. I felt so lonely. I spent a lot of time sitting in my room.' He found the workers 'nice enough' and looked after his physical needs well but he does not remember any taking a particular interest in his school work. His room had no desk and he had to do homework sitting on his bed. 'But I stuck it out.'

Despite these barriers, B was successful in education, got good grades in external examinations and received unconditional offers from several universities to study mathematics. He attributes his success to a combination of personal determination, encouragement from his current foster carers and support in school:

> 'To be fair about my parents, they instilled in me a value of education and I want to make something of myself, despite everything. I want to be able to say I came from something difficult but I can make something of myself. Social work helped me out a lot but I needed to go for it. I want to be an example.'

One factor that undoubtedly helped was the local authority's willingness to pay for travel by taxi to maintain a settled school life during several care placements. This meant getting up early and having long days, a challenge to which B responded by becoming organised and determined. He is grateful to his foster carers for being encouraging, for example, providing a laptop, while 'not putting too much pressure on me'. The most important thing is that 'foster carers should be happy with what you do; nothing should be a failure. Give children time – patience is a big thing.'

Two other factors appear to have been important in supporting B's education. The independent foster care placement agency used by the local authority provided an education liaison specialist to work with the school and B's carers. Also, the support of a senior member of staff in the school was 'the best thing that happened to me':

> 'She made sure that everything was all right at home. She went out of her way to help and attended all my care reviews. She kept a record of my progress. I felt if I ever needed her she would step in. There were times when she pleaded with the head when my behaviour meant I was nearly at exclusion. She was so proud of me.'

In B's last year of school, approaching 18, additional stressors began to impact on his studies. There were 'always things going on in the background, like meetings [in connection with his immigration status] and struggling to stay in the country'. B was granted temporary leave to remain in the UK for three years beyond 18 on humanitarian protection grounds on condition that he had no access to public funds, though he was free to seek employment. The universities' offers were changed from unconditional to conditional, the condition being that he could show the ability to pay international fees. At the time of interview, within two weeks of university term starting, B felt in limbo and was highly anxious about his future. Having been sustained by a strong belief in the value of education, working hard at his studies, and achieving, it seemed that his efforts were not to be rewarded. B's solicitor made an application for a review of the immigration decision on the grounds that there were no living relatives in the country of birth which, if successful, would allow access to support for fee payment and living expenses. B also applied to his chosen university for an international student scholarship to cover international fees and some living expenses. At the time of writing, the authors learned that this application had been successful, removing the anxiety over fees, but leaving questions to be resolved over continuing immigration status (particularly since leave to remain was due to end before the expected end of the degree course) and accommodation.

Considerations for supporting education

The research by Wade and colleagues identified five important factors associated with educational progress (Sirriyeh and Wade 2013). These were: (i) not considered to have emotional or behavioural difficulties; (ii) having a range of hobbies and interests; (iii) fewer past placement moves; (iv) some evidence of positive social work planning; and (v) helpful contact with the social worker.

Social workers were valued for facilitating access to good schools, resources, such as laptops, and funding for courses. Teachers, language support staff and foster carers were, perhaps unsurprisingly, more influential in providing direct help with education.

Several reports have highlighted what might be considered good practice in providing support in education for refugee and asylum-seeking young people, whether living with their family or arriving as unaccompanied migrants (for example, Jackson *et al.* 2005; Candappa *et al.* 2007). These include the following:

+ Providing effective welcome and induction procedures in schools.

+ Making special efforts to demonstrate an ethos of inclusion and respect, including strategies aimed at helping other pupils and their parents to be supportive and welcoming to asylum-seeking children, for example by buddying or peer mentoring and by using opportunities to value cultural diversity through personal and social education lessons.

+ Addressing English language needs in ways which are sensitive to the young person's learning needs across the curriculum, for example without being withdrawn from other subjects or remaining in specialist language units for longer than is judged necessary to cope in mainstream school.

+ Monitoring progress, achievement and attainment, ensuring that education receives high priority in multi-agency planning and reviews, and recognising the normalising routine of education which can help young people to settle and make sense of their new lives.

+ Providing specialist training and support for teachers, and opportunities to share practice during in-service training days and at seminars and conferences.

+ Timely anticipation of the effects of immigration issues in planning for post-school education.

+ Making the most of the high level of motivation reported by many of these young people and encouraging them to realise their ambition of going to university.

+ Putting them in touch with advocacy organisations and arranging effective legal representation if they are threatened with deportation.

Concluding thoughts

Children and young people who have uncertain immigration status face additional barriers in the care system with implications for their educational success. Yet this group are often extremely determined to make a success of education, often against considerable linguistic and informational odds. This value attached to education is often derived from their birth parents. In many ways, the supports are those which should be available for all children in care, such as encouragement from carers, practical help, suitable facilities for doing homework, good communication between the agencies and co-ordinated arrangements in school. In addition, it is vital to have access to specialist advice and services from refugee agencies, particularly where young people are planning to progress in education beyond school.

Practice points

- ◆ Think child first and not asylum seeker or refugee. All under-18-year-olds are entitled to protection under domestic legislation and international agreements.

- ◆ Schools should not simply assume that a pupil is receiving appropriate advice; they should actively confirm this with social work agencies and help the child to access advice directly if this has not been arranged (because immigration status has important implications for post-school education when a young person turns 18).

- ◆ Encourage educational ambition. Asylum-seeking young people who are looked after often provide a model of educational dedication and motivation for other young people in care.

Useful resources

- ◆ The Refugee Council website provides useful facts about asylum in the UK and links to other sources (www. refugeecouncil.org.uk). See also the Scottish Refugee Council (www.scottishrefugeecouncil.org.uk) and the Welsh Refugee Council (www.welshrefugeecouncil.org.uk).

- ◆ Briefings on migration to the UK are published annually by The Migration Observatory at the University of Oxford (http://migrationobservatory.ox.ac.uk).

- ◆ The Scottish children's charity Aberlour provides a guardianship service in partnership with the Scottish Refugee Council for children who arrive in Scotland unaccompanied and separated from their family. For more details see the Scottish Guardianship website (www.aberlour.org.uk/how_we_help/services/248_scottish_guardianship_service). The website also hosts a protocol of best practice agreed between the Scottish Guardianship Service, Scottish local authorities and the UK Border Agency, and in particular lists the responsibilities of guardians and social workers at various critical stages of the asylum process, including looked after children reviews and liaison with education services.

+ The British Association for Adoption and Fostering (BAAF) report, *Fostering Unaccompanied Asylum-seeking Young People* (Wade *et al.* 2012), is a detailed and readable account of the authors' research on the experiences of asylum-seeking young people, including progress in and barriers to accessing education. The full report is available to purchase from BAAF and a summary can be downloaded from the Social Policy Research Unit at the University of York (www.york.ac.uk/inst/spru).

CHAPTER 13

Putting It All Together
Taking a Strategic Approach

This chapter reviews the main points of the book and argues that to make a step change in the education of children in care a different approach is needed.

KEY POINTS

- Ample policy aimed at improving educational outcomes for young people in care has had a limited impact.

- While education is improving for children in care, the gap between young people in care and all young people is not narrowing, as education is improving for all young people.

- The trend is similar for children on free school meals, a proxy for children from families on low income.

- A different strategic approach is needed that views care and education as inseparable and integrates concepts and practices.

- Young people need fewer substantial changes during the leaving care process to enable them to focus on studying or training.

- Learning placements enable children and everyday experts to look forward and focus on strengths and interests.

- Educational thinking for children in care must start early, for very young children, and at the point of placement planning.

Introduction

Despite near universal recognition of the importance of securing an education for children in care, few gain 'good' qualifications at school or attend higher education. The standards expected of this group appear to be lower than for any other defined group. There has been a plethora of official guidance, and some admirable policy measures, but these have, to date, had only a limited impact. Education is, of course, more than gaining qualifications and it would be a mistake just to focus on this outcome: enjoyment of learning, being introduced to new subjects and modes of learning, improved self-esteem through acquiring skills and knowledge, and a sense of reward from working with others are also extremely important. Some young people in care as children find their educational niche later on in life and overcome their earlier difficulties (Cherry 2013; Ashcroft 2013; Mallon 2007) but the proportion is unknown and probably small.

However, the UK is a party to the UN Convention on the Rights of the Child, and, therefore, access to education is a right for all children and young people up to the age of 18. Education should be directed to 'development of the child's personality, talents and mental and physical abilities to their fullest potential' (UNCRC 1989 Art 28, 29). There are implications in this commitment for the school attendance of children in care, and for access to the full range of subjects in order for them to develop to their 'fullest potential'. It is not acceptable for children looked after by the state, by virtue of abuse and neglect from their early childhood, to be screened out of mainstream schooling, offered inadequate support to compensate for their earlier adversity and educated in unsympathetic or inflexible organisational environments.

Throughout this book we have argued that a holistic perspective and practice is needed for the education of children in care to become a reality for all. We have documented many initiatives in England, Wales and Scotland that have recognised the issue of lack of participation and underachievement and taken steps to address it. Education policy is devolved to the nations of the UK and all four countries have well-elaborated legislation and policy in respect of the education of children in care but reports consistently find that implementation is very variable.

Meshing universally provided education with highly targeted care services is complex. It draws to our attention policy developments in other spheres, for example the diversification of schools and school providers, such as those in England, who, albeit bound by a common admissions code if receiving public money, may have different priorities, such as maximising scores in published league tables rather than retaining and working with children who may have multiple problems. There are also significant financial pressures on all public services. Children's services departments in local authorities in England have been relatively protected from budget cuts (Audit Commission 2013; Donovan 2013), but with rising numbers of children in care, demand is such that there are examples of local authorities moving responsibility for looked after children from qualified social workers to non-qualified staff, and bearing down on the costs of commissioned residential and specialist foster placements (Donovan 2013). Some measures introduced by the Labour government in England (1997–2010) which benefited children in care and their education, such as the Education Maintenance Allowance, have been discarded or watered down. The work of designated teachers and Virtual School Heads may be undermined by overload and reduced resources. The latter have responsibility for managing the spending of the financial resource for children in care, the Pupil Premium.

But acquiring knowledge, skills and educational qualifications is still the most effective means of achieving economic self-reliance, and goes a long way towards enhanced self-esteem. As well as having a strong learning identity, and valuing education for its own sake, many of the young people interviewed for the YiPPEE study said they were motivated to achieve in education in order not to repeat the life course of their parents, which had brought them into care in the first place (Jackson and Cameron 2014). They wanted a clean break from their past and to be recognised for their own achievements. The question is, how do we maximise the number of young people in care who can make the most of their abilities, and enjoy their right to education?

At present, certainly in England, the gap in educational achievement between children in care and that of all young people shows little sign of narrowing, despite the many initiatives tried. Practice is improving, but the impact on children's test results at ages 7, 11 and 16 is only keeping pace with improvements for all children, as we reported in Chapter 3. The same trend is apparent when comparing children on free school meals, a proxy for those on low income, with those who are not. On the whole, children from low income backgrounds gain fewer qualifications than those from higher income backgrounds and the gap has not narrowed, despite some progress in achievement for the very poorest.

The Fair Education Alliance, a coalition of 25 organisations committed to addressing educational inequality, stated in June 2014: 'Last year 65% of children not on free school meals achieved 5 GCSEs at grade A*–C – but for poorer children, this shockingly drops by 10% even in the area of success that is inner London, and then to a gap of 32% in the seemingly affluent South East. The gap is at its widest in Wales, where there is a 40% gap between the success of pupils from disadvantaged background and their wealthier peers.' For children in care, the gap is about 43 percentage points in England (DfE 2013a) and, in Scotland, where a different method of calculating is used, the gap is also wide (Scottish Government 2014).

These findings underline the importance of the home environment – or learning placements, for children in care – in addressing educational inequality. For looked after children, despite numerous policy initiatives in all parts of the UK, being in the care of the state rarely turns around educational inequality sufficiently to reflect the 'government's deep determination to give every child, whatever their start in life, an equal chance to make the best of themselves' (DfE 2014b), even though the fact of being in care means they are no longer subject to extreme deprivation as they may have been previously.

Action to address educational inequality is needed at all levels, including addressing poverty and, for children in care, mental health difficulties and structural problems such as placement instability. Once young people leave foster or residential placements, there is also a need for better and more supportive housing. Those wider issues, however, are beyond the scope of this book.

We argue that for young people in care to thrive, learn and emerge from care with the level of education and skills they need to achieve a good quality of adult life, they need both learning placements and caring schools. This means a thorough examination of practice in both care and education services. It means that those who look after children in care are 'experts in everyday life'; they use all opportunities to be in dialogue with children, to make meaning out of everyday events, to calculate and imagine in collaboration, to exercise empathy and set high expectations of both children, as achievers, and themselves, as continually learning, reflecting on and analysing practice.

Likewise, 'caring schools' implies not just caring about looked after children in terms of procedures, but having an ethos of ethical care that runs through the whole school, generating a sense of belonging to, and mutual respect for, all its members. Within this environment, looked after children are less likely to feel visible and vulnerable and more likely to own their learning in that particular space. We have reiterated throughout this book the centrality of trusting relationships for learning, and this is just as important in a school setting as in placements or support services.

In this final chapter we take the opportunity to explore three themes, which, at the level of strategy and implementation, have the potential to strengthen the educational fortunes of children in care. Mike Stein (2006) argued that young people leaving care fell into three groups: moving on; survivors; and strugglers. Those moving on were more likely to be able to access further and higher education, had more stable and secure relationships and had a gradual process of leaving care. Survivors had had more instability in their lives through changes of placement and periods of homelessness, and tended to have a 'tough' or self-reliant self-image, but support services tended to have a positive impact on them. The third group, strugglers, were the most disadvantaged, and care placements were unable to compensate for their earlier difficulties; they were lonely, isolated, and tended to alienate support, although it was important that someone was there for them. In our discussion of each theme, we point out what might be needed for a young person in each of these groups to thrive.

Theme one: Compressed transitions work against education

The phrase 'compressed and accelerated transitions' (Stein 2002, p.68) has acquired international recognition for its capture of the multiple responsibilities and challenges young people face during the phase of leaving care. To Stein's list of 'leaving foster care and residential care and setting up home, leaving school and entering the world of work (or more likely, being unemployed and surviving on benefits), and being parents – at a far younger age than other young people' we would add entering further or higher education, possibly coping with the uncertainties of their migrant status, or living in areas of poor housing with limited transport. For many young people, the complications of their birth families also come back into the frame when they leave care, as well as potentially continuing relations with substitute parents, relatives and friends. Many also have continuing mental health difficulties and face the change of status and access to services that comes with moving from 'child' to 'adult' in the health service.

One major strategy for promoting continuing educational engagement must be to lessen the compression of these responsibilities and challenges over such a short period of time.

In England, there has been a general move towards leaving care at 18 or later. In 2011, 63 per cent of young people leaving care at the ages of 16+ were aged 18 or older. This lengthening of the period in care is reinforced in the 'staying put' policy of enabling young people to stay with foster carers after their 18th birthday. However, this still means that 37 per cent of young people are leaving care at age 16 or 17. In 2011, nearly a third of these young people moved into independent living (DfE 2012a). These were likely to be 'survivors' or 'strugglers', whose needs are more complex and greater, rather than those 'moving on', who are likely to be staying in care.

There are two main reasons why this must be addressed. First, a recent change in the law in England requires young people to participate in education or training up to the age of 18 years. Ejecting young people from the practical support of a care environment while at the same time requiring them to participate in education or training is contradictory if not perverse. Second, we know that many young people in care are delayed in acquiring educational qualifications and at the ages of 16 and 17 they need additional support to focus on their studies and skill development at a time when there are often multiple distractions, as in the case of Donna in Chapter 3. This delay can happen to young people, whether they are moving on, survivors or strugglers. Such additional support may mean developing more hybrid and flexible 'care and support' arrangements, where the expected relationship is not 'attachment' but commitment and practical help. Support is needed not just from leaving care teams, valuable as they are, but also from 'everyday experts' who are available to young people at all times of day or night. Those who are survivors or strugglers will be difficult to help and are often inaccessible to formal services; hence the need for more flexibility in what is provided. It may also mean taking inspiration from the Danish system of boarding schools, which offer a year of focused academic and social education for any student in a set age bracket, and were highly valued by children in the YiPPEE study in Denmark (Jackson and Cameron 2014).

At present, 'pathway planning' begins when young people in care reach their 16th birthday and is reviewed every six months. Aside from thinking about where they are to live, the plan includes young people's health, education, training and development, contact with family and their financial management. A serious question must arise as to whether and how this age stage of planning for the future maps onto what happens in educationally committed homes across the land. Of course, not thinking about the future is not an option, but in the interests of 'decompressing' transitions, plans for 16- and 17-year-olds should focus on education and training, and health, and require local authority social workers and leaving care support workers routinely to meet living and accommodation costs in accordance with their corporate parent responsibilities.

Theme two: Looking forward

One of the advantages of an educational approach to care placements is that it offers young people the opportunity to look forward and for professionals to see them as agents of their own lives from the moment of initial contact, rather than dwelling on the difficulties of the past. While, of course, many young people have mental health difficulties and may need access to specialist help, the everyday encounters with adults charged with their care and education in foster care, residential care and elsewhere (such as secure units and youth offending institutions, as well as supported living hostels) must see them as 'rich' with possibilities for their lives if they can find the key to unlock their interests and strengths. This may not happen overnight, but the everyday expert can use their relationship-building skills to set high expectations of being together, enjoyment and trust. This perspective puts the responsibility for establishing a relationship with the everyday expert, who needs to be equipped with the skills and knowledge to do so, and to be able to interpret young people's behaviour within a wide framework of possibilities – to be open minded and non-judgemental but also to dig deep to understand where the child or young person is coming from, through reflection in the staff group or with other professionals, and shared activities, rather than direct questioning of the young person.

A social pedagogue trained in Germany, and employed in residential care in England, participated in a study conducted by one of the authors and was asked how professionals with her training go about developing a relationship with young people. She gave an example of such a forward-looking approach. She replied:

> 'I start by getting on the floor, doing things. Drawing, they realise I can draw and I'll draw them or they draw too. [We do] little things to gain access [to them. We might play] board games with a colleague. We start things and they join in, laugh together, and then we can ask questions about their everyday life. If they are in trouble at school, we don't talk about it straightaway, we focus on the good stuff. [We try to find out] what gives their life meaning. [We] may ask to see pictures they have, to show an interest in their life. [We] use our own creativity. We don't overwhelm them with expectations. They have often been responsible for their own family, with parents who drink, younger siblings, and so on, so in residential care we allow them to be kids again, play with toys, cuddly toys, pictures, videos and so on.'

The emphasis in this account is on developing a relationship through doing things together that are enjoyable, and that enable the child to talk about the aspects of their lives that are going well, or less badly, than others, centred on their interests rather than focusing on problems. The social pedagogue also recognised the possibility that the young people have been shouldering many responsibilities and that the care environment can be a relief from that, although young people may continue to worry about what they have left behind.

The emphasis, for the social pedagogue, is to build a relationship based on mutuality. The social pedagogue continued to say that a good relationship is one:

'where we can speak to each other or discuss without shouting… If we can disagree and show the reasons and tell why we disagree. In a nice way, without foul language. If they start to say what their mother said on the phone, or that they are hiding alcohol. If they start to open up or choose to sit next to you at table, or if you are cooking and they choose to join in. If they choose your company or ask "when you are back on", or tell you about their nightmares.' (Cameron, n.d.)

The benefit for a young person's education of having an educationally framed relationship with an everyday expert is that they have a thorough knowledge of a young person's strengths and interests, acquired through doing things together. Building a sense of 'strengths' among those survivors who are used to thinking of themselves as 'tough' and self-reliant will require imaginative and collaborative thinking, and might, for example, require thinking about 'outward bound' type experiences to build a sense of interdependence and team work as well as leadership skills. For those who are strugglers, it might mean starting with music or art, built around structures for reliable communication: knowing they can meet a key worker at a set time and place.

This knowledge is invaluable when it comes to representing them in school or educational environments, as the everyday expert can physically or empathetically 'accompany' the young person through the transition from care to school, or between school environments, and help them to reflect on the experience afterwards. A foster carer from Scotland interviewed for this book helped a young person to manage school when she worked out that a handkerchief impregnated with her perfume was a source of comfort to her foster daughter:

'I had a young girl of 15, her placement had broken down and she came to me in an emergency while they looked for a [residential] unit for her. She would only manage one afternoon a week in school. She was in a behavioural unit, and she was not allowed to leave the unit. If she was to go anywhere she had to be escorted. She would swear, scream, shout. They were frightened of her. They could not manage her. Her life was chaotic, going to school was the last thing on her mind. Lots of violence and drugs in her background.

She could not handle school at all. She would get on the bus, get into school and be there half an hour, screaming at me down the phone, calling the teachers names. I would say calm down, breathe, she would end up getting the bus home. I thought I needed something to calm her down. I got a packet of hankies. I like perfume, the kids like it too. I chose one of the perfumes that she liked, and said when she is in school and getting stressed and wanting to throw something, or swear, she was to take out the hanky, smell it, you will get my smell, and think "what would [foster carer] say to me now", think home, think of something nice, think of the weekend. She used it a lot. She had missed a lot of years from baby time. When she was in school and feeling unsafe, she linked the hanky to somewhere safe. She used it, she rang me up to tell me that she had used it.'

This line of thinking was not to conclude that the girl's past difficulties made education or care an insurmountable problem, but to find ways to connect or accompany the girl between home and the challenging environment of school. This looking forward, building on the knowledge of what the girl liked, was crucial to enabling the girl to focus on school in a more constructive way.

Overall, what needs to happen is that everyday experts need the knowledge and skills, and imagination, supported by a facilitative care and education system, to see young people as rich and rewarding, rather than necessarily problematic.

Theme three: Education to the fore throughout childhood

The third theme urges policy makers and practitioners to integrate thinking about education right from the start of children's lives and the beginning of placements. Children's centres and other early childhood education and care services have played an important role in offering an educational framework to families with young children, as they mesh family support with more formal 'learning' and care. Since 2010, the number of children's centres has contracted, and the range of services on offer has diminished. Children's centres are now aimed at 'improving outcomes for young children and their families, with a particular focus on the most disadvantaged families' and fewer childcare places are available (cf. Moss 2013).

As we saw in Chapter 7, it is not known to what extent young children in care access formal educational settings such as children's centres or nurseries. They are entitled, by the age of two, to part-time Early Childhood Education and Care (ECEC) and the extra resources available through, for example, the Pupil Premium Plus in England. But the main responsibility for the educational development of young children in care rests with what we have called 'everyday experts', usually foster carers. Their role, even if it is a temporary placement awaiting adoption, must be to excite the young child about the possibilities of the world and their place in it. This means providing opportunities to explore and exercise their curiosity, providing a rich and sensory environment, engaging in conversational exchanges from the earliest months and later, welcoming their endless questions. Young people who are moving on are likely to have been able to learn with and through adults who gave them opportunities like these. The principle is of thinking 'education in its broadest sense', and as something that happens in all settings and environments, not just in schools, nurseries or centres, and throughout childhood. It may be a lack of these very early experiences that seems to make it so hard for children who come into care later, and are survivors or strugglers when leaving care, to become confident learners.

As we have reiterated throughout the book, education is too important to be left solely to schools, and the education of children in care relies on educationally competent practitioners. There are implications for the recruitment and training of foster carers and residential care workers, for the way the roles are framed in official guidance and standards, and for the support of practitioners in their own learning and in rethinking their role and purpose.

We argue that foster carers and residential care workers should be educationally capable of operating at about Foundation Degree level (Level 5)/Higher National Certificate or above; that is, they should have a good level of basic education including English and maths. At present, most foster care training is pitched at lower levels than this, usually around Level 2 or 3, and does not lead to qualifications. One professional course for foster carers and residential workers, at the University of the West of England, offers a series of six day-long workshops in order for practitioners to 'develop new ideas, skills and capacities for working and living with troubled children.'[1] Although valuable, it does not lead to a qualification. Completing a qualification should offer a participant the opportunity to explore their practice in a learning environment in terms of not only health and safety, but also how to build educationally focused relationships, how to foster a sense of belonging for children in their homes, how to understand and make sense of the complex lives that young people's histories bring to the care environment, as well as how to 'be alongside' young people, to play, take risks and enable them to feel they are valued individuals.

Recruiting foster carers and residential workers should take into account their ability to offer such educationally competent practice and not just to support schools with their educational responsibility. Homework can become a conflict zone if exhortations to complete it are not backed up by understanding and practical help. If carers are not equipped to do this themselves they need to seek help from the Virtual School Head and arrange supplementary tuition where necessary. Current shortages of supply of foster carers and residential care workers tend to lead to lowering of entry conditions, based on the 'caring' role, with the implication that this is different from 'education'. We would argue that education and care must be seen as one, an integral part of the day-to-day existence that is foster care or group care living.

There are implications here for how everyday experts are supported and trained throughout their careers. One way forward would be to learn from the social pedagogy pilot and demonstration programmes in residential and foster care services in England and Scotland since 2009, which have been very successful in introducing educationally competent practice approaches that build practitioners' sense of professional confidence and of themselves as learners (Berridge *et al.* 2011; Vrouwenfelder 2013; Smith and Skinner 2013;

---

1   New Practice Skills for Foster Carers and Children's Residential Care Workers (http://courses.uwe.ac.uk/UZVRDT30M/2014#coursecontent).

McDermid *et al.* 2014), and this is a critical first step in building the educational confidence of the children they look after.

Concluding thoughts

Effective interventions to support looked after children in school are in their infancy (Liabo *et al.* 2013). We already know a great deal about what gets in the way of children's educational participation and engagement while they are in care and there are some promising results from new approaches, especially if they can be sustained over time. Studies of care leavers have repeatedly found that care and education services matter enormously to young people's fortunes. Providing stability, relationships characterised by commitment and emotional warmth, high expectations and 'being alongside' young people, can make a world of difference to their ability to make the most of their lives as they grow up. At school and college, what young people seem to want most is respect for their individuality and at the same time invisibility for their care status, non-stigmatising help to enable them to catch up with their peers and make the most of their talents. In this book we have focused on one aspect of the task of guiding practitioners in children's all-round upbringing in local authority care and we have focused, in the main, on the many encouraging practical examples from England and Scotland. Much of the educational and care practice we advocate has common ground with what happens in families and schools for a wide spectrum of children. What is different is making sure it happens for every child in care.

REFERENCES

Abbott, L. and Nutbrown, C. (eds) (2001) *Experiencing Reggio Emilia*. Buckingham: Open University Press.

Ainley, P. and Bailey, B. (1997) *The Business of Learning. Staff and Student Experiences of Further Education in the 1990s*. Herndon, VA: Books International.

Ainscow, M. and Sandill, A. (2010) 'Developing inclusive education systems: the role of organisational cultures and leadership.' *International Journal of Inclusive Education 14*, 4, 401–416.

Alexander, R. (ed.) (2010) *Children, their World, their Education: Final Report and Recommendations of the Cambridge Primary Review*. London: Routledge.

Anderson, B. and Blinder, S. (2014) Who Counts as a Migrant: Definitions and their Consequences. Available at www.migrationobservatory.ox.ac.uk, accessed on 9 January 2015.

APPG (All-Party Parliamentary Group) (2012) *Education Matters in Care: A Report by the Independent Cross-Party Inquiry into the Educational Attainment of Looked After Children in England*. London: University and College Union (UCU).

Archer, L., Hutchings, M. and Ross, A. (2003) *Higher Education and Social Class: Issues of Exclusion and Inclusion*. London: Routledge Falmer.

Arnold, J.C. (2014) *Their Name is Today: Reclaiming Childhood in a Hostile World*. New York: Plough Publishing House.

Ashcroft, B. (2013) *Fifty-one Moves*. Hook, Hants: Waterside Press.

Audit Commission (2013) *Tough Times 2013: Councils' Responses to Financial Challenges from 2010/11 to 2013/14*. Available at www.audit-commission.gov.uk/wp-content/uploads/2013/11/Tough-Times-2013-Councils-Responses-to-Financial-Challenges-w1.pdf, accessed on 9 January 2015.

Babb, P. (2005) *A Summary of Focus on Social Inequalities*. Available at www.ons.gov.uk/ons/rel/social-inequalities/focus-on-social-inequalities/2004-edition/focus-on-social-inequalities---a-summary-of-focus-on-social-inequalities.pdf, accessed on 9 January 2015.

Ball, S., Maguire, M. and Macrae, S. (2000) *Choice, Pathways and Transitions Post-16: New Youth, New Economies in the Global City*. London: Routledge Falmer.

Barlow, W. (2011) 'Using educational drama to improve outcomes for looked-after children.' *Scottish Journal of Residential Child Care 11*, 2, 24–35. Available at www.celcis.org/media/resources/publications/SIRCCFinalAutumn2011.pdf, accessed on 9 January 2015.

Bath Spa University (2012) In Care In School: Staff Training and Support. Bath: Author. Available at www.incareinschool.com/resources/booklets/icistraining.pdf, accessed on 30 January 2015.

Benson, C. (1996) 'Resisting the Trend to Exclude.' In E. Blyth and J. Milner (eds) *Exclusion from School: Interprofessional Issues for Policy and Practice*. London: Routledge.

Bentley, C. (2013) 'Great Expectations: Supporting "Unrealistic" Aspirations for Children in Care.' In S. Jackson (ed.) *Pathways through Education for Young People in Care: Ideas from Research and Practice*. London: British Association for Adoption and Fostering.

Benton, T. and White, K. (2007) *Raising the Achievement of Bilingual Learners in Primary Schools: Statistical Analysis*. DCSF Research Report 006. London: DCSF. Available at http://webarchive.nationalarchives.gov.uk/20130401151715/http://www.education.gov.uk/publications/eOrderingDownload/DCSF-RR006.pdf, accessed on 9 January 2015.

Berridge, D., Biehal, N., Lutman, E., Henry, L. and Palomares, M. (2011) *Raising the Bar? Evaluation of the Social Pedagogy Pilot Programme in Residential Children's Homes*. DfE Research Report DFE-RR148. London: HMSO.

Berridge, D., Dance, C., Beecham, J. and Field, S. (2008) *Educating Difficult Adolescents: Effective Education for Children in Public Care or with Emotional and Behavioural Difficulties*. London: Jessica Kingsley Publishers.

BIS (2013) *Widening Participation in Higher Education 2013*, Department for Innovation, Business and Skills, BIS/13/P155.

Bloomer, K. (2013) *By Diverse Means: Improving Scottish Education, The Commission on School Reform Final Report*. Edinburgh: Centre for Scottish Public Policy and Reform Scotland.

Blyth, E., and J. Milner (1996) *Social Work with Children: The Educational Perspective*. London: Longman.

Borders, L.D. and Leddick, G.R. (1987) *Handbook of Counseling Supervision*. Alexandria, VA: Association for Counselor Education and Supervision.

Borthwick, S. and Donnelly, S. (2013) *Achieving Early Permanence for Babies and Young Children*. London: British Association for Adoption and Fostering.

Broad, B. (1998) Young People Leaving Care: Life after the Children Act 1989. London: Jessica Kingsley Publishers.

Brodie, I. (2001) *Children's Homes and School Exclusion: Redefining the Problem*. London: Jessica Kingsley Publishers.

Brooks, G. (2002) *What Works for Children with Literacy Difficulties? The Effectiveness of Intervention Schemes*. DfES RR 380. Available at http://dera.ioe.ac.uk/4662/1/RR380.pdf, accessed on 9 January 2015.

Brown, L. (2011) An audit of the needs of 268 children attending pupil referral units in 4 local authority areas. London: National Children's Bureau. Available at www.ncb.org.uk/media/580252/matching_needs_and_services.pdf,

Brown, R. (2010) *Snail Trail*. London: Andersen Press.

Browne, K. (2005) 'A European survey of the number and characteristics of children less than three years old in residential care at risk of harm.' *Adoption & Fostering 29*, 4, 23–33.

Brownlees, L. and Finch, N. (2010) *Levelling the Playing Field: A UNICEF UK Report into Provision of Services to Unaccompanied or Separated Migrant Children in Three Local Authority Areas in England*. London: UNICEF UK.

Bruce, T. and Spratt, J. (2008) *Esssentials of Literacy from 0–7*. London: Sage.

Bruner, J. (1977) 'Early Social Interaction and Language Acquisition.' In H.R. Schaffer (ed.) *Studies of Mother-Infant Interaction*. London: Academic Press.

Budge, D. (2011) *Case Study on the Impact of Institute of Education Research into 'Going to University from Care'*. London: Institute of Education, University of London.

Cairns, K. (2013) 'The Effects of Trauma on Children's Learning.' In S. Jackson (ed.) *Pathways through Education for Young People in Care: Ideas from Research and Practice*. London: BAAF.

Cambridge Primary Review (2011) *Towards a New Primary Curriculum*. Available at http://cprtrust.org.uk/wp-content/uploads/2014/06/CURRICULUM_BRIEFING_REVISED_2_11.pdf, accessed on 9 January 2015.

Cameron, C. (n.d.) *Understandings of Relational Practice with Children in the Care of the State in Belgium, Denmark and Germany: The Contribution of Concepts and Theories*. Unpublished data, Anglia Ruskin University.

Cameron, C., Jackson, S., Hauari, H. and Hollingworth, K. (2010) *WP5 UK Report: Young People from a Public Care Background: Pathways to Further and Higher Education in England: A Case Study*. Available at http://tcru.ioe.ac.uk/yippee/Portals/1/WP5report%20UKFINAL%2025.01.11.pdf, accessed 9 January 2015.

Candappa, M., Ahmad, M., Balcata, B., Dekhinet, R. and Gocmen, D. (2007) *Education and Schooling for Asylum Seeking and Refugee Students in Scotland: An Exploratory Study*. Edinburgh: The Scottish Government.

Cassen, R. and Kingdon, G. (2007) *Tackling Low Educational Achievement*. York: Joseph Rowntree Foundation. Available at www.jrf.org.uk/sites/files/jrf/2063-education-schools-achievement.pdf, accessed on 9 January 2015.

Chambers, H. (2005) *Carers Can! Play and Be Creative with Children and Young People*. London: National Children's Bureau.

Chambers, H. (2013) *The SPDN in Hackney on 14 May, 2013*. Available at www.thempra.org.uk/SPDNmeeting8.htm, accessed on 9 January 2015.

Cherry, L. (2013) *The Brightness of Stars: Stories of Adults who Came Through the British Care System*. Banbury, Oxfordshire: Wilson King Publishers.

Children's Commissioner for England (2012) *They Never Give Up on You: Office of the Children's Commissioner's School Exclusions Inquiry*. London: Office of the Children's Commissioner.

Children's Commissioner for England (2013a) *Always Someone Else's Problem: Office of the Children's Commissioner's Report on Illegal Exclusions*. London: Office of the Children's Commissioner.

Children's Commissioner for England (2013b) *They Go the Extra Mile: Reducing Inequality in School Exclusions*. London: Office of the Children's Commissioner.

Clayden, J. and Stein, M. (2005) *Mentoring Young People Leaving Care: Someone for Me*. York: University of York.

Collins, M.E., Spencer, R. and Ward, R. (2010) 'Supporting youth in the transition from foster care: formal and informal connections.' *Child Welfare 89*, 1, 125–143.

Connelly, G. (2013) 'Improving the Educational Outcomes of Looked After Children in Scotland.' In S. Jackson (ed.) *Pathways through Education for Young People in Care: Ideas from Research and Practice*. London: British Association for Adoption and Fostering.

Council for Disabled Children (2014) *A Step by Step Guide to EHC Plans*. Available at www.councilfordisabledchildren.org.uk/resources/cdcs-resources/a-step-by-step-guide-to-ehc-plans, accessed on 9 January 2015.

Courtney, M.E., Dworsky, A., Cusick, G.R., Keller, T., Havlicek, J. and Perez, A. (2007) *Midwest Evaluation of Adult Functioning of Former Foster Youth: Outcomes at Age 21*. Chicago: University of Chicago, Chapin Hall Center for Children.

Cummings, C., Dyson, A., Mujis, D., Papps, I. *et al.* (2007) *Evaluation of the Full Service Extended Schools Initiative: Final Report*. DfES Research Report 852. London: DfES. Available at www.bredeschool.info/sites/bredeschool.dev/files/evaluation%20of%20tull%20service%20extended%20school%20final%20report.pdf, accessed on 9 January 2015.

Dahlberg, G. and Moss, P. (2005) *Ethics and Politics in Early Childhood Education*. London: Routledge Falmer.

Darling, N. (2005) 'Participation in extracurricular activities and adolescent adjustment: cross-sectional and longitudinal findings.' *Journal of Youth and Adolescence 34*, 5, 493–505.

Daykin, N., Orme, J., Evans, D., Salmon, D., McEachran, M. and Brain, S. (2008) 'The impact of participation in performing arts on adolescent health and behaviour: a systematic review of the literature.' *Journal of Health Psychology 13*, 2, 251–264.

(DCSF) Department for Children, Schools and Families (2007) *Care Matters: Time for Change*. London: DCSF.

Demie, F. and Mclean, C. (2007). 'The achievement of African heritage pupils: good practice in secondary schools.' *Educational Studies, 33*,4, 415-434.

Denholm, A. (2006, 1 February) 'Violent pupils allowed back to school: Tougher action demanded.' *The Herald*.

DH (1991a) *The Children Act 1989 Guidance and Regulations: Volume 6 Children with Disabilities*. London: HMSO.

DH (1991b) *The Children Act 1989 Guidance and Regulations: Volume 3 Family Placements*. London: HMSO.

DH (1991c) *The Children Act 1989 Guidance and Regulations: Volume 4 Residential Care*. London: HMSO.

DH (1998) Quality Protects. London: DH.

DH (2000) *Guidance on the education of children and young people in public care, LAC (2000)*13, London: DH.

Derluyn, I. and Broekaert, E. (2008) 'Unaccompanied refugee children and adolescents: the glaring contrast between a legal and a psychological perspective.' *International Journal of Law and Psychiatry 31*, 4, 319–330.

Desforges, C., with Abouchaar, A. (2003) *The Impact of Parental Involvement, Parental Support and Family Education on Pupil Achievement and Adjustment: A Literature Review*. RR 433. London: DfES.

DfE (2010) *Care Planning, Placement and Case Review (England) Regulations, March 2010*. London: Department for Education.

DfE (2011) *Children's Homes: National Minimum Standards*. Available at http://webarchive. nationalarchives.gov.uk/20130401151715/https://www.education.gov.uk/publications/ eOrderingDownload/NMS%20Children's%20Homes.pdf, accessed on 9 January 2015.

DfE (2012a) *Care Leavers in England Data Pack, October 2012*. Available at http://media. education.gov.uk/assets/files/pdf/c/care%20leavers%20data%20pack%20final%20 29%20oct.pdf, accessed on 9 January 2015.

DfE (2012b) *Training, Support and Development Standards for Foster Care: Guidance*. Available at www.gov.uk/government/uploads/system/uploads/attachment_data/file/192340/ foster_care_tsd_standards_guidance.pdf, accessed on 9 January 2015.

DfE (2012c) *Exclusion from Schools and Pupil Referral Units in England: A Guide for Those with Legal Responsibilities in Relation to Exclusion*. London: Department for Education. Available at www.education.gov.uk/consultations/downloadableDocs/Exclusion%20 Guidance%20-%20Consultation%20Version.pdf, accessed on 9 January 2015.

DfE (2013a) *Outcomes for Children Looked After by Local Authorities in England, as at 31 March 2013*. SFR 50/2013. Available at www.gov.uk/government/uploads/system/uploads/ attachment_data/file/264385/SFR50_2013_Text.pdf, accessed on 9 January 2015.

DfE (2013b) *Participation in Education, Training and Employment by 16–18 year olds in England*. Available at www.gov.uk/government/uploads/system/uploads/attachment_ data/file/209934/Participation_SFR___end_2012_-_FINALv2.pdf, accessed on 9 January 2015.

DfE (2014a) *Outcomes for Children Looked After by Local Authorities in England* as at 31 March 2014, SFR 49/2014. Available at www.gov.uk/government/statistics/outcomes-for-children-looked-after-by-local-authorities, accessed on 14 March 2015.

DfE (2014b) *Children Looked After in England (Including Adoption and Care Leavers) Year Ending 31 March 2014*. SFR 36/2014. Available at www.gov.uk/government/uploads/ system/uploads/attachment_data/file/359277/SFR36_2014_Text.pdf, accessed on 9 January 2015.

DfE (2014c) Promoting the Education of Looked After Children: Statutory Guidance for Local Authorities. London: Department for Education. Available at www.gov.uk/ government/uploads/system/uploads/attachment_data/file/335964/Promoting_the_ educational_achievement_of_looked_after_children_Final_23-....pdf, accessed on 30 January 2015.

DfE website (n.d.) www.gov.uk/government/organisations/department-for-education, accessed on 9 January 2015.

Department for Education and Skills and Department of Health (2000) Guidance on the Education of Children and Young People in Public Care. London: DfES & DH.

DfES (Department for Education and Skills) (2003) *Education Protects: The Role of the School in Supporting the Education of Children in Public Care*. London: DfES.

DfES (2005) *Statutory Guidance to the Children Act 2004*. London: DfES.

DfES (2006) *Care Matters: Transforming the Lives of Children and Young People in Care* (Green Paper). London: DfES.

Donovan, T. (2013) 'Protection for adults but cuts for children: how Osborne's plans affect social care.' *Community Care 28 June*. Available at www.communitycare.co.uk, accessed on 29 January 2015.

Dorling, F. and Hurrell, A. (2012) *Navigating the System: Advice Provision for Young Refugees and Migrants*. London: Coram Children's Legal Centre.

Douglas, J.W.B. (1964) *The Home and the School: A Study of Ability and Attainment in the Primary Schools*. London: Macgibbon and Kee.

Driscoll, J. (2011) 'Making up lost ground: supporting the educational attainment of looked after children beyond Key Stage 4.' *Adoption & Fostering 35*, 2, 18–30.

DuBois, D.L., Portillo, N., Rhodes, J.E., Silverthorn, N. and Valentine, J.C. (2011) 'How effective are mentoring programs for youth? A systematic assessment of the evidence.' *Psychological Sciences in the Public Interest 12*, 2, 57–91.

Duffy, B. (1998) *Supporting Creativity and Imagination in the Early Years*. Buckingham: Open University Press.

Eisenstadt, N. (2011*) Providing a Sure Start: How Government Discovered Early Childhood*. Bristol: The Policy Press.

Elfer, P., Goldschmied, E. and Selleck, D. (2012) *Key Persons in the Early Years: Building Relationships for Quality Provision in Early Years Settings and Primary Schools*. Abingdon: David Fulton Publishers.

Epstein, A. (2003) *How planning and reflection develop young children's thinking skills*. Available at www.naeyc.org/files/yc/file/200309/Planning&Reflection.pdf, accessed on 29 January 2015.

European Commission (2012) *Youth on the Margins of Society: Policy Review of Research Results*. Brussels: European Union Directorate General for Research and Innovation, Socio-Economic Sciences and Humanities.

Eurydice (2013) *The Structure of the European Education Systems 2013/14: Schematic Diagrams*. Available at http://eacea.ec.europa.eu/education/eurydice/documents/facts_and_figures/education_structures_EN.pdf, accessed on 9 January 2015.

Evans, J. (2010) *Not Present and Not Correct: Understanding and Preventing School Exclusions*. Ilford, Essex: Barnardos.

Evans, R. (2000) *The Educational Attainments and Progress of Children in Public Care*. PhD Thesis. Coventry: University of Warwick Institute of Education.

Featherstone, B., White, S. and Morris, K. (2014) *Re-imagining Child Protection: Towards Humane Social Work with Families*. Bristol: Policy Press.

Feinstein, L. (2003) *Very Early Evidence, Centrepiece*. Available at http://cep.lse.ac.uk/pubs/download/CP146.pdf, accessed on 9 January 2015.

Feinstein, L. and Brassett-Grundy, A. (2005) *The Life Course Outcomes for Looked After Children: Evidence from the British Cohort Study 1970*. London: Institute of Education.

Finn, M. (2008) *Evaluation of the Reading Rich Programme*. Edinburgh: The Scottish Government. Available at www.scotland.gov.uk/Publications/2008/07/14103033/0, accessed on 9 January 2015.

Firth, H. and Horrocks, C. (1996) 'No Home, No School, No Future: Exclusions and Children who are "Looked After".' In E. Blyth and J. Milner (eds) *Exclusion from School: Inter-professional Issues for Policy and Practice*. London: Routledge.

Fletcher-Campbell, F. (1997) *The Education of Children who are Looked-After*. Slough: National Foundation for Educational Research.

Forbes, R. (2004) *Beginning to Play: Young Children from Birth to Three*. Maidenhead: Open University Press.

Forrester, D. (2008) 'Is the care system failing children?' *The Political Quarterly 79*, 2, 206–211.

Fostering Network (2014) *The Skills to Foster – Complete Course pack (Third Edition)*. Available at www.fosteringresources.co.uk/?cid=1&sid=12&pid=500&p=0, accessed on 9 January 2015.

Froebel Trust (2013) *Discovered Treasure: The Life and Work of Elinor Goldschmied 1910–2009*. Roehampton: Froebel Institute.

Furnivall, J., McKenna, M., McFarlane, S. and Grant, E. (2012) *Attachment Matters for All: An Attachment Mapping Exercise for Children's Services in Scotland*. Glasgow: CELCIS and Scottish Attachment in Action.

Garfat, T. (2005) *Reflective Child and Youth Care Practice, The International Child and Youth Care Network*. Available at www.cyc-net.org/cyc-online/cycol-0605-editor.html, accessed on 9 January 2015.

Geary, D.C. and Bjorklund, D. (2000) 'Evolutionary developmental psychology.' *Child Development 71*, 1, 57–65.

Giedd, J.N., Blumenthal, J., Jeffries, N.O., Castellanos, F.X. *et al.* (1999) 'Brain development during childhood and adolescence: a longitudinal MRI study.' *Nature Neuroscience 2*, 10, 861–863.

Gillies, D. (2013) 'The Politics of Scottish Education.' In T.G.K. Bryce and W.M. Humes (eds) *Scottish Education: Third edition, Beyond Devolution*. Edinburgh: Edinburgh University Press.

Gilligan, R. (2013) 'Spare-time Activities for Young People in Care.' In S. Jackson (ed.) *Pathways Through Education for Young People in Care: Ideas from Research and Practice.* London: BAAF.

Goddard Blythe, S. (2009) *Attention, Balance and Co-ordination: The A.B.C. of Learning Success.* Chichester: Wiley-Blackwell.

Golden, S., O'Donnell, L., Benton, T. and Rudd, P. (2006) *Evaluation of Increased Flexibility for 14 to 16 Year Olds Programme: Outcomes for the First Cohort.* DfES Research Report RR668. London: National Foundation for Educational Research.

Goldschmied, E. and Jackson, S. (2004) *People Under Three: Young Children in Day Care* (2nd edition). London: Routledge.

Goodman, A. and Gregg, P. (2010) *Poorer Children's Educational Attainment: How Important are Attitudes and Behaviour?* York: Joseph Rowntree Foundation.

Gopnik, A. Meltzoff, A. and Kuhl, P. (1999) *How Babies Think: The Science of Childhood.* London: Weidenfeld & Nicholson.

Gosling, M. (2013) *Alternative Education Provision in London: scoping report.* The Research Base. Available at http://theresearchbase.com/reports/ewExternalFiles/Alternative%20Education%20Provision%20in%20London%20V1.0.pdf, accessed on 30 January 2015.

Green, A. and Lucas, N. (eds) (1999) *FE and Lifelong Learning: Realigning the Sector for the twenty-first Century.* London: University of London, Institute of Education.

Griffiths, R. (2013) 'The Letterbox Club: Educational Possibilities in a Parcel.' In S. Jackson (ed.) *Pathways through Education for Young People in Care: Ideas from Research and Practice.* London: British Association for Adoption and Fostering (BAAF).

Griffiths, R. (2014) *Difficulties in Number Experienced by Children aged 7 to 11 in Public Care in England.* PhD Thesis. Cambridge: University of Cambridge, Faculty of Education.

Grossman, J. and Rhodes, J. (2002) 'The test of time: predictors and effects of duration in youth mentoring relationships.' *American Journal of Community Psychology 30*, 2, 199–219.

Hallam, S. (2010) *'Transitions and the Development of Expertise', Vernon Wall Lecture.* Paper presented at British Psychological Society, Leicester.

Halvorsen, T. (2014) 'Bridging the divide between education and social work in order to improve the prospects of looked after children.' *Scottish Journal of Residential Child Care 13*, 2, 1–11.

Hannan, D.F., Raffe, D. and Smyth, E. (1996, September) *Cross-national Research on School to Work Transitions: An Analytical Framework.* Background Paper prepared for the Planning Meeting for the Thematic Review of the Transition from Initial Education to Working Life.

Hauari, H., with Cameron, C. (2014) 'England: A Targeted Approach.' In S. Jackson and C. Cameron (eds) *Improving Access to Further and Higher Education for Young People in Public Care: European Policy and Practice.* London: Jessica Kingsley Publishers.

Hart, N. (2013) 'What helps children in a pupil referral unit (PRU)? An exploration into the potential protective factors of a PRU as identified by children and staff.' *Emotional and Behavioural Difficulties, 18*, 2, 196–212.

Hauari, H., Hollingworth, K., Glenn, M., Cameron, C., and Jackson, S. (2010) *Analysis of National Statistics and Survey of Local Agencies to Establish a Baseline of Post-Compulsory Educational Participation Among Young People from a Public Care Background.* London: Institute of Education. Available at http://tcru.ioe.ac.uk/yippee/Portals/1/Workpackage%204%20UK%20report.pdf, accessed on 9 January 2015.

Her Majesty's Inspectors of Schools and Social Work Services Inspectorate (2001) *Learning with Care: The Education of Children Looked After Away from Home by Local Authorities.* Edinburgh: HMI and SWSI. Available at www.educationscotland.gov.uk/Images/5679text_tcm4-712681.pdf, accessed on 9 January 2015.

Herrera, C., Sipe, C.L. and McClanahan, W.S. (2000) *Mentoring School-age Children: Relationship Development in Community-based and School-based Programs.* Philadelphia: Public/Private Ventures.

Higgins, S. and Elliott Major, L. (2012) *Pupil Premium Toolkit, Feedback.* Available at http://educationendowmentfoundation.org.uk/toolkit/feedback, accessed on 9 January 2015.

Hill, V. (2014) personal communication.

HM Government (2014) *Children and Families Act.* Available at www.legislation.gov.uk/ukpga/2014/6/contents/enacted, accessed on 15 March 2015.

HMSO (1989) *The Care of Children: Principles and Practice in Regulations and Guidance.* London: HMSO.

Hodgson, A. and Spours, K. (2011) 'Rethinking general education in the English upper secondary system.' *London Review of Education.* Available at http://eprints.ioe.ac.uk/6771/1/Hodgson2011Rethinking205.pdf, accessed on 9 January 2015.

Hollingworth, K. (2012) 'Participation in social, leisure and informal learning activities among care leavers in England: positive outcomes for educational participation'. *Child & Family Social Work 17,* 4, 438–447.

House of Commons Education Committee (2014) *Into Independence, Not Out of Care: 16 Plus Care Options.* Second Report of Session 2014–15 (259). London: The Stationery Office.

Jackson, B. and Marsden, D. (1962) *Education and the Working Class.* London: Routledge and Kegan Paul.

Jackson, S. (1987) *The Education of Children in Care.* Bristol: University of Bristol.

Jackson, S. (2000) 'Promoting the Educational Achievement of Looked-After Children.' In T. Cox (ed.) *Combating Educational Disadvantage: Meeting the Needs of Vulnerable Children.* London: Falmer Press.

Jackson, S. (2007) 'Care Leavers, Exclusion and Access to Higher Education.' In D. Abrams, J. Christian and D. Gordon (eds) *Multidisciplinary Handbook of Social Exclusion Research.* Chichester: Wiley.

Jackson, S. (2010) 'Reconnecting care and education: from the Children Act 1989 to Care Matters.' *Journal of Children's Services 5,* 3, 48–60.

Jackson, S. and Ajayi, S. (2007) 'Foster care and higher education.' *Adoption & Fostering 31,* 1, 106–117.

Jackson, S. and Cameron, C. (2013) 'Leaving Care: Looking Ahead and Aiming Higher.' In S. Jackson (ed.) *Pathways through Education for Young People in Care: Ideas from Research and Practice.* London: BAAF.

Jackson, S. and Cameron, C. (2014) *Improving Access to Further and Higher Education for Young People in Care: European Policy and Practice.* London and Philadelphia: Jessica Kingsley Publishers.

Jackson, S. and Forbes, R. (2014) *People Under Three: Play, Work and Learning in a Childcare Setting.* London: Routledge.

Jackson, S. and Martin, P.Y. (1998) 'Surviving the care system: education and resilience.' *Journal of Adolescence 21,* 560–583.

Jackson, S. and Sachdev, D. (2001) *Better Education, Better Futures: Research, Practice and the Views of Young People in Public Care.* Ilford: Barnardos.

Jackson, S. and Simon, A. (2006) 'The Costs and Benefits of Educating Children in Care.' In E. Chase, A. Simon and S. Jackson (eds) *In Care and After: A Positive Perspective.* London: Routledge.

Jackson, S., Ajayi, S. and Quigley, M. (2003) *By Degrees: the First Year – From Care to University.* London: National Children's Bureau/ The Frank Buttle Trust.

Jackson, S., Ajayi, S. and Quigley, M. (2005) *Going to University from Care.* Final report of By Degrees Project. London: Institute of Education.

Johansson, H. and Höjer, I. (2014) 'A Long and Winding Road.' In S. Jackson and C. Cameron (eds) *Improving Access to Further and Higher Education for Young People in Public Care: European Policy and Practice.* London: Jessica Kingsley Publishers.

Joint Committee on Human Rights (2013) *Human Rights of Unaccompanied Migrant Children and Young People in the UK.* London: The Stationery Office. Available at www.publications.parliament.uk/pa/jt201314/jtselect/jtrights/9/9.pdf, accessed on 9 January 2015.

Kelly, Y., Kelly, J. and Sacker, A. (2013) 'Changes in bedtime schedules and behavioral difficulties in 7 year old children.' *Pediatrics*, October, 1096.

Kendall, L., O'Donnell, L., Golden, S., Ridley, K. *et al.* (2005) *Excellence in Cities: The National Evaluation of a Policy to Raise Standards in Urban Schools 2000–2003.* DfES Research Report 675A. London: DfES. Available at http://webarchive.nationalarchives.gov.uk/20130401151715/http://www.education.gov.uk/publications/eOrderingDownload/RR675a.pdf, accessed on 9 January 2015.

Kendall, S., Straw, S., Jones, M., Springate, I. and Grayson, H. (2008) *A Review of the Research Evidence: Narrowing the Gap in Outcomes for Vulnerable Groups.* Slough: National Foundation for Educational Research.

Kintrea, K. St. Clair, R. and Houston, M. (2011) *The Influence of Parents, Place and Poverty on Educational Attitudes and Aspirations.* York: Joseph Rowntree Foundation.

Kirton, D. (2013) 'What is work? Insights from the evolution of state foster care.' *Work, Employment and Society 27*, 4, 658–673.

La Mendola, W. (2011) 'Child welfare and technology.' *CW 3600*, Spring.

Lawner, E. and Beltz, M. (2013) *What Works for Mentoring Programs: Lessons from Experimental Evaluations of Programs and Interventions.* Child Trends Research Brief. Available at www.childtrends.org/wp-content/uploads/2013/03/Child_Trends-2013_03_28_RB_WWMentor.pdf, accessed on 9 January 2015.

Learning and Skills Council (2009) *Identifying Effective Practice in Raising Young People's Aspirations.* Available at http://dera.ioe.ac.uk/11137/1/nat-raising_aspirations-re-24sep2009-v1-1.pdf., accessed on 30 January 2015.

Lessing, D. (1994) *Under My Skin, Volume One of My Autobiography, to 1949.* London: Harper Collins.

Liabo, K., Gray, K. and Mulcahy, D. (2013) 'A systematic review of interventions to support looked after children in schools.' *Child and Family Social Work, 18*, 341–353

Liddell, G. and Macpherson, S. (2013) *Post-16 Education (Scotland) Bill, SPICE Briefing 13/05.* Available at www.scottish.parliament.uk/ResearchBriefingsAndFactsheets/S4/SB_13-05.pdf, accessed on 9 January 2015.

Linnane, C. (2008) 'Encouraging reading among children in care: the Edinburgh Reading Champion Project.' *Scottish Journal of Residential Child Care 7*, 2, 25–27.

Livingstone, D.W. (2006) 'Informal Learning: Conceptual Distinctions and Preliminary Findings.' In Z. Bekerman, N. C. Burbules and D. Silberman-Keller (eds) *Learning in Places: The Informal Education Reader.* New York: Peter Lang.

Macfarlane, K., Casley, M., Cartmel, J. and Smith, K. (2014) 'Understanding the "how": a model of practice for critical reflection for children's services practitioners.' *Journal of Playwork Practice 1*, 1, 47–59.

Mahoney, J.L. (2000) 'School extracurricular activity participation as a moderator in the development of antisocial patterns.' *Child Development 71*, 2, 502–516.

Mallon, J. (2007) 'Returning to education after care: protective factors in the development of resilience.' *Adoption & Fostering 31*, 1, 106–117.

Matthews, A. (2012) *Landing in Dover: The Immigration Process Undergone by Unaccompanied Children Arriving in Kent.* London: Office of the Children's Commissioner for England.

Maynard, T. and Powell, S. (eds) (2014) *An Introduction to Early Childhood Studies (third edition).* London: Sage.

McAra, L. and McVie, S. (2010) 'Youth crime and justice: key messages from the Edinburgh Study of Youth Transitions and Crime.' *Criminology and Criminal Justice 10*, 2, 179–209.

McDermid, S., Tapsfield, R. and Trivedi, H. (2014) *Head, heart, hands: Social pedagogy in UK foster care*, presentation at Safeguarding Children: Everybody's Business Conference, Centre for Child and Family Research, Loughborough University. Loughborough University 4 July.

McGuinness, L., Stevens, I. and Milligan, I. (2007) *Playing It Safe? A Study of the Regulation of Outdoor Play for Children and Young People in Residential Care.* Glasgow: Scottish Institute for Residential Child Care.

McLeish, J. (2009) 'Forest playground is a natural start.' *Times Educational Supplement Scotland*, 29 April.

McQuillan, R. (2014, May 17) 'Explorer Craig Mathieson has conquered the poles: now he's changing young lives.' *The Herald Magazine*.

Meltzer, H., Gatward, R., Corbin, T., Goodman, R. and Ford, T. (2002) *The Mental Health of Young People Looked After by Local Authorities in England*. London: TSO.

Miles, K. (2011) 'Using attachment theory in mentoring.' *Nursing Times 107*, 38, 23–25.

Morrison, C. (2012) *Exclusions in Scotland's Schools: One Year On, Where Are We Now?* Edinburgh: Pupil Inclusion Network Scotland.

Moss, P. (2013) 'Early Childhood Policy in England 1997–2013: Anatomy of a missed opportunity.' *Early Childhood Education, 22*,4,346-58.

Mougne, C. (2010) *Trees Only Move in the Wind: A Study of Unaccompanied Afghan Children in Europe*. Geneva: UNHCR.

Mozilla Foundation (n.d.) Open Badges. Available at http://openbadges.org, accessed on 9 January 2015.

Munro, E. (2011) *The Munro Review of Child Protection: Final Report: A Child-centred System*. Available at www.gov.uk/government/uploads/system/uploads/attachment_data/file/175391/Munro-Review.pdf, accessed on 9 January 2015.

Murray, L. and Andrews, A. (2000) *The Social Baby*. Richmond, Surrey: CP Publishing.

Nandy, L. (2007) *Going It Alone: Children in the Asylum Process*. London: The Children's Society.

Noddings, N. (1992) *The Challenge to Care in Schools: An Alternative Approach to Education*. New York: Teachers College Press.

Nutbrown, K., Clough, P., and Selbie, P. (2012) *Early Childhood Education: History, Philosophy and Experience*. London: Sage.

O'Connor, T. and Colwell, J. (2002) 'The effectiveness and rationale of the "nurture group" approach to helping children with emotional and behavioural difficulties remain within mainstream education.' *British Journal of Special Education 29*, 2, 96–100.

OECD (2012) *Programme for International Student Assessment (PISA) Results from PISA 2012*. UK Country Note. Available at www.oecd.org/unitedkingdom/PISA-2012-results-UK.pdf, accessed on 9 January 2015.

Ofsted (2010) *The Special Educational Needs and Disability Review: A Statement is Not Enough*. Available at http://dera.ioe.ac.uk/1145/1/Special%20education%20needs%20and%20disability%20review.pdf, accessed on 9 January 2015.

Ofsted (2011) *National Minimum Standards for Foster Care*. London: Ofsted.

Ofsted (2012) *The Impact of Virtual Schools on the Educational Progress of Looked After Children*. London: Office for Standards in Education, Children's Services and Schools (Ofsted).

OPM (2013) *Evaluation of CCE/NCB Arts and Cultural Activities Project with Looked After Children*. London: OPM. Available at www.ncb.org.uk/media/925803/cce-ncb_evaluation_final_report.pdf, accessed on 30 January 2015.

Osborne, C., Alfano, J. and Winn, T (2013) 'Paired Reading as a Literacy Intervention for Foster Children.' In S. Jackson (ed.) *Pathways through Education for Young People in Care: Ideas from Research and Practice*. London: BAAF.

OUP (2013) *Reading With Children – The 7 year Ditch!* Available at https://global.oup.com/education/content/primary/news/primary_news_books_bedtime?region=internationalternational, accessed on 9 January 2015.

Pagani, L., Fitzpatrick, C. *et al.* (2010) 'Prospective associations between early childhood television exposure and academic, psychosocial and physical well-being by middle childhood.' *Archives of Pediatrics and Adolescent Medicine 164*, 5, 425–431.

Parker, R. and Gorman, M. (2013) 'In Care, In School: Giving Voice to Children and Young People in Care.' In S. Jackson (ed.) *Pathways through Education for Young People in Care: Ideas from Research and Practice*. London: BAAF.

Parnell, R. (2011) *The Adolescent and Children's Trust (TACT)* evidence. Office of the Children's Commissioner's Inquiry on School Exclusions. Available at http://tactcare.org.uk/data/files/resources/office_of_the_childrens_commisioners_inquiry_on_school_exclusions.pdf, accessed on 30 January 2015.

Parsons, C. and Castle, F. (1998) 'The cost of school exclusion in England.' *International Journal of Inclusive Education 2*, 4, 277–294.

Payne, J. (2003) *Choice at the End of Compulsory Schooling: A Research Review.* Nottingham: DfES.

Pecora, P. (2012) 'Maximising educational achievement of youth in foster care and alumni: factors associated with success.' *Children and Youth Services Review 34*, 6, 1121–1129.

Poulton, L. (2012) *Looked-after Children and Literacy: A Brief Review.* London: National Literacy Trust.

Poyser, M. (2013) 'Is Inclusion Always Best for Young People in Care? A View from the Classroom.' In S. Jackson (ed.) *Pathways through Education for Young People in Care: Ideas from Research and Practice.* London: BAAF.

Prensky, M. (2010) *Teaching Digital Natives.* Thousand Oaks, CA: Corwin.

Pugh, G. and Statham, J. (2006) 'Interventions in Schools in the UK.' In C. McAuley, P.J. Pecora and W. Rose (eds) *Enhancing the Well-being of Children and Families through Effective Interventions: International Evidence for Practice.* London: Jessica Kingsley Publishers.

Rapley, G. and Murkett, T. (2008) *Baby-led Weaning.* London: Ebury Press.

Rich, D., Casanova, D., Dixon, A., Drummond, M.J., Durrant, A. and Myer, C. (2005) *First Hand Experience: What Matters to Children: An Alphabet of Learning from the Real World.* Clopton, Suffolk: Rich Learning Opportunities.

Roulstone, S., Law, J. *et al.* (2011) *Investigating the Role of Language in Children's Early Educational Outcomes.* Bristol: University of the West of England.

Ryan, M. (ed.) (2011) *Carers Can! Foster Singing.* London: National Children's Bureau.

Salmon, D. and Rickaby, C. (2014) 'City of one: A qualitative study examining the participation of young people in care in a theatre and music initiative.' *Children & Society, 28*, 1, 30-41.

Sammons, P., Sylva, K., Melhuish, E., Siraj-Blatchford, I. *et al* (2007) *Influences on Children's Development and Progress in Key Stage 2: Social/Behavioural Outcomes in Year 5.* DCSF Report 007. London: DCSF. Available at http://dera.ioe.ac.uk/7906/7/DCSF-RR007.pdf, accessed on 30 January 2015.

Schaps, E., Battistich, V. and Solomon, D. (2004) 'Community in School as Key to Student Growth: Findings from the Child Development Project.' In J. Zins, R. Weissberg, M. Wang and H. Walberg (eds) *Building Academic Success on Social and Emotional Learning: What Does the Research Say?* New York: Teachers College Press.

Schugerensky, D. (2006) 'This is Our School of Citizenship: Informal Learning in Local Democracy.' In Z. Bekerman, N. C. Burbules and D. Silberman-Keller (eds) *Learning in Places: The Informal Education Reader.* New York: Peter Lang.

Scotland's Commissioner for Children and Young People (2008) *Sweet 16? The Age of Leaving Care in Scotland.* Edinburgh: SCCYP.

Scottish Executive (2002) *National Care Standards Scotland.* Edinburgh: The Scottish Government.

Scottish Government (2008a) *Core Tasks for Designated Managers in Educational and Residential Establishments in Scotland.* Edinburgh: The Scottish Government. Available at www.scotland.gov.uk/Publications/2008/09/09143710/0, accessed on 9 January 2015.

Scottish Government (2008b) *These Are Our Bairns: A Guide for Community Planning Partnerships on Being a Good Corporate Parent.* Edinburgh: The Scottish Government. Available at www.scotland.gov.uk/Publications/2008/08/29115839/0, accessed on 9 January 2015.

Scottish Government (2011) *Included, Engaged and Involved: A Positive Approach to Managing School Exclusions.* Edinburgh: The Scottish Government. Available at www.scotland.gov.uk/Publications/2011/03/17095258/0, accessed on 9 January 2015.

Scottish Government (2014) *Educational Attainment.* Edinburgh: The Scottish Government. Available at www.scotland.gov.uk/Publications/2014/09/6499/2, accessed on 9 January 2015.

Scottish Institute for Residential Child Care (2010) *Go Outdoors! Guidance and Good Practice on Encouraging Outdoor Activities in Residential Child Care.* Glasgow: SIRCC.

Scottish Refugee Council (2012) *Inquiry into the Human Rights of Unaccompanied Migrant Children and Young People: Evidence Submitted by Scottish Refugee Council.* Glasgow: Scottish Refugee Council.

Seddon, C. (2011) 'Lifestyles and Social Participation'. *Social trends* 41. London: Office for National Statistics. Available at www.ons.gov.uk/ons/rel/social-trends-rd/social -trends/social-trends-41/lifestyles, accessed on 11 March 2015.

Simpson, D. (2013) *The Therapeutic Potential of Bedtime Reading in Residential Child Care from the Perspective of Young People and Residential Workers within a Social Pedagogy Framework.* Unpublished Undergraduate Dissertation, University of Strathclyde.

Sinclair, G. (2014) 'Please listen: A drama created by Kibble Education and Care Centre.' *Scottish Journal of Residential Child Care,* 13, 1, 23–27. Available at www.celcis.org/media/resources/publications/2014_vol13_No1_sinclair_please_listen.pdf, accessed on 30 January 2015.

Sinclair, I., Gibbs, I. and Wilson, K. (2004) *Foster Carers: Why They Stay and Why They Leave.* London: Jessica Kingsley Publishers.

Sirriyeh, A. and Wade, J. (2013) 'Education Pathways for Lone Asylum-seeking and Refugee Young People.' In S. Jackson (ed.) *Pathways through Education for Young People in Care: Ideas from Research and Practice.* London: BAAF.

Smith, M. (1997) 'Friedrich Froebel.' *Informal Education.* Available at http://infed.org/mobi/fredrich-froebel-frobel, accessed on 9 January 2015.

Smith, M. (2004) *Nel Noddings, The Ethics of Care and Education, the Encyclopaedia of Informal Education.* Available at http://infed.org/mobi/nel-noddings-the-ethics-of-care-and-education, accessed on 9 January 2015.

Smith, M. (2013) 'Forgotten connections: reviving the concept of upbringing in Scottish child welfare.' *Scottish Journal of Residential Child Care* 12, 2, 13–29.

Smith, M. and Skinner, K. (2013) *Evaluation of Early Adopters SP Project in Suffolk County Council 2012–13.* Edinburgh: University of Edinburgh.

Social Exclusion Unit (2003) *A Better Education for Children in Care.* London: Office of the Deputy Prime Minister.

Spector, K. (2014) *Advocacy in Education: When Education Rights are Held by Parents and Not Children: A Look at the Issues Arising for Children Generally and for Looked After Children in Particular.* Unpublished MA Thesis. London: Institute of Education.

Spencer, R. Collins, M.E., Ward, R. and Smashnaya, S. (2010) 'Mentoring for young people leaving foster care: promise and potential pitfalls.' *Social Work* 55, 3, 225–234.

Social Services Inspectorate (SSI) and Department of Health (1993) *Corporate Parents: Inspection of Residential Child Care Services in 11 Local Authorities.* London: SSI.

Starks, L. (2013) *Assessing the Impact of the Buttle UK Quality Mark in Higher Education.* London: Buttle UK.

Stein, M. (2002) 'Leaving Care.' In D. McNeish, T. Newman and H. Roberts (eds) *What Works for Children.* Milton Keynes, UK: Open University.

Stein, M. (2006) 'Research review, young people leaving care.' *Child and Family Social Work* 11, 3, 273–279.

Stein, M. (2012) *Young People Leaving Care: Supporting Pathways to Adulthood.* London: Jessica Kingsley Publishers.

Stevenson, J. and Willott, J. (2007) 'The aspiration and access to higher education of teenage refugees in the UK.' *Compare: A Journal of Comparative and International Education* 37, 5, 671–687.

Strand, S. (2010) 'Do some schools narrow the gap? Differential school effectiveness by ethnicity, gender, poverty, and prior achievement.' *School Effectiveness and School Improvement* 21, 3. Available at http://dx.doi.org/10.1080/09243451003732651, accessed on 9 January 2015.

Streeter, A. (2012) *A Study into the Effectiveness of the 'In Care, In School Resources' in De-stigmatising Looked After Children, and Raising the Awareness of their Real Situation Amongst their Peers.* PGCE Assessment Assignment. Bath: Bath Spa University, Centre for Education Policy in Practice.

Sutton, C., Utting, D. and Farrington, D. (2004) *Support from the Start: Working with Young Children and their Families to Reduce the Risks of Crime and Anti-Social Behaviour.* DfES Research Report 524. London: DfES. Available at www.crim.cam.ac.uk/people/academic_research/david_farrington/rb524.pdf, accessed on 30 January 2015.

Sylva, K., Melhuish, E., Sammons, P., Siraj-Blatchford, I. and Taggart, B. (2004) *Effective Pre-school Education: the Effective Provision of Pre-school Education (EPPE) Project. A Longitudinal Study Funded by the DfES 1997–2004: Final Report.* London: DfES. Available at http://eprints.ioe.ac.uk/5309/1/sylva2004EPPEfinal.pdf, accessed on 30 January 2015.

Taylor, C. (2006) *Young People in Care and Criminal Behaviour.* London: Jessica Kingsley Publishers.

The Children's Society (2012) *Into the Unknown: Children's Journeys through the Asylum Process.* London: The Children's Society.

Thomas, M.S.C. and Johnson, M.H. (2008) 'New advances in understanding sensitive periods in brain development.' *Current Directions in Psychological Science 17*, 1–5.

Tideman, E., Vinnerljung, B., Hintze, K. and Isaksson, A.A. (2013) 'Improving Foster Children's School Achievements: Promising Results from a Swedish Intensive Study.' In S. Jackson (ed.) *Pathways through Education for Young People in Care: Ideas from Research and Practice.* London: BAAF.

Tomlinson, S. (1982) *A Sociology of Special Education.* London: Routledge.

Trevarthen, C. (2004) *Learning About Ourselves from Children: Why a Growing Human Brain Needs Interesting Companions.* Hokkaido: Hokkaido University Graduate School of Education.

United Kingdom Supreme Court (2011) Judgment: ZH (Tanzania) (FC) (Appellant) v Secretary of State for the Home Department (Respondent).

Universities UK (n.d.) Available at www.universitiesuk.ac.uk, accessed on 9 January 2015.

Vander Ven, K. (2003) 'Bedtime story, a wake up call – and serve it with a cup of cocoa.' *The International Child and Youth Care Network,* Issue 51.

Vosniadou, S. (2001) *How Children Learn.* International Academy of Education. Available at http://unesdoc.unesco.org/images/0012/001254/125456e.pdf, accessed on 9 January 2015.

Vrouwenfelder, E. (2013) 'Contextualising the findings – the Orkney Social Pedagogy Evaluation.' *Scottish Journal of Residential Child Care 12*, 2.

Vygotsky, L. (1978) *Mind in Society.* Cambridge MA: Harvard University Press.

Wade, J., Biehal, N., Farrelly, N. and Sinclair, I. (2010) *Maltreated Children in the Looked After System: A Comparison of Outcomes for Those Who Go Home and Those Who Do Not.* Available at www.gov.uk/government/publications/maltreated-children-in-the-looked-after-system-a-comparison-of-outcomes-for-those-who-go-home-and-those-who-do-not, accessed on 9 January 2015.

Wade, J., Sirriyeh, A., Kohli, R. and Simmonds, J. (2012) *Fostering Unaccompanied Asylum-seeking Young People.* London: BAAF.

Walker, C., and Winter, J. (2014) *Becoming Reflexive Researchers: An Experiment in Research Collaboration.* Unpublished. London: Thomas Coram Research Unit, Institute of Education, University of London.

Walker, T. (2001) 'The Place of Education in a Mixed Economy of Child Care.' In S. Jackson (ed.) *Nobody Ever Told Us School Mattered.* London: BAAF.

Ward, H. (2009) 'Patterns of instability: moves within the English care system: their reasons, contexts and consequences.' *Child and Youth Services Review 31*, 1113–1118.

Ward, H., Brown, R. and Westlake, D. (2012) *Safeguarding Babies and Very Young Children from Abuse and Neglect.* London and Philadelphia: Jessica Kingsley Publishers.

Webb, R. and Vulliamy, R. (2004) *A Multi-agency Approach to Reducing Disaffection and Exclusions from School.* York: University of York.

Welbourne, P. and Leeson, C. (2013) 'The Education of Children in the Care System: A Research Review.' In S. Jackson (ed.) *Pathways through Education for Young People in Care: Ideas from Research and Practice.* London: BAAF.

Wetz, J. (2009) *Urban Village Schools: Putting Relationships at the Heart of Secondary School Organisation and Design.* London: Calouse Gulbenkian Foundation.

Wetz, J. (2011) 'Relationships as a springboard for learning.' *Human Scale Education.* Available at www.publications.parliament.uk/pa/cm201012/cmselect/cmeduc/writev/1515/att24. htm, accessed on 14 March 2015

White, A. (n.d.) *Case Study 2: An Evidence-Based Practice Review Report Theme: School Based Interventions for Emotional and Behavioural Development. Are Nurture Groups Effective Interventions for Improving the Social and Emotional Functioning of Participating Pupils in UK Primary Schools?* Available at www.ucl.ac.uk/educational-psychology/resources/ CS2White.pdf, accessed on 9 January 2015.

Whitebread, D. (2011) *Developmental Psychology and Early Childhood Education.* London: Sage.

Who Cares? Trust (2012) *Open Doors, Open Minds.* London: The Who Cares? Trust.

Wolf, A. (2011) *Review of Vocational Education – The Wolf Report.* Available at www.gov.uk/ government/uploads/system/uploads/attachment_data/file/180504/DFE-00031-2011. pdf, accessed on 9 January 2015.

Wood, C. and Caulier-Grice, J. (2006) *Fade or Flourish: How Primary Schools can Build on Children's Early Progress.* London: Social Market Foundation. Available at www.smf. co.uk/publications/fade-or-flourish-how-primary-schools-can-build-on-childrens-early-progress, accessed on 9 January 2015.

Wright, F. (2012) 'Social work practice with unaccompanied asylum-seeking young people facing removal.' *British Journal of Social Work 44,* 4, 1027–1044.

Young, I. M. (1997) *Intersecting Voices: Dilemmas of Gender, Political Philosophy and Policy.* Princeton, NJ: Princeton University Press.

Younger, M., Warrington, M. *et al.* (2005) *Raising Boys' Achievement.* University of Cambridge, Faculty of Education, Dfes Research Report 636.

SUBJECT INDEX

AUTHOR INDEX